'This is a very kind book. It is kind to the reader because it is so clear, informative, and hopeful; it is eminently kind to the mothers, babies, and toddlers. The way in which a mother's critical observation of her baby or herself can be turned into a more generous view and thereby change mother-child interactions is stunning. May this methodology spread, as it will change many lives.'
**Anne Alvarez**, *consultant Child and Adolescent psychotherapist, Tavistock Clinic, London; author,* The Thinking Heart

'This thoughtful guide embodies the author's profound understanding of mother-child relationships in the critical first three years of a child's life. The specific support, educational, and psychodynamic intervention components that create a reflective space are carefully described and richly illustrated. This book is so readable and informative, it can enrich a broad range of practitioners, and parents themselves.'
**Tessa Baradon**, *Parent-Infant Project, Anna Freud Centre; co-director, International Training School for Infancy and Early Years*

'This wonderful book fills an important gap in the current literature on parenting interventions. The *Guide* derives much of its power from the wealth of narratives describing the way the group-leader recruits mothers' memories from their own childhoods to give meaning to current problems with their babies and toddlers thereby offering insight to all group members.'
**Alexandra Harrison**, *training and supervising analyst, Boston Psychoanalytic Society and Institute; assistant professor of Psychiatry, Harvard Medical School; founder, Supporting Child Caregivers - Infant-parent mental health training non-profit throughout the world*

'This wonderfully valuable book is an eminently practical guide. Its distinctiveness is in the detailed vignettes that describe the complex challenges at each age and the unique way developmental information is integrated with psychodynamic intervention. This book is for experienced clinicians and early career professionals.'
**Wendy Olesker**, *training and supervising adult and child analyst, New York Psychoanalytic Institute; editorial board,* Psychoanalytic Study of the Child

'The *Mother-Baby-Toddler Group Guide* is straightforward in its outline, yet at the same time is a multilayered and intricate template that offers depth and nuance as it powerfully weaves together many ideas about fostering resilience in mothers, babies, and toddlers. The many vignettes provide vivid illustration of the intense emotions mothers experience and how the integrated educational and psychodynamic group-process provides understanding and time to reflect.'
**Rita Reiswig**, *co-director, The Anni Bergman Parent-Infant Program, Contemporary Freudian Society and IPTAR; psychoanalyst for adults, adolescents, and children*

# Mother-Baby-Toddler Group Guide

This book is a comprehensive guide for leading mother-baby-toddler groups, a text for teaching child development, and a handbook for early intervention.

The guidelines provide a detailed psychodynamic approach to resolve typical developmental and mothering difficulties that arise during the first three years of life. As mothers' thoughts about their babies and toddlers ricochet between the past, the present, and the future, mothers' childhood memories are activated and out of awareness influence mother-child interactions. Specific interventions that generate mothers' self-reflection and insight are delineated. Group questions are organized by age and psychodynamic theme. Compelling vignettes illustrate synergies between the supportive and educational group-process, and the psychodynamic interventions with each mother-child dyad. Difficulties are resolved before they escalate into disorders. This is the first psychodynamic group guide to extend the infant mental health focus on treatment, to include prevention.

Experienced clinicians, students, psychologists, psychiatrists, social workers, and others interested in infant mental health and mothers' wellbeing will find the specific guidelines practical, informative, and illuminating.

**Ilene S. Lefcourt** established the Sackler Lefcourt Center for Child Development in 1982. She was the director, led the mother-baby-toddler groups, and provided developmental consultation to parents for over 35 years. She taught child psychiatry residents and parent-infant psychotherapy trainees about her work. She has been a faculty member at the Columbia University Center for Psychoanalytic Training and Research Parent-Infant Program since 1995. Ms. Lefcourt is currently in private practice in NYC. She is the author of *Parenting and Childhood Memories: A Psychoanalytic Approach to Reverberating Ghosts and Magic.*

# Mother-Baby-Toddler Group Guide

## A Psychodynamic Approach

Ilene S. Lefcourt

LONDON AND NEW YORK

First published 2023
by Routledge
4 Park Square, Milton Park, Abingdon, Oxon OX14 4RN

and by Routledge
605 Third Avenue, New York, NY 10158

*Routledge is an imprint of the Taylor & Francis Group, an informa business*

© 2023 Ilene S. Lefcourt

The right of Ilene S. Lefcourt to be identified as author of this work has been asserted in accordance with sections 77 and 78 of the Copyright, Designs and Patents Act 1988.

All rights reserved. No part of this book may be reprinted or reproduced or utilised in any form or by any electronic, mechanical, or other means, now known or hereafter invented, including photocopying and recording, or in any information storage or retrieval system, without permission in writing from the publishers.

*Trademark notice*: Product or corporate names may be trademarks or registered trademarks, and are used only for identification and explanation without intent to infringe.

*British Library Cataloguing-in-Publication Data*
A catalogue record for this book is available from the British Library

*Library of Congress Cataloging-in-Publication Data*
Names: Lefcourt, Ilene S., 1946– author.
Title: Mother-baby-toddler group guide : a psychodynamic approach / Ilene S. Lefcourt.
Description: New York, NY : Routledge, 2023. | Includes bibliographical references and index.
Identifiers: LCCN 2022019738 (print) | LCCN 2022019739 (ebook) |
ISBN 9781032351384 (hbk) | ISBN 9781032351391 (pbk) |
ISBN 9781003325482 (ebk)
Subjects: LCSH: Mother and child. | Child development.
Classification: LCC HQ759 .L435 2023  (print) |
LCC HQ759  (ebook) | DDC 155.6/463–dc23/eng/20220714
LC record available at https://lccn.loc.gov/2022019738
LC ebook record available at https://lccn.loc.gov/2022019739

ISBN: 9781032351384 (hbk)
ISBN: 9781032351391 (pbk)
ISBN: 9781003325482 (ebk)

DOI: 10.4324/b23150

Typeset in Garamond
by Newgen Publishing UK

# Contents

| | |
|---|---|
| *About the author* | ix |
| *Foreword by Daniel Schechter, MD* | x |
| *Preface* | xi |
| *Acknowledgements* | xiv |

## SECTION I
## Guideline principles                                              1

Introduction                                                         3
  *Part 1: Mothers' childhood memories 3*
  *Psychodynamics of everyday life 5*
  *Group-leader approach 9*
  *Part 2: Group goals and group-process 12*
  *Child development information and group questions 17*

1  Psychodynamic themes                                             22

2  Mother-child proximity                                           57
   *Vignette 63*

## SECTION II
## Mother-baby-toddler beginning groups                             67

3  Beginning groups                                                 69
   *Pre-enrollment visits 69*
   *Group composition and group schedules 70*
   *Pre-group mother-child visits 71*
   *Vignettes 72*
   *First three group sessions 80*
   *Child development information and group questions 82*

## SECTION III
**Child development information and group questions**    **85**

4   2 to 10-months    87
*Child development information and group questions 87*
*Vignettes 100*

5   11 to 19-months    109
*Child development information and group questions 109*
*Vignettes 121*

6   20 to 28-months    128
*Child development information and group questions 128*
*Vignettes 140*

7   29 to 36-months    148
*Child development information and group questions 148*
*Vignettes 161*

## SECTION IV
**In conclusion**    **177**

8   Individual sessions with a group mother    179
*Vignette 180*

9   Ending groups    184

*Glossary*    185
*Suggested reading*    189
*Index*    192

# About the author

**Ilene S. Lefcourt** established the Sackler Lefcourt Center for Child Development in 1982. She was the director, led the mother-baby-toddler groups, and provided developmental consultation to parents for over 35 years. She taught child psychiatry residents and parent-infant psychotherapy trainees about her work. She has been a faculty member at the Columbia University Center for Psychoanalytic Training and Research Parent-Infant Program since 1995. Ms. Lefcourt is currently in private practice in NYC. She is the author of *Parenting and Childhood Memories: A Psychoanalytic Approach to Reverberating Ghosts and Magic*.

# Foreword

*by Daniel Schechter, MD*

During my psychiatric and psychoanalytic training, so many years ago, I was supervised by Ilene S. Lefcourt and we co-led a mother-baby group. Currently, I am the Medical Director of Perinatal and Early Childhood Ambulatory Care and Research at Lausanne University Hospital in Switzerland. Throughout these years, the infant mental health field has continued to grow. Research has expanded, training programs have been established, and clinical services have increased. This extremely clear and richly illustrated Mother-Baby-Toddler Group Guide captures the details and fundamental psychodynamic principles of Ms. Lefcourt's work and is at the core of infant mental health efforts today.

What I have learned from Ilene S. Lefcourt and am still learning through this volume, is golden when it comes to working with mother-child dyads in groups and individually. Above all, this Guide is a treasure for clinicians and trainees with an interest in thinking about the specifics of a psychodynamic approach. The approach highlights the value for mothers, babies, and toddlers of a supportive group setting. It integrates educational material for mothers with psychodynamic intervention. The mother-baby-toddler relationship flourishes, baby and toddler development is fortified, and the building of connections among mothers, their babies, and toddlers is promoted. A time and space for reflection on the inner world of mothers and their little ones is created.

Such groups can enrich ongoing psychotherapies for mother, child, or both, can catalyze further intervention for those who need it, and for some mothers can represent the only journey to explore their own and their child's mind and development. There are precious few books written to accompany clinicians into the playroom and address the nitty-gritty of how to work with mothers, babies, and toddlers in a group modality, how to meet the challenges, and how to seize magic moments that arise in this very special form of intervention. This book does so with attention to each period of development from 2 to 36 months of age. The author is a compelling and careful writer on the topic and so the book is also a pleasure to read as we intensify our efforts to do more for mothers, babies, and toddlers.

# Preface

The *Mother-Baby-Toddler Group Guide (MBTG Guide)* offers a psychodynamic approach to understanding mothers' emerging childhood memories and their impact on mother-child interactions. In Selma Fraiberg's resounding words, "In every nursery there are ghosts."

The first three years of a child's life are an important time for both the mother and the child. The maturational thrust is powerful; there are also significant vulnerabilities. Mothers' childhood memories are activated and relived with their babies and toddlers, sometimes out of the mother's awareness. Some of the enactments benefit the mothers and children, others are disturbing, and some are potentially damaging.

Mother-child interactions during this early phase that meet the developmental needs of babies and toddlers lay an important foundation for infant mental health and maternal well-being. When mothers are supported, are provided child development information about their babies' and toddlers' developing minds, and when mothers acquire insight – emotionally significant new shared meanings about the ways in which their own childhood memories are influencing their interactions with their children, mothers are better able to resolve typical emerging difficulties. While the focus of the *MBTG Guide* is on mothers and their children; many of the ideas also apply to fathers and other significant relationships for babies and toddlers.

The *MBTG Guide* is based on observations at the Sackler Lefcourt Center for Child Development from 1982 to 2020. The Center, a neighborhood program in New York City, was established to fill a gap between pediatric well-baby-care and child psychiatry. Within this gap is where the typical struggles of mothers, babies, and toddlers emerge: the inconsolable crying of babies, temper tantrums of toddlers, and the loneliness, anxiety, and everyday stress of mothers. These typical difficulties may not be pathological, but they are painful and can affect mothers' well-being and children's development.

Most mother-infant mental health programs have been for the treatment of high-risk populations. A new population for psychodynamic mother-baby-toddler groups was identified for this program. A developmental problem or mothering difficulty was not required. Mothers' stated reasons for joining included: to meet other mothers, to learn more about child development and mothering, and to have a playgroup for their children. The wish to be "a good mother," often the wish either to be a better mother than her own, or to be as good a mother as her own, was expressed and was a frequent motivation. The women were primarily self-referred after having heard about the program from friends; they were married, college graduates. Their countries of origin, religions, careers, and ages varied. They had between one and three children.

The mother-baby-toddler groups had support, educational, and dyadic intervention components. The groups were designed to:

1. Support mothers during the first three years of their children's lives
2. Teach the fundamentals of early development focused on the underlying meanings of babies' and toddlers' behavior and how the meanings of their behavior relate to their developing minds
3. Understand the links between each mother's childhood memories and her current perceptions of and interactions with her child
4. Provide play activities for the children (the play part of the program and the play-leader's role are not described in the *MBTG Guide*)

The *MBTG Guide* is based on leading groups for over 35 years with more than 1,000 mothers, their babies, and toddlers. The approach evolved from psychoanalytic theories of development, psychodynamic interventions with adults, and their application to the early mother-child relationship. The approach was based on the Guideline principles summarized on page 21.

The Center was a site for child psychiatry residents and parent-infant psychotherapy trainees to learn more about typical early development, the first three years of motherhood, and the developing mother-child relationship. The groups served as a model for mother-baby-toddler groups that were established with other populations in other settings: a psychoanalytic institute, a community center for financially disadvantaged mothers, and a residential treatment program for mothers and their babies who were at risk for abuse and neglect, many of whom had been remanded by the courts. Interventions described in the *MBTG Guide* have also been successful during individual parent consultations.

The child development information and group questions in Chapters 3 through 7 were used at the Center to facilitate group discussion, to provide support, to explore mothers' childhood memories, and to generate mothers' self-reflection. These are the essential elements of the group-process. The main perspective of the child development information is the inner world of babies and toddlers: their developing sense of self, attachment relationships, thoughts, feelings, and wishes.

The *MBTG Guide* describes group-leader interventions to promote the supportive and educational group-process, and when difficulties arise, interventions with individual mother-child dyads to explore the connections between a mother's interactions with her child and her childhood memories. The group questions and child development information presented by the group-leader provide a bridge between the group-process and interventions with individual mother-child dyads. Synergies between the group-process and the process with an individual mother-child dyad will be illustrated.

The *MBTG Guide* demonstrates that mothers' motivation for self-reflection is heightened in the context of the early mother-child attachment relationship. New solutions to long-standing internal conflicts and interpersonal difficulties can be achieved; unfulfilled yearnings can be gratified. A foundation for the fulfillment of maternal satisfaction and children's security of attachment can be established. During the first three years of life, typical child development and mothering difficulties can be resolved before they escalate, become entrenched, and evolve into disorders.

A premise of this book is that group-leaders who use the *MBTG Guide* are professionally trained and follow the ethical and professional standards of their discipline. If a mother reports something or does something that is potentially dangerous, appropriate action should be taken to ensure the safety of everyone concerned. For example, if a mother reports that her toddler climbed unsupervised into the crib of her newborn, and that she is worried that her toddler wanted to hurt the baby, or a mother mentions that her child walked out the front door which she does not always lock and that it was a good thing she heard him knocking, or a comment about the dog growling when the baby goes next to the dog's food. This book does not replace professional training. When psychiatric, psychological, or developmental evaluations are indicated, an appropriate referral should be made.

Some of the ideas throughout the *MBTG Guide* appeared in *Parenting and Childhood Memories: A Psychoanalytic Approach to Reverberating Ghosts and Magic*. The *MBTG Guide* revisits some of those stories with further discussion of theory and technique to illustrate the guidelines. New stories are added. The identities of the mothers and children who inspired the stories are disguised. The vignettes are fictionalized composites. Two goals are important in telling these stories: to maintain the essence of what occurred and to protect the privacy of the mothers and children.

# Acknowledgements

I wish to thank the families who participated in Center programs. This book describes our exciting work together and the guidelines that emerged. Writing the *MBTG Guide* has been a challenging endeavor. Mother-baby-toddler groups are complex; early development is exciting, at times perplexing, and non-linear; mothering is formidable. The past, the present, and the future rapidly intertwine. The *MBTG Guide* is an attempt to portray a deeply satisfying, complicated process in an organized way. It would not have been possible without the contributions of esteemed colleagues. I leaned heavily on the infant mental health literature, especially the contributions of Alicia Lieberman, PhD. I would like to highlight the enormous help I got from Susan Coates, PhD; Gail Davis; Judith Levitan, MSW; Robert Michels, MD; Alyson McCormick, MSW; Patricia Nachman, PhD; Wendy Olesker, PhD; Daniel Schechter, MD; Theodore Shapiro, MD; Meriamne Singer, MD; Mark Sorenson, MD; Nadia Brushweiler-Stern, MD; and Myrna Weissman, PhD. In addition, I would like to thank Betsy Lynn for her organizational and editorial assistance throughout, and Kate Hawes and the Routledge team for supporting this work from vision to publication.

# Section I

# Guideline principles

Section I discusses the psychodynamic foundation of the *Mother-Baby-Toddler Group Guide*. The support and educational components are described and illustrated. The group-leader approach is outlined. The centrality of the mother-child attachment relationship is highlighted. Synergies between group-process and group-leader interventions with each mother-child dyad to explore the meanings of the mother's childhood memories and their influence on current mother-child interactions are discussed.

# Introduction

**Part I: Mothers' childhood memories**

The *Mother-Baby-Toddler Group Guide* (*MBTG Guide*) is about the difficulties children birth to 3 years and their mothers typically confront, and ways in which they can be resolved. There are support, educational, and mother-child psychodynamic intervention components. The *MBTG Guide* describes the group- process that motivates mothers to discover underlying meanings of their own and their children's behavior, and the impact of their own childhood memories on current mother-baby and mother-toddler interactions.

When a woman becomes a mother, dreams of the future and memories of the past are aroused. The moment-to-moment oscillating attention elicited by her baby changes her mental landscape. Her thoughts ricochet between the past, the present, and the future. Divergent feelings are intense and excitedly fluctuate. Mothers' attachment needs to their babies are activated. Mothers' childhood memories that may have been deeply buried are awakened and influence mother-child interactions. A woman's identity takes on new facets. Her primary intergenerational relationship identity shifts from "I am my mother's daughter" to "I am the mother of my child." A mother's potential for an expanding positive sense of self is activated. Her expanding sense of self is derived from her attachment to her baby, pride in being a mother, pleasurable mother-child interactions, and her mothering goals. An expanding sense of self fuels her readiness for insight – emotionally significant new shared meanings. Current mother-child interactions that are contributing to difficulties can be resolved.

*Marlene gazed longingly across the room at 10-month-old George and said, "I feel like I'm not George's mother. He thinks the nanny is his mother. He laughs with her in a way that he never laughs with me. I've turned his care completely over to her." Marlene's painful words marked the beginning of our exploration of her childhood memories and her conflicts about being a mother, of which she was unaware.* (This vignette is discussed in Chapter 4, page 107)

# 4  Guideline principles

At the core of the approach presented in the *MBTG Guide* are the following four main ideas.

1. Mother-child attachment is a powerful relationship dynamic that promotes robust child development and sensitive mothering
2. Out of awareness, mothers' childhood memories influence their interactions with their babies and toddlers
3. When typical child development difficulties and mother-child interaction problems arise, mothers with children under 3 years are available to self-reflection about the links between their childhood memories and their interactions with their children
4. A supportive group-process focused on child development, the mother-child relationship, and mothers' childhood memories facilitates the self-reflection of each mother and the emergence of emotionally significant new shared meanings that can lead to change

When a baby is born, either first-born or later born, the mother's life changes; what is on her mind and what she does. The enormity of the care her baby needs for survival and for thriving is daunting. Questions and concerns about her baby and about her mothering abound. Mothers pursue child development information and seek out other mothers. Inspired by her new perspective, her childhood memories acquire new meanings. The wish to provide the best for her child and to be the best mother she can be consolidates. It is typically a period of both intense pleasures and vulnerability to anxiety and depression.

Mothers and their children benefit from child development information when it leads to informed child rearing approaches, age-appropriate expectations, and the confidence that knowledge can bring. There is an abundance of child development information available in books, articles, and on the internet. Advice to mothers is forthcoming from experts, family, friends, and strangers. Mothers' personal competing ideas, past experiences, and childhood memories can interfere with the usefulness of information or advice if it activates unresolved conflicts or disturbing memories that are not addressed. The *MBTG Guide* delineates interventions that create a working alliance between each mother and the group-leader to address mothers' thoughts and feelings that interfere with the usefulness of valid child development information. The *Guide* sketches child development information for the group-leader to present that is coordinated with group questions to raise. The information combined with the questions and evoked memories promotes group discussion and generates group support leading to each mother's self-reflection. As part of this process, the information can be more useful.

## Psychodynamics of everyday life

All behavior is motivated and has conscious and unconscious meanings. This is a main tenet of a psychodynamic approach. Mothers' interest in the meanings of their children's behavior and their own behavior with their children is easily aroused. The meanings begin to make sense to them as they observe their children, and as they reflect on their own wishes, fears, conflicts, fantasies, and childhood memories: the psychodynamics of everyday life for mothers, babies, and toddlers.

The following vignette, about a mother and her 3-month-old-baby, illustrates the emergence of a mother's core theme, the educational and support components of the group-process, and interventions that link the mother's childhood memories with current mother-baby interactions. Conceptualizing a mother's core theme, or what is sometimes called a dynamic formulation, is a way for the group-leader to organize the mother's narrative and mother-child interactions in a cohesive, concise way, and helps to structure interventions. A core theme is a psychodynamic construct about the mother's conscious and unconscious conflicts. The core theme can be refined or changed as is useful. Examples of core themes that appear throughout the *MBTG Guide* are listed on page 9. A Vignette summary precedes each vignette and highlights the psychodynamics illustrated.

## Regina and Candi

> **Vignette summary**
>
> **Child's age** – 3-months
> **Mother-child interaction** – At times impatient, critical, and angry – negative attributions to baby
> **Presenting problem** – Self-critical and negative attributions to baby, "I'm not a natural mother."
> **Childhood memory** – "My mother only cared about how I behaved, not about how I felt."
> **Mother's core theme** – Conflict between empathy for her child and behavioral goals
> **Primary defense mechanism** – Enactment of childhood memory, identification with the aggressor
> **Organizing fantasy** – "If my child does not behave, I am a bad mother."
> **Intervention** – Interpretation of links between mother's childhood memories and difficulty integrating her behavioral goals with empathy for child
> **Resolution** – Mother's increased empathy for child, less self-critical. Mother and child have fewer and briefer struggles

*During a first mother-baby group, 3-month-old Candi began to cry. Regina, Candi's mother, explained, "See, this is what happens. She's very difficult." After a few minutes of loud crying, Regina stood up and began walking back and forth, gently rocking Candi in her arms. After a few more moments Regina said, "Maybe I should leave."*

*The other mothers urged Regina to stay and commiserated with her distress. Additional group-leader support and child development information enabled her to stay, "You are welcome to stay. During our group, the babies are going to do all the things they do – cry, poop, eat, spit-up, sleep, smile, coo, and more. Babies 3-months are learning how to transition from awake to sleep and sleep to awake. They are learning about what it feels like to poop and to burp. They may have strong reactions to these internal experiences and may for a while. They are also learning about what it feels like to be in a mother-baby group for the first time." This allusion to the mothers' feelings and implicitly to mother-baby mutual arousal triggered the mothers' recognition of some discomfort and a shared laugh. Everyone seemed to relax. The following highlighted the anticipated group-process, "These may be some of the meanings of Candi's crying. We are going to talk a great deal this year about the meanings beneath the surface of the babies' behavior: what we imagine and what research has found."*

In what seemed to me like a few minutes, but what might have seemed to Regina like forever, Candi calmed and then fell asleep in her mother's arms. Regina was in a sweat as she criticized herself, "I guess I'm just not a natural mother. I need to teach her to behave better." Regina's negative attributions to Candi then spewed out, "She looks like a crazy baby. Her stringy blonde hair is so wild."

Regina's negative attributions when she was feeling inadequate herself were not confined to Candi's hair and sanity. Regina minimized her own painful feelings about herself as an inadequate mother and bolstered her positive feelings by negative attributions to Candi. Recognizing when a mother's feelings about herself have activated criticism of and anger towards her baby to defend herself against her own painful feelings promotes the group-leader's ability to empathize with the mother and to formulate support, educational, and psychodynamic interventions.

During the next several weeks Regina's core theme emerged: conflict between her behavioral goals for Candi and her empathy for Candi's distress. Regina's negative attributions to Candi were triggered when her core theme was activated. The ways in which this core theme was rooted in Regina's childhood memories also became clear. For example, when Candi was 7-months Regina described separations at the gym day-care center, "She's impossible, she needs to behave better, she screams when I leave her." The following intervention included: child development information, empathy for both Candi and Regina, and the interpretation of affect; "Babies that are Candi's age often cry when separated from Mommy or before Mommy leaves. They feel frightened. Babies gradually learn about separations and develop strategies for coping: just like adults. It sounds like Candi's cries are also painful for you. Babies remind their mothers of feelings they also have. Candi has a strong attachment to you, which is a good thing. Babies need their mommies so much and love them so much that they sometimes have strong reactions to separations. When babies are distressed, it is more difficult for them to remember you, and to know that you will return. Let's think about what might help Candi to adapt to this separation which is important to you and stressful for you both."

Asking the other mothers how their babies were reacting to separations promoted group discussion and support. They all described similar separation reactions. Babies' crying when separated from Mommy was normalized. Additional child development information included, "Play can help babies to adapt to separation. Peek-a-boo is a game of separation. The separation is brief, and the reunion is joyful. Peek-a-boo delights babies and evolves into hide-and-seek during the first three years and helps babies and toddlers to learn that even when they cannot see you they are loved and safe, and they can expect you to return. I then asked Regina, "Does Candi have a special toy, or a toy you play with together that she can keep with her when separated from you that might make it easier for her?" Regina responded, "My mother only cared about how I behaved, never about how I felt."

Regina's response to the intervention that included: child development information, empathy for Candi, and reference to Regina's own painful feelings that were evoked by Candi's cries helped Regina to recognize her own empathy for Candi and assimilate the developmental information, and awakened childhood memories. Asking about a *specific memory when a mother reports a general memory helps to evoke associated feelings attached to a specific memory. I asked Regina, "Do you remember a specific example of your mother only caring about how you behaved, not about how you felt?" Regina quickly responded, "I was in a school play and as I was walking on stage, I told my mother I was very nervous. She told me that there is nothing to be nervous about, I have a nothing part." The following interpretation connected Regina's memory to her current interactions with and attitudes towards Candi, "It seems as if that memory of feeling nervous walking on stage and your memory of your mother's response interferes with your awareness of Candi's feelings. Your memory may also interfere with feeling good about yourself."*

*As the weeks passed there were increasing opportunities to identify Regina's empathic soothing and loving delight with Candi, and Candi's responses to her mother of being soothed, shared pleasure, and safety. When Candi's behavior triggered Regina's rejecting and punitive reactions, she was able to recognize the link to her own childhood memories filled with feeling inadequate, alone, and painfully not understood. Regina became better able to integrate her behavioral goals for Candi with empathy for Candi's inner experience. We had never talked about Candi's hair again; however, when she was 1.5-years Regina said, "I used to hate her hair, I thought it was wild and crazy, now I see it as her own unique style, I love it!"*

*When Candi was approaching 2.5-years their struggles were around learning to use the potty. Candi tried, but sometimes failed. Regina became angry and impatient. Candi appeared painfully criticized and dejected. Regina's behavioral goal for Candi to use the potty and her own feelings of inadequacy to teach her, at times prevented her from having empathy for Candi's experience of the process. However, when asked what she thought Candi was feeling when she wet or soiled her panties, Regina agreed, "I know Candi wants to please me, she is trying, and feels ashamed and nervous when I reprimand her, which probably makes it more difficult for her to feel good about herself and learn to use the potty." Regina was able to expand her behavioral focus to include Candi's emotional needs for feelings of self-worth even when she made a mistake, recognition that she was trying, and understanding when her fears about wetting and soiling her clothes intensified when reprimanded. Regina became better able to integrate her behavioral goals with her empathy for Candi. While each phase of development during Regina's first three years of motherhood had difficulties related to this core theme, her feelings of inadequacy, and easily triggered anger at Candi lessened; the struggles between them were modulated. Candi thrived. Regina was proud of Candi and satisfied with herself.*

## Mothers' core themes summary (examples)
1. Conflicts between empathy for her child and behavioral goals
2. Ambivalence about how close to be or how distant to be from her child
3. Attachment to her own mother conflicting with her attachment to her child
4. Wishes to provide the best for her child conflicted with envy of her child having things she did not or does not have
5. Ambivalent feelings about the child that she has, conflicted with the idealized child that she wishes she had
6. Difficulty resolving the schism between the mother she wishes to be, with the mother she believes she is
7. Wishes to protect her own mother from pain, conflicted with getting comfort for her own pain
8. Attachment needs to her child, conflicted with revived fears of attachment
9. Conflicts between work and family life

## Group-leader approach

Curiosity to understand characterizes the group-leader's approach. Sustained curiosity is the lens through which all observations are made and all interventions are formulated. Because of the close link between curiosity to understand and empathy, curiosity helps to establish and to build a working alliance between the group-leader and each mother. The group-leader's curiosity activates each mothers' curiosity to understand more about herself and her child. Curiosity is also a driving force motivating children's play. When curiosity predominates the group-leader's approach, untimely and disturbing interpretations, advice tinged with criticism, and other disruptive interventions are minimized. Curiosity to understand is a primary motivation to be protected, nurtured, and activated. The scope of group-leader curiosity is summarized on page 12.

While observing mother-child interactions and listening to a mother's narrative, the group-leader is watching in real time what has been conceptualized as the intergenerational transfer of trauma, and the intergenerational correlation between a mother's mental representations of attachment and the attachment category of her child. Curiosity helps to elucidate the moment-to-moment everyday details.

The group-leader maintains a shifting yet simultaneous focus on each mother, each child, and each mother-child dyad, and at the same time on the group. This ongoing shifting attention, with empathy for each, is mostly out of awareness. Awareness of this dynamic process is required when the group-leader's personal reactions are biasing the process and threaten to rupture a working alliance.

Throughout the *MBTG Guide*, the importance of the group-leader building and maintaining a working alliance with each mother is highlighted. When working alliance ruptures occur, they need to be repaired. Misunderstandings can be clarified; group-leader empathic failures may need apologies. The group-leader's attention to emerging potential fractures is required when there are differences of opinion between a mother and the group-leader, when power struggles between a mother and the group-leader are occurring, or when the group-leader is partial to affinities within the group. These kinds of potential ruptures in the working alliance sometimes can be averted if they are made explicit. For example, *"We have a strong difference of opinion and we each have evidence to support our view."*

Differentiating between what is observed and the personal meaning to the group leader of what is observed is paramount. For example, *the mother yelled at her child is an observation; the mother was angry at her child is an interpretation of its meaning.*

A dramatic example of a group-leader's inability to recognize her own personal feelings that triggered a confrontation with a mother and ruptured the emerging positive working alliance follows. The group-leader's fundamental approach of curiosity to understand had broken down. *A mother had described the following routine with her 32-month-old twin daughters, "Every evening before bedtime Daisy, Remi, and I cuddle on my bed and watch a short video. While we are watching, they pleasure themselves. We are very close, and they are totally comfortable. I think it is good for their sexual development that they are not ashamed. It was the opposite in my family."*

*The mother was intent on continuing this routine with her daughters, and the group-leader wanted to challenge her decision. The group-leader believed that the mother was disavowing her own sexual arousal and pleasure watching her children masturbate and had lost sight of the mother's acknowledged shame about her own sexuality. The group-leader confronted her, "It seems like you also get sexual pleasure from the routine you describe." The mother protested and the group-leader insisted. The mother withdrew from the group.*

*The group-leader was not able to recognize that it was her own personal reaction to the mother's description of the routine and her own intense feelings that were determining her approach with the mother. She was ignoring the mother's use of disavowal as a defense to protect herself from humiliation. The group-leader was unable in the moment to be curious about the meaning of the mother's disavowal. She did not explore any details of the routine that the mother had described, or the mother's allusion to her own sexual shame. The group-leader's own childhood memories, which included sexual over-stimulation, fueled her confrontation with the mother. The group-leader's insistence on the mother's disavowed sexual arousal ruptured their emerging working alliance and triggered the mother's withdrawal from the group.*

*The mother's description of her routine with her little girls may have been the mother's attempt to evaluate the group-leader's attitudes about masturbation, to assess her own safety in the group to talk about what was on her mind without being challenged or criticized, or to find out more about whether what she was doing with her daughters would have the outcome that she intended. The mother may have been asking for help with her own sexual problems. The group-leader's response was based on her own feelings and impeded further exploration with the mother. Supervision helped the group-leader understand what had transpired.*

All group-leaders have themes that trigger strong personal reactions. Personal feelings can be used to increase understanding of a mother and a child, or they may motivate disruptive interventions as occurred in the above example. When personal feelings are interfering, the needed shifting and simultaneous identifications and empathy for both the mother and the child does not occur. Recognizing a mother's primary defense mechanisms used to mitigate her emotional pain helps to promote the group-leader's empathy for the mother and to ward off enactments of the group-leader's personal feelings that interfere. Defense mechanisms are summarized on page 56 and defined in the glossary. Added to the list of usual defense mechanisms is: enactment of a childhood memory to defend against painful affect.

Group-leaders' impulses to give advice and reassurance also need to be understood. Sometimes they are triggered by the group-leader's personal feelings of anxiety or anger and are untimely for the mother.

Another important aspect of the group-leader's working alliance is to minimize mothers' dependency on and idealization of the group-leader, both of which may be gratifying to the group-leader but may interfere with mother-baby-toddler group goals. *Opportunities to address mothers' idealizing of the group-leader arise when mothers say for example, "You always know the best thing to say to a child." A useful response is some version of, "It is easier to understand a child when described by a mother, than it is when interactions are happening with all the intense feelings."*

Consistent with group goals and the group-process is the group-leader not referencing personal information. The one exception to this might be when asked, "Do you have children?" Whether the answer is yes or no, answering can convey a recognition of the unique significance of the experience of having a child. At the core of the question is, "Can you understand me?" The ultimate answer to this question will be demonstrated over time. Undoubtedly, feeling understood will fluctuate. Another motivation for a mother asking the group-leader this question is an attempt to create an aspect of symmetry in their relationship. After answering yes or no, some version of the following addresses both meanings, *"I can understand why you are asking me; having a child has such a strong influence on how we think and feel about child development and mothering. We talk about many aspects of your life, your child, and your childhood memories. I do not believe that talking about me is helpful to understand as much as we can about you and your child."* If a mother is in conflict about a decision and asks about what the group-leader did in a similar situation, the following is useful, *"What I did in this kind of situation may not be right for you or your child. We will try to understand together what is best for you and your child."*

The efficacy of interventions with individual mothers to explore the impact of a childhood memory on a mother-child interaction is promoted by the group-process. The main element of the group-process among the mothers is support, including the support of shared experience. The educational component of the group-process, in addition to being inherently useful, can mitigate the stress of ongoing self-reflection when it is painful. The shifting focus on each mother provides the other mothers a respite from being the focus of attention. Synergies between the group-process and group-leader interventions with an individual mother-child dyad are illustrated throughout the *MBTG Guide*.

### Group-leader approach summary

1. **Curiosity to understand** the meaning to the mother of her statements, questions, concerns, and childhood memories
2. **Curiosity to understand** the underlying meaning of an observation of a mother, of a child, and of a mother-child interaction
3. **Curiosity to understand** a mother's response to things the group-leader and the other mothers say and do
4. **Curiosity to understand** how a mother's behavior, thoughts, and feelings, and their meaning to the mother, relate to the mother's childhood memories
5. **Curiosity to understand** how a baby or toddler reacts and adapts to his or her mother
6. **Curiosity to understand** the group-leader's own personal reactions to a mother, child, or mother-child interaction

## Part 2: Group goals and group-process

### Support

A primary goal of mother-baby-toddler groups and a core part of the group-process is support: group-leader support and support among the mothers. Support enhances mothers' abilities to care for their babies and toddlers in ways that promote emotional development and security of attachment. Support enriches mothers' pleasure with their children and mothering satisfaction. At the core of support is feeling understood. The group-leader Support summary appears on page 17.

During the first three years of life, the vigorous developmental progression of babies and toddlers, and the profound growth potential of their mothers is activated. Fantasies about the mother she wants to be and the actual mother she thinks she is can become more aligned. Ideas about perfect mothers and bad mothers evolve. This process of aligning memories of the past, wishes for the future, and current mother-child interactions is influenced by supportive interactions among the mothers, group-leader interventions, and as a derivative of mothers' self-reflection and insight. The ongoing group-process of emotionally significant new shared meanings emerges. The concept of the good-enough mother is embraced. As a mother once explained, "With a silent smile, I often remember what a truly un-intuitive mother I was, and yet felt assured it was ok."

The group-leader's recognition of a child's positive response to a mother's attuned and empathic interaction with her child affirms and validates the mother's behavior, and increases the likelihood of it re-occurring. These frequent supportive interventions highlight for each mother the importance to her child of her sensitive responsiveness.

Babies' and toddlers' demands for gratification of needs and wishes are insistent. During the first three years there are inherent challenges and stresses to mutually regulated developmental tasks such as weaning, impulse control, emotion regulation, etc. Additional stress for mothers includes sleep deprivation, interference with previously established patterns of eating, toileting, and sexual intimacy; disrupted work and leisure activities; intrusions and shifts in relationships. The group-leader's acknowledgement of these stresses makes them more tolerable.

Events such as the death of a loved one, illness, accidents, divorce, change of children's caregivers, work demands, and the birth of a sibling stress family life and may be difficult for young children. Extraordinary events like September 11th and the Covid pandemic stress parents and impact their young children. Addressing ways to help babies and toddlers to cope and recognizing indications of their resilience are part of the supportive group-process.

Support includes the acknowledgement of the painful feelings typical of the experience of mothering: for example, feelings of anxiety, boredom, loneliness, inadequacy, guilt, envy, and anger towards one's own child. It also includes recognizing aggressive and sexual fantasies, fears, and impulses when they arise. Acknowledging their ubiquity lessens the stigma that mothers attach to them.

*The mother of a 3-month-old told the group that every time she walked past a door holding her baby, she thought about the possibility of his head banging against the door frame. Another mother then reported that every time she closed the car door, she imagined that she had slammed it on her baby's hand. The following intervention highlighted the ubiquity of these frightening thoughts, their adaptive function, memories that might trigger them, and related feelings that intensify them, "These kinds of thoughts for mothers are frightening and typical for mothers with babies this age. In some ways they increase mothers' vigilance to protect their babies. Frightening thoughts of hurting your baby may be triggered by your own childhood memories of accidents. Your own accident may not be thought of in the moment, but the feelings may have been evoked. Angry feelings that mothers' typically have towards their babies can intensify their horror about these kinds of thoughts. These images and thoughts usually diminish as babies develop."*

Mothers' discoveries that others have similar thoughts about hurting their babies, the exploration of related childhood memories, and comments that include a reference to universalizing mothers' angry feelings towards their babies that can be horrifying are supportive. Identifying mothers' angry feelings towards their babies as the cause of these fears, though they might contribute to them, is secondary to supporting the mothers' wishes to protect their babies. On the other hand, if there is any concern about a mother's impulse to hurt her baby, a psychiatric referral or other action is needed.

Each mother has her own personal mothering style, aspects of which may be shared with others, but the essence of which is unique. Personal authenticity is an inherently valuable attribute and can be supported even when other changes may be desirable. In a mother's words, *"What a truly unnatural mother I was, very different from the other mothers, in many ways I was ridiculous. And while you saw that, you simultaneously made me feel, I'm ok."* Whatever the external behavior that is adopted by an adult or is required of a child, and however optimal it may be in the moment to be inauthentic, knowing one's own authentic feelings and thoughts is important.

The personal style of mothers with their babies and toddlers is evolving. Sometimes mothers read something, observe another mother, or hear something in a mothers' group and adopt it, but it does not feel quite authentic to themselves. *Group questions that address this theme include, when have you tried something you heard that did not feel authentic when you did it? When do you want your child to be polite rather than authentic? When are you inauthentic with your child? When are you angry, sad, or bored with your child and try to conceal it?"*

Sometimes a mother's envy of her child is triggered and creates conflict about giving to her child things she did not have when she was a child and still may not have. Mothers may be envious of emotional, relational, or economic things. Acknowledging mothers' envy can be supportive and promote self-reflection. For example, *during a group discussion about mothers' envy of their children, Jemma described her pleasure that Marco's father played with him, but that their playing together also triggered painful memories of her father playing with her twin brother and not with her. While talking about her childhood memories Jemma had an insight, "I just realized, that when my husband is playing with Marco, I often ask him to walk the dog."*

Mothering involves difficult decisions. Support can facilitate the decision-making process by enabling mothers to acknowledge and accept the painful consequences of certain decisions, or to recognize the unconscious conflicts and related childhood memories that may be underlying, without awareness, certain decisions, or indecision. Sometimes mothers are in conflict about what they think is best for their child and what is best for their own relationship with another mother, or with their husbands, or partners. Exploration of this conflict can be supportive. For example, *Lexington thought that a one-hour play date was optimal for 20-month-old Seth, but she did not want to appear rejecting of her friend even though after an hour the children's play always dissolved into physical fighting. Exploration of Lexington's conflict revealed its connection to childhood fights with her older sister, which were the price she paid for being able to play with her.*

When a mother is confused and disturbed by an interaction with her child, having a way to understand it can be supportive. *Deidra frequently said things to Mandie that she thought were mean, and she did not know why she kept doing it. The following intervention linked a childhood memory to current mother-child interactions, "From what you have told us about your mother, 'mean' is the way that you remember she spoke to you sometimes. It is as though you are talking to Mandie in your mother's voice. It may be a way to feel close to your mother as you separate because you are now Mandie's mother." Deidra's positive self-feelings were supported in that she was helped not to feel like a mean person herself, but rather wanting to feel close to her mother with whom she was also angry. Interpreting Deidra's wish to be close to her own mother but not to be like she described her, helped Deidra to talk to Mandie in the way that she wanted, not "mean."*

When a mother is self-critical about making comparisons between herself and other mothers or between her child and other children, and says, "I always compare them, I know I shouldn't," telling her the following can be supportive: "When there are two things in the same category: two apples, two children, or two ideas, we compare them. A mother's comparison of her child to others is a potentially valuable way for mothers to monitor their babies' and toddlers' development and intervene early when needed. Comparing yourself to other mothers is potentially a way to learn. What is disturbing sometimes about making comparisons is the underlying meanings of the comparisons, which often include painful feelings. Maybe we can understand more clearly the meaning to you of the specific comparison you are making."

The group-leader supports the mothers' hopes for their babies and toddlers in ways that also nurture the babies' development. For example: *Libby, the mother of 10-month-old Johnny, was eager for him to crawl. She placed him in the middle of the room and walked away as she said, "I know he can crawl; he even can pull himself up to stand. He just does not want to do it. He clings to me all the time. Maybe he's just lazy." Johnny remained still and looked down at the floor as his mother walked away. He did not reach for a toy or approach his mother. Libby's phrase, "He clings to me all the time" may have suggested her underlying conflict about Johnny separating. The following intervention supported the mother's goal and addressed her underlying conflict, "I wonder whether for Johnny to crawl he needs to lean on you, feel your strength, and borrow some of it for himself. As he crawls away from you, he will feel emotionally close to you." In response to this statement that highlighted Libby's strength in contrast to the weakness in the form of laziness that she had attributed to Johnny, and included that Johnny will remain emotionally close to her as he crawls away, Libby returned to Johnny and sat next to him on the floor. Johnny placed his hands on his mother's thigh, straightened his arms, and propped his torso up. He turned, crawled to the other side of the room, and then back to his mother.*

## 16  Guideline principles

*The intersubjective details of this mother-baby interaction were not observable. The mother-baby interactions that preceded Johnny propping himself up on his mother and crawling could not be seen. The intervention that included Libby had strength, Johnny could share some of her strength, and they would remain emotionally connected when he crawled away was effective because it referred to meanings of crawling of which the mother had been unaware.*

When typical problems arise and mothers seek an explanation of why their child has the problem, it may be supportive to reframe the question and implied self-accusation, *"We may not be able to know why your child has this problem, but we can work together to try to figure out what you can do to help."*

When group support takes the form of reassurance in efforts to alleviate one mother's anxiety, it may interfere with the exploration of concerns. Sometimes what mothers think is supportive to each other is a defensive strategy to cope with their own escalating anxiety that needs to be acknowledged.

*Colette told the group that 2-year-old Kenzie had been evaluated and her speech was delayed. The mothers jumped in quickly to reassure her. Colette persisted, "I'm worried because Kenzie has a slight hearing loss and might need tubes surgically implanted in her ears. Maybe she will need hearing aids." The mothers grasped for reassuring evidence that Kenzie would be ok, "My niece didn't talk until she was 2.5 and now she's on the debate team." The following interpretation addressed the anxiety that was triggered among the mothers, "Colette has raised a serious concern that she has. Colette's concern seems to trigger so much anxiety in everyone. It sounds like everyone is trying to reassure Colette, to feel better themselves. I'm not sure Colette feels reassured." Colette added, "When I was 10, I had a bad lisp and needed to see a speech therapist. I was so embarrassed, it was awful." The influence of Colette's childhood memory on her current concerns and interactions with Kenzie could now be explored and understood.*

Group mothers primarily support each other. At times they may feel competitive, angry, critical, envious, inadequate, guilty, superior, or inferior, but they remain fundamentally supportive to each other. When angry, critical, or dismissing interactions are triggered among the mothers, the group-leader needs to intervene and acknowledge or interpret what is occurring and facilitate a repair of the ruptured group support. For example, *when Daphne alienated herself from the group by dramatizing her neglectful attitudes towards 2-year-old Jolie, the following interpretation modulated the impact, "Daphne, I think you are unaware of how horrifying to other mothers some of the things you say are. Or maybe you want to shock them and frighten them the way you have been frightened, and the way you sometimes frighten Jolie."*

The support component of mother-baby-toddler groups is essential. It is fundamental to the establishment and maintenance of a working alliance between the group-leader and each mother and among the mothers. The usefulness of providing child development information, and exploring the underlying meanings of the children's behavior, and links between a mother's childhood memories and current mother-child interactions, rests on the positive working alliance. A valuable component of the alliance includes the group-leader's respect for the challenges that mothers face and their struggles to meet them. This collaborative relationship between the group-leader and the mothers is created and sustained by the support derived from feeling understood and the emergence of new shared meanings. Group support is essential to create the safety needed for mothers to openly explore connections between childhood memories and current mother-child interactions and to speak about painful, humiliating, and frightening feelings.

## *Group-leader support summary*

1. Identify babies' and toddlers' responsiveness to mothers' attunement and empathy
2. Acknowledge mother-child interactions that communicate mothers' delight in their children's agency and assertiveness
3. Acknowledge stresses that are inherent to mothering
4. Recognize life events that are stressful to babies and toddlers, and ways to mitigate the stress
5. Acknowledge mothers' typical feelings of anger, boredom, anxiety, guilt, and envy in response to their babies and toddlers
6. Recognize mothers' aggressive and sexual feelings evoked and impulses triggered towards their children
7. Identify the unrecognized meanings of mothers' indecision when faced with choices
8. Acknowledge mothers' hopes for their children and validate ways to achieve them that promote the children's development
9. Reframe mothers' self-blame and search for reasons why, into we can work together to find a solution
10. Expand comments and questions raised by a mother to include its general applicability to child development and mother-child interactions
11. Identify the links between mothers' childhood memories and mother-child interactions

## Child development information and group questions

The *MBTG Guide* child development information and group questions are categorized by age and psychodynamic theme in Chapters 4 through 7. There is an ongoing interweaving of questions and concerns raised by the mothers and the child development information and group questions introduced by the group-leader. Mothers' answers to the questions reflect what have been called working models or mental representations of self, her child, and the mother-child relationship.

The group-leader's response to a mother's question or comment is formulated to explore her concerns, and in addition to expand for group discussion the multiple meanings, complexity, and general applicability of the specific question or concern. This process promotes group participation and the exploration of a wide range of topics. This approach also highlights that most child development and mothering questions do not have simple answers and are shared by others. Group-leader responses that focus on related child development research can highlight the scientific importance and complexity of a mother's question.

When the mothers are discussing a topic exclusively in terms of adults, describing its application to babies and toddlers expands the theme and includes the immediacy of the feelings that have been aroused. For example, *during an emotional group discussion about the mothers appearing competent and confident to others when they themselves feel incompetent and insecure, the following broadened the discussion, "Babies and toddlers also may appear differently to others than they themselves feel. For example, toddlers may appear defiant or brave when they do something they have been told is dangerous. However, they may do it because they are afraid and want to do it successfully to reassure themselves. What are some examples when your child appeared on the surface to feel differently than you discovered?"* Maintaining attention to the children and how they fit into what is on the mothers' minds is an important role of the group-leader. In Alicia Lieberman's words, we *"Make Room for Baby."*

Validated child development information can enrich mothering capacities when it includes a developmental understanding of the thoughts, feelings, wishes, fears, and conflicts among them that motivate babies' and toddlers' behavior. When underlying meanings of behavior cannot be known, what is imagined by the mother influences mother-child interactions and therefore the development of her baby and toddler's mind. The child development information and group questions can expand mothers' imaginings in ways that promote development-facilitating mother-child interactions.

Central to the ways in which *MBTG Guide* child development information is formulated, and the group questions structured, are their references to mothers' related childhood memories. Group questions that include references to childhood memories can be inherently supportive even when they may also be disturbing. For example, *"Children adapt to their mothers. What about you will your child need to adapt to? What about you is your child adapting to now? What did you need to learn to adapt to your mother?"*

A mother's rejection of child development information can be explored and understood in terms of her memories, goals, and observations of her child. For example, *the following child development information was presented: different children and children at different ages react differently to seeing their parents naked. Tania insisted that she believed in family-nudity. She did not want her children raised in a "sexually up-tight home like her parents'." She wanted her children to be more sexually uninhibited than she was. The following group-question extended the discussion to focus on the children's reactions to parental nudity, "How are the children reacting when they see you and your husband naked?" Answers included, no reaction, trying to touch their parents' genitals and the parents' prohibitions, peeing on the floor, biting, 2-year-old Anthony holding his penis all the time, and other indications of over-stimulation. Focusing on the importance of the children's reactions and what their reactions mean, in addition to the mothers' childhood memories and goals, can guide parents' decisions, and make the developmental information more useful.*

The *MBTG Guide* psychodynamic themes that categorize the information and questions are relevant from birth to 3 years of age, and in some ways throughout life. There is enormous overlap among the theme categories. Mother-child interaction is the main theme. The other themes matter because of their impact on mother-child interactions. The breadth and depth of the mother-baby-toddler group endeavor matters because it influences mother-child interaction. The psychodynamic themes are summarized on page 22 and are discussed in Chapter 1.

The child development information and the group questions fluctuate between surface, easily accessible topics, for example play, to deeper more conflictual or high arousal topics, for example topics related to separation and loss. On the other hand, themes that are more surface and affectively neutral for one mother, may be high arousal for another.

What the group-leader chooses from among the questions and information, and in what order, is based on observations of a child, mother, or mother-child interaction. The observation may be a development-facilitating mother-child interaction or indicative of a problem. A group question is a way to address it. At the beginning of each group, if a mother has not initiated discussion, the group-leader initiates group discussion by presenting child development information as an introduction to raising a group question. Many of the questions may be useful to raise at multiple ages, multiple times.

While mother-baby-toddler groups are like other groups in many ways, they are significantly different in terms of phase of life and the compelling impact of the developing mother-child bond. Emerging group problems and transitions are addressed by the exploration during groups of the specific situation and related childhood and teenage memories of friendships and other group experiences, including family. For example, *through tears Stella criticized the play-leader for paying more attention to all the other children compared to her son, Logan. When asked why she thought this was happening she answered, "I don't know, but that's the way it was in my family. My sister always got more attention than I did. She had cerebral palsy, so she needed more attention, but still. It also happened when I was in school. The teachers paid more attention to everyone else." The following intervention linked her childhood memories to her current feelings, "It sounds like your painful childhood feelings are being triggered now with Logan."*

The psychodynamic approach, group-process, and group-leader interventions described throughout the *MBTG Guide* mitigate problems frequently encountered in groups and provide an approach for addressing them if they begin to arise. Absences, a new member joins, confidentiality is breached, conflict among the mothers, hitting or biting among the children, a group member does not talk, talks too much, or is a self-designated co-leader are potential group disruption triggers that need to be addressed.

**To summarize:** During mother-baby-toddler groups, there is an ongoing intermingling of mothers' observations, questions, and concerns; the child development information and group questions raised by the group-leader; and the exploration of each mother's childhood memories, their meanings, and their impact on mother-child interaction. Each of these elements contributes to the group-process. Synergies between these elements create the power of psychodynamic mother-baby-toddler groups to achieve group goals. Group goals are summarized below and the Group-process that is initiated by the group-leader is summarized below.

### Mother-baby-toddler group goals summary

1. Mothers are supported
2. Mothers' knowledge of early child development is increased
3. Mothers' understanding of the underlying meanings of their own and of their children's behavior is increased
4. Mothers acquire insight – new shared meanings, about the connections between their childhood memories and their mother-child interactions
5. Empathic, attuned mother-child interactions are increased
6. The children's development and security of attachment and the mothers' pleasure, satisfaction, and well-being are promoted
7. Emerging difficulties are resolved

### Mother-baby-toddler group-process initiated by the group-leader summary

1. Identify the challenges and pleasures of raising children birth to 3 years
2. Identify mother-child interactions that promote security of attachment and development
3. Identify mother-child interactions that indicate each mother's ability to understand her child and to respond empathically
4. Provide child development information
5. Raise generalized questions for group discussion based on phase of development, a comment or question raised by one mother, an observed attuned mother-child interaction, or a difficulty of one mother or child
6. Normalize mothers' phase of life anxieties, self-criticisms, and the impact of childhood memories on mother-child interactions
7. Explore, clarify, and interpret unrecognized and unacknowledged conflicts, wishes, fears, and underlying meanings of an individual child's or mother's behavior

## Guideline principles summary

1. During the first three years of motherhood, mothers are motivated to understand more about themselves and their children
2. Behavior can be understood in terms of its conscious and unconscious meanings, its developmental context for babies and toddlers, and phase of life context for mothers
3. Play, alone and with others, is an essential way in which babies and toddlers learn about themselves, others, and the world around them, and reveals their inner life
4. Mothers' abilities to care for their babies and toddlers are enhanced when the essential nature of their task is recognized and acknowledged by others
5. Mother-child attachments are powerful relationship dynamics
6. Reflecting on one's own thoughts and feelings, and those of others, are important aspects of mental life
7. Mother-child proximity during groups facilitates mothers' self-reflection leading to insight
8. Mothers' understanding of their childhood memories and their influence on attributions to and interactions with their babies and toddlers enable them to resolve emerging difficulties
9. The group-process promotes the efficacy of interventions with each mother-child dyad
10. Explore a specific memory related to a generalized memory reported by a mother
11. Explore and identify connections between an individual mother's childhood memory and her attributions to her child and current mother-child interactions

# Chapter 1

# Psychodynamic themes

Chapter 1 discusses the 15 psychodynamic themes that are fundamental to the approach of the *MBTG Guide*. The themes are used to organize the child development information and group questions presented in Chapters 4 through 7. Frequent mother-child interactions that arise during groups and ways to think about them are discussed. Familiarity with the themes and the examples are useful to implement the guidelines.

Psychodynamic themes are used to organize the *MBTG Guide* child development information and group questions. The themes will be familiar; their application to understanding and promoting the mother-baby-toddler group-process may be new and will be highlighted. While the psychodynamic themes overlap and merge, one theme will be central to a child development idea or group question. These themes are also at the back of the group-leader's mind while listening to the mothers and watching the children. The 15 themes incorporate the psychodynamics of everyday life for mothers, babies, and toddlers.

The psychodynamic themes are listed below. The following discussion and examples of each theme illustrate group-leader interventions. The *MBTG Guide* definition of psychodynamic is: the mental processes underlying behavior and their impact on behavior. Included are conscious and unconscious thoughts, feelings, memories, intentions, fantasies, and wishes, and the conflicts among them.

## Psychodynamic theme summary

1. Mother-child interaction
2. Mother-child attachment
3. Mother-child communication
4. Mothers' childhood memories
5. Separation
6. Play

7. Aggression
8. Body awareness
9. Children's interactions with other children
10. Emotion regulation
11. Gender
12. Underlying meanings of behavior
13. Internal conflict
14. Mother-child differences
15. Learning

**To repeat for emphasis** – Mother-child interaction is the main psychodynamic theme. The other themes matter because of their impact on mother-child interactions. The breadth and depth of the mother-baby-toddler group endeavor matters because it influences mother-child interaction.

## Psychodynamic themes

### *Mother-child interaction*

Mother-baby and mother-toddler interactions are intersubjective, physical, verbal, and non-verbal. They have underlying psychodynamics: memories, thoughts, feelings, intentions, and wishes. Interactions are motivated, have conscious and unconscious meanings, and occur on a spectrum of feelings of connectedness. An important aspect of mother-child interactions is the mother's attachment to her child, and a main feature is the influence of interactions on the nature of the child's developing mind, including security of attachment and sense of self.

Mother-baby and mother-toddler interactions lead to expectancies. Babies and toddlers make mental predictions based on their experience, and the expectancies they create influence their future experience. Expecting safety, shared pleasure, and gratification promotes experiencing it. For example, *the baby cries, hears Mommy's voice, "I'm coming," baby stops crying, Mommy arrives. The satisfied expectation intensifies the pleasure of reunion with Mommy.* Satisfied expectancies increase the security that comes with knowing and promote adaptation. Another version of this is toddlers' pleasure in repeatedly being read the same book. What comes next is expected.

Mother-child interactions reflect aspects of the mother's mental representations or internal working models of self, self-as-mother, and the mother-child relationship. They reflect the mother's mental representations of attachment. They also reflect the mother's mental representations of her child. Mother-child interactions influence the child's evolving mental representations of self, mother, and their relationship. *Related group questions at all ages are: What would be your child's definition of a mother? What will become your child's self-description?* These questions invite mothers to think about her child's developing mental representations related to their interactions.

Mother-child interactions that support a child's agency, autonomy, control, and assertiveness are identified during groups. In other words, interactions that contribute to the development of these traits in the babies and toddlers and to these traits as part of their developing sense of self are identified by the group-leader. For example, *"I noticed you looked delighted and praised Jessie for being able to take her own shoes and socks off, even though you wanted her to keep them on, which helped her easily accept you putting them back on because she felt proud of herself and competent. She also knew that you were proud of her."*

Intersubjective, joint focus of attention interactions initiated by a baby pointing are powerful mother-child interactions that are endlessly repeated. For example: *the baby points to the light. Mommy says some version of, "Yes, I see the light." Both mother and baby know that they are both looking at the same thing. In addition, they both know that the other knows, that they both know.* How do they know this with such certainty? This kind of intersubjective self-with-other experience will continue throughout life and will include the certainty of being understood. So much is happening emotionally, mentally, and interpersonally in this brief interaction triggered by the baby pointing.

Mother-baby and mother-toddler narrative co-construction of a memory is a shared symbolic pointing to a past event and is another version of joint focus of attention. It is a joint focus of attention to a mental act: remembering. Mothers, babies, and toddlers co-constructing shared memory narratives, though their contributions are different at different ages, can begin a process to help even very young children to modulate painful feelings, and to mentally organize elements of an event and their experience of it. For example, *"The lion roared so loud, you got scared. How loud did the lion roar?"* 1-year-old Piper roared, *"Grrrr."*

Intersubjective joint focus of attention, social referencing, and feelings of emotional connectedness can also occur during limit-setting and support the child's developing security of attachment and positive sense of self when confronted with mother's disapproval. When babies crawl towards a potted plant and stop, get Mommy's attention, smile, and then accelerate towards the plant, they are signaling their intention to touch the plant and scoop the dirt out of the pot. It is a kind of pointing to a future event, without the finger gesture. This complex, nuanced mother-baby intersubjective interaction includes: the baby's memory of the limit, the non-verbal signal to Mommy of an intention, the expectation of being stopped, the conflict between doing what will please Mommy and the wish to please oneself knowing it will displease Mommy, and the motivation to assert autonomy by touching the plant. It is an interpersonal creative compromise between conflicting wishes and an amalgamation of a multitude of thoughts and feelings. Once the baby gets Mommy's attention, the baby quickly moves towards the plant. These are subtle back and forth interactions between mother and baby that reflect a merging of external behavior, internal mental processes, and mother-baby communications.

When the complexities of a mother-baby interaction are understood this way, possibilities of responding can expand beyond external behavior to include aspects of the baby's inner experience, *"I see you remember the plant and the dirt are not for touching. I know you want to touch them. I'm going to help you to stop yourself."* Babies' complex thinking and internal conflict about pleasing themselves, asserting their autonomy, pleasing Mommy, and learning the limit can be processed together.

After numerous repetitions of this kind of mother-child interaction about behavior and its meaning, while maintaining feelings of self-worth, babies can internalize the limit, make it their own, and stop themselves. In time the impulse to touch the plant will seem to have evaporated. This process is different from obedience. In obedience, behavior is controlled primarily to avoid a consequence, for example time-out, or Mommy's anger and baby's reactive fear. Most early childhood learning that relates to behavior is also about developing inner mental structures that support behavioral learning. Learning the behavior in the context of mothers' positive regard and support not only reinforces learning the behavior, but also adequately maintains the child's developing positive sense of self in the context of behavioral disapproval. Positive regard in the context of behavioral disapproval promotes frustration tolerance, impulse control, value systems of right and wrong, the ability to tolerate ambivalence, and the capacity for empathy. These mental processes contribute to the ability to tolerate the inherent, most powerful consequence: the mother's disapproval which becomes the baby's self-disapproval. These inner mental processes are the pillars of behavior.

Mother-toddler shared wish fulfilling fantasies can provide a substitute for actual fulfillment, *"It might be great to have all the cookies in the world!"* Sometimes adding a touch of reality pleasure is useful, *"Of course, we want grandma to have some of the cookies so she can give them to us!"* Children catch on quickly to the power and pleasure of wishful thinking. *When Jimmy was asked, "If you could make one wish, what would it be?" Jimmy answered, "I would wish for one million wishes." Some wishes need to be renounced, "I understand right now you want to marry me, but you are my son and will always be, even when you grow up."*

Sometimes in addition to changing their children's behavior, mothers want to change the thoughts and feelings that motivate the behavior. Differentiating between their children's behavior that they want to change and their children's thoughts and feelings that they want to change is useful. It is easier to change behavior when feelings are acknowledged and accepted, and thoughts are processed. For example, *"I know you want more cookies, tomorrow you can have more. No more cookies now."*

As in all love relationships, mother-child ongoing pleasurable interactions have ruptures that require repair. With babies the ruptures can be brief and easily repaired. When a baby grabs Mommy's eyeglasses and Mommy takes them back, the baby may cry but when a substitute is offered the baby's smile returns. The baby's attention has shifted. Being able to shift attention lays a foundation for frustration tolerance which includes a delay of gratification or acceptance of a substitute gratification. Helping to shift a baby's attention is a different notion than distracting a baby. The idea of shifting attention is often misunderstood as distracting or confusing the baby, or in the extreme, "wipe out the memory" of what the baby wants, or sometimes to convince the baby that the thing has disappeared. These distinctions in the mother's mind between shifting her baby's attention and distracting or confusing her baby may be useful.

As children get older, the ruptures can be more intense and take longer to repair. A 2-year-old's kicking and screaming protests can last 20 minutes or longer and may have a residual impact on the mother's responsiveness to her child. For example, *Skyler described what happened when she prevented her 22-month-old son from running into the street, "Peter got so angry. He was hitting me, so I held his hands and then he bit me. I was so angry, I yelled at him and pushed him away. He started to cry and then wanted me to hold him. I was not ready; I was still so angry. I didn't even want to talk to him." At this moment Skyler remembered that whenever her mother was angry at her when she was a little girl, her mother always gave her the "silent treatment." The link between her memory about her mother's "silent treatment" and her interaction with Peter was easily recognizable to her; it had already come to the front of her mind as she spoke the words, "I didn't even want to talk to him." Skyler also noted that she sometimes gives the "silent treatment" to her husband, and it enrages him.*

*The idea that children sometimes learn the "silent treatment" from their own mothers helped to temper Skyler's rage at Peter and helped her to modify her interactions with her husband. The idea that children learn things like the "silent treatment" from their parents, even things that had made them feel rejected and angry, motivated her to stop doing it; she did not want to do it to Peter or teach it to him. It also helped her to feel that it was something she had learned, rather than an inherent part of herself. In addition, Skyler became curious about how her mother had learned it. Skyler's expectations of rupture and repair cycles with Peter, without the "silent treatment," helped the repairs between them to go more smoothly. Painful childhood memories of the "silent treatment" from parents and siblings were described by the other mothers. Group support deepened.*

Mother-child teaching-learning interactions by imitation and identification are occurring all the time, often without awareness. Another example: *32-month-old Troy, with a serious expression, began to repeatedly bend his arm at the elbow, fold it across his body, and look at his wrist. His mother was curious and somewhat concerned because Troy did it so often it started to look as though he had developed a tic. She inquired, "Troy, what are you doing?" Troy replied, "I don't know, but you do it all the time." Troy's mother realized that he had been carefully observing her look at her watch and was doing what he had seen her do.*

## Mother-child attachment

Mother-child attachment is at the center of a baby and toddler's inner world. Their attachment relationship contributes to the mother's capacity for empathic sensitivity to her child and her own sense of well-being. A child's feelings of safety, a mother's responsiveness when feelings of safety are threatened, and experiences of being delightfully enjoyed, understood, and empathically responded to, promote the child's security of attachment and positive sense of self.

Much behavior of toddlers can be understood in terms of attachment needs and autonomy strivings that support each other and the tensions between them.

*Paco's delight when he learns to jump escalates when his mother shines with pride and pleasure as she watches him. Hazel's sense of power and self-satisfaction is intensified as she whacks the ball on the banging toy and her mother squeals with excitement and approval. In contrast, in moments when attachment needs and autonomy strivings clash, the following can happen. Mateo was 18-months and desperately wanted to tie his own shoes all by himself, just like his big sister. He was unable, though he persisted gallantly. In a rush to meet friends at the park, his mother gently tried to offer some assistance. Angry and asserting his autonomy, Mateo smacked her in the face. Startled and angry, his mother yelled at him. Mateo did not want to hurt his mother, he loved her. Her disapproval and the threat of losing her love was terrifying. Mateo started to cling to her and cry; his attachment needs felt threatened. Perhaps he also felt some remorse.*

During groups, everyday mother-baby-toddler attachment interaction details are magnified. The group-leader drawing attention to them can increase exploration. For example, *Georgina had described Ginger's explosive and at times unexplained vomiting, but we had yet to understand more about it. During groups, Georgina and Ginger's interactions always appeared gentle and attuned. When Ginger was 16-months, Georgina decided to let her cry herself to sleep and as the group was ending mentioned, "She frequently vomits while crying." The following week, as they were entering the mother-toddler room, seeking a secure base, Ginger slightly and fleetingly reached up to hold her mother's hand. Georgina did not respond. Describing the mother-child interaction that had occurred opened exploration: "It looked like Ginger gave a very weak signal to you when she wanted to hold your hand to feel safe walking into a loud, crowded room." Georgina responded, "She vomits all the time, all of a sudden, out of nowhere." Georgina sounded angry and her response suggested that she was aware of Ginger's attempt to hold her hand but did not want to. The following intervention addressed Georgina's implicit conflict about responding: "Whether Ginger's signals are weak or strong, and whether you decide to give her what she wants or not to, you can let her know that you understand what she wants. Feeling understood by you may help her, especially when she does not get what she wants." Georgina responded, "She needs to learn, she can't have everything she wants."*

*Georgina's reaction to Ginger's secure base attachment behavior when she reached up to hold her mother's hand was related to painful memories of her own emotional neglect and her wish to teach her daughter she cannot have everything she wants. We identified the multitude of ways in which children can learn they cannot have everything they want and simultaneously can feel safe and secure. Georgina began to recognize and acknowledge Ginger's attachment behavior. For example, "I know you want to hold my hand now, it's so loud, but I am going to help you walk in all by yourself." Over the next several weeks, Ginger's unexplained explosive vomiting diminished and then stopped, although she maintained a low threshold for vomiting.*

Many of the developmental and mothering difficulties illustrated in the *MBTG Guide* describe mother-child attachment problems. Some triggered by mothers' unresolved mourning, reactivated childhood terror, the result of maternal depression, and thoughts and feelings rooted in childhood memories.

## *Mother-child communication*

Babies express their feelings of pleasure and distress. When mothers respond, their expressions develop into communications. Toddlers begin to communicate ideas, wishes, and intentions. Mothers' communications to their babies and toddlers are explicit, implicit, verbal, non-verbal, physical, emotional, and intersubjective. Contradictions in mother's communications are explored and underlying psychic conflicts are revealed. The complexity of mother-child communications and children's adaptation to communication contradictions are talked about during groups.

A frequent communication contradiction that may reflect mothers' conflicts about setting limits occurs when mothers prohibit children from doing something and then tell their children, "If you do it again…" For example, *in a lively group discussion about setting limits, Cassie talked about her frustration with Jud, "I told Jud, there is no drawing on the table. If you draw on the table one more time, I will take the crayons away, and just as I expected, he did it again."* Some version of this mother-child communication is reported frequently and may be related to mothers' conflicts about setting the limit.

The following developmental information and group-leader questions explore mothers' communication contradictions and underlying conflicts: *"When you do not want your child to do something, let's think about why a plan is made for what will happen when your child does do it. Does planning for it, rather than preventing it, increase the likelihood that your child will do it again? Babies and toddlers often need help to stop themselves. For example, some version of the following may be a clearer communication of your expectation. While taking the milk away, 'I am not going to let you spill your milk. I will help you to stop yourself. You can have the milk back when you want to drink it.'"*

Sometimes mothers will say in response to comments like this, further revealing their conflict about setting the limit, *"It would not be fair if I did not tell her what will happen if she does it again."* Additional exploration and the incorporation of childhood memories includes: *"Maybe you are not sure about the limit. Maybe you think the limit itself is unfair. Sometimes when mothers are setting limits, they are reminded of limits they thought were unfair when they were little girls. Or it seemed unfair that their parents had more power than they did. Now, having more power than your child may seem unfair. Of course, having more power than the children, if not abused, enables us to care for them. Sometimes mothers feel it is unfair that they get to sleep with their husband or partner and the children sleep alone, or they get to drink wine and the children don't. What are some other limits that seem unfair? How do they relate to your childhood?"* For some mothers, memories of their own mothers' permissiveness are idealized and create limit-setting conflicts. For others, memories of harsh limits are triggered.

In addition to limit-setting communications to children, the mothers' own behavior in response to limits imposed on adults, for example speed limits, broadens the discussion, increases empathy, and clarifies communications. For example, *in the middle of a group discussion about limits for adults, Meri said, "I have tried to set a limit for my husband for years. I always tell him not to eat food off my plate. It's disgusting."* Meri then described how her mother and father always eat off each-other's plates, *"It's like they are having sex at the table right in front of everybody."* Connecting this new meaning that Meri blurted out to her reaction to her husband eating off her plate prompted Meri's realization that her angry disgust reaction to her husband was an expression of her feelings of disgust towards her parents. Meri's intense reaction to her husband abated and she began to share food with her 15-month-old daughter whom several weeks before she had described as a *"picky eater"* who also liked to eat off her plate. Her daughter's repertoire of liked foods expanded, and meal-time pleasure for all increased. In addition, Meri discovered new sexual pleasures with her husband.

For some mothers, apologizing to their children is a frequent communication and drawing attention to it can be useful. *Viviana said to Griffin as she restrained him, "I'm sorry, but you cannot write on the wall."* The following intervention facilitated exploration: *"I noticed that you apologized to Griffin for telling him that he cannot write on the wall and for stopping him."* Viviana explained, *"My mother never apologizes for anything. When I was 12 years old, she cut my hair so short. I hated it, she said it would just be a trim, and she never apologized for that or for anything."* Exploration of the connection between Viviana's memory and her interaction with Griffin followed, *"I wonder how that memory influences you to apologize to Griffin."* Viviana responded, *"I always apologize for everything; even when it's not my fault. I know I'm doing the right thing stopping Griffin."* The following intervention expanded the connection between Viviana's memories of her mother and apologies to Griffin, *"It sounds like you are making up for all the apologies that were not made to you and all the apologies you may think you owe."* Many examples of mothers' gratuitous apologies followed. Group discussion extended to children's apologies as reflections of remorse or social decorum, and the useful distinctions between them.

For some mothers, the harsh communications they remember are repeated with their children. For example, *during a group discussion about teaching children to use the potty, Ryleigh described that her almost 3-year-old daughter Eloise was wetting her "beautiful bed" every night, "I'm so angry at her, I yell at her, but it doesn't help. I don't want to yell at her. I feel like punishing her, but I don't want to do that either. I don't know what to do." In association to what she had just said, Ryleigh shamefully confessed, "When I was 11 years old, I was visiting my cousin who lived on a farm. She had a beautiful bed with a pink satin cover and white organza canopy. It was the most beautiful bed that I had ever seen. There was a gasoline pump on the property that the children were not allowed to touch. I filled a watering can with the gasoline and poured it on my cousin's bed. It was a filthy mess. The punishment was severe." Ryleigh described the details of being locked in a shed, alone all night. Linking her memory of her mother's anger, the harshness of the punishment, and her terror, to her current angry yelling at Eloise promoted new shared meanings, "It seems as though fragments of your memory; the anger, fear, shame, and helplessness are being repeated with Eloise. You are angry, Eloise is frightened, and you both feel helpless and ashamed. There is no gasoline, no pink satin bed cover, and no shed. There are sheets wet with urine. Eloise's 'beautiful bed' is a mess."*

*This was the beginning of the exploration of Ryleigh's communications to Eloise that revealed aspects of her identification with memories of her mother's punitive anger. The intensity of Ryleigh's childhood envy and her own angry mess that had been displaced towards Eloise reverted to her* childhood memory. *Ryleigh's harshness in response to wet sheets lessened, she helped Eloise get to the potty in the middle of the night, and in a short while Eloise slept through the night and her bed stayed dry.*

Learning to talk includes communicating thoughts, feelings, wishes, and intentions, and being understood. Often mothers are the only ones who understand their toddlers' emerging language. When mothers are uncertain about the meaning of their babies' or toddlers' utterance, they rely on the context to attribute meaning. The approximation of a word, in combination with the mother's enunciation of the word and attribution of meaning to it, create a new word for the baby. In this way, the language acquisition process is about communication between mother and baby; it is an interpersonal process about feeling understood and meaning making.

In general, children use the words that their mothers use. In every family, with great delight, there are some words, maybe one maybe three, sometimes more, that the family uses that were coined by the baby. For example, pisketti for spaghetti.

Children gradually learn the power of words, and in many ways words are powerful. However, when feelings are intense or overwhelming, words do not come easily to toddlers, and do not satisfy. The refrain "use your words" is heard from adults for several years with young children. Sometimes words are not enough to convey the desired meaning even for adults, "I'm speechless" is also often heard.

## Mothers' childhood memories

During the first three years of motherhood, both explicit declarative and implicit procedural childhood memories are triggered by mother-child interactions. Explicit memories include associated wishes, conflicts, and feelings about events. They have narrative truth, not necessarily historical truth. They are crafted portrayals of experience that illuminate personal meanings. For example, when adult siblings have different memories of the same childhood event. The aim of explicit memories is mental processing and representation organization of lived experience, adaptation, internal conflict resolution, and a positive sense-of-self. Implicit memories include emotions, bodily sensations, learned body procedures like riding a bike, and interpersonal ways of being with another that are connected to past relationships or events that are re-experienced or re-lived. Both kinds of memories are triggered and without awareness may be enacted during mother-baby and mother-toddler interactions.

The feeling parts of mothers' activated childhood memories are intensified during mother-child interactions. Memories arouse mothers' passionate love and tenderness. They also evoke heightened anger, fear, and helplessness. For the mother, the present experience with her baby or toddler obscures the past. During the intensity of the present moment, reliving the past may replace remembering. When a memory is being repeated in a mother-child interaction – it's "pastness" fades. When mothers acquire insight about the influence of their childhood memories on current mother-child interactions, difficulties can be resolved.

Mothers' emerging concerns about "spoiling" their babies and toddlers may be related to their own childhood memories. Concerns may be focused on showing affection, children having their own way, or the acquisition of things. The terms "spoiling" and "spoiled child" are frequently used and have variable meanings. The traits that adults do not like in children that fall under the rubric of "spoiled" and prompt the attribution are a sense of entitlement, selfishness, and unrelenting demands. These traits may be acquired from a variety of experiences. They are often viewed as the result of overindulgence but may also be acquired by experiences of deprivation.

A mother's concerns about "spoiling" her 6-month-old baby, and underlying conflicts about responding to her baby's cries were activated in the following example. *Looking sad and far away Zina wondered, "When I'm in a different room and Callie cries, I am not sure I should go to her. I don't want to spoil her." Exploration of the meaning of her concern started with, "Why do you think she is crying?" Zina's answer was quick and sounded reminiscent, "I don't know, but I feel like she is calling me a bad mother." An interpretation of a link to childhood memories promoted Zina's self-reflection, "Maybe you are remembering your mommy calling you a bad little girl." Through tears Zina said, "I guess Callie needs me." Further exploration revealed Zina's memories of her own mother being a "bad mother."*

A mother's conflicts about gratifying her baby or toddler that are motivated by envy may contribute to fears of "spoiling." Concerns about "spoiling" are sometimes a rationalization for depriving a child. Mothers' childhood memories of unmet emotional needs can influence ideas about children being "spoiled" by having things.

*Miranda felt that she was never valued or approved of by her mother, "I don't think my mother ever really liked me. We are very different." Miranda worried that her daughter would be "spoiled" if she bought her the doll she wanted for Christmas, her favorite ice cream, or the pet she longed for. The issue was not whether Miranda bought these items or not, the issue was what was motivating her decision: fear of "spoiling." Linking Miranda's painful yearnings related to her own unmet emotional needs, with her concerns about "spoiling" her daughter by buying things, lessened her concerns about "spoiling" and enabled her to make decisions about ice cream, a family pet, and Christmas gifts based on other criteria.*

Babies and toddlers have many needs and increasing wishes. When a toddler has a limited ability to tolerate the inevitable frustration of wishes, and a mother has a limited ability to tolerate her child's distress when frustrated, excessive gratification of the child's wishes can occur. The child can then become frightened by an amount of power that causes Mommy's submission, as well as the mother's anger that is triggered by her own compliance. Differentiating between a child's needs and a child's wishes, and identifying a mother's related childhood memories that make it hard for her to say no and tolerate her child's distress, can help to resolve this cycling difficult dynamic.

Sometimes a new meaning of a long-standing, recurring memory is triggered. *During an excited group discussion about parents' sex lives when they have young children, Claudia recounted a fanciful childhood memory, "When I was about 8 years old, I was alone in the kitchen and there was a knock on the screen door. The Easter Bunny was right there. He was standing on two legs, straight up, much taller than I was, holding a basket with two brightly colored eggs in a nest of brown grass. I know this sounds impossible, but my memory is clear, it feels like it really happened. I ran upstairs to my parents who were still in bed and told them about this amazing thing that I saw."*

*The women in the group offered possible rational explanations, "A grown-up may have been dressed in a bunny costume." "It could have been a toy bunny." Claudia insisted, "It was real, it was alive, I know it sounds impossible, but the memory feels real." Claudia had repeated this memory to others many times and was always told, "It never happened." Being told it never happened and believing herself that it sounded unrealistic had never changed her feelings about the memory being real. Claudia's memory had narrative truth, not historical truth.*

*Our lively group discussion continued about whether parents lock the bedroom door when they have sex, have sex when sharing a room with their children, or when the children are sleeping in their bed with them. Bright-eyed and animated, Claudia chimed in, "This never occurred to me before. My parents always told me that I once walked in on them when they were having sex, but I never remembered it. Maybe the unrealistic Easter Bunny was my way of remembering the unimaginable, incomprehensible sight of my parents having sex."*

The excitement Claudia felt during the group discussion had triggered her recurring Easter Bunny memory. Her experience being a mother with young children had created a different context for the emergence of the new meaning that she attributed to her memory: seeing her parents having sex. Specific images in Claudia's memory supported her sexual interpretation: two brightly colored eggs, the brown grass, her parents in bed, and the size of the bunny "standing straight up" that placed his genitals at Claudia's eye level. The details of Claudia's memory were consistent with her new sexual interpretation.

Claudia's fanciful memory of an Easter Bunny had seemed real to her for many years, was frequently called to mind, and was accompanied by a detailed memory narrative. The new meaning Claudia attributed to her memory, seeing her parents having sex, was being enacted when she and her husband were having sex and their bedroom door was left open to their children. After Claudia attributed the new meaning to her memory, she and her husband began to close their bedroom door.

A mother's emerging fear may be a reactivated memory and can herald renewed working through. *Kari joined a mother-baby group with her twins Carson and Cassandra who were 10-months. As they approached 1-year, Kari developed a fear that they would be kidnapped. When she saw a car drive slowly past their house, she felt convinced of the danger; although she also believed it probably was not true. When the children were in the garden and Kari saw the car drive past her house several times, she became panicky.*

*Kari had been adopted when she was a newborn and grew-up being frequently told that her adoption did not become final until she was 1-year, the same age her twins would soon be. In other words, Kari's memory was also about her mother's anxiety that her baby, Kari, might be taken away and be reunited with her biological mother. Embedded in Kari's memory was also the idea that her adoptive mother had taken another woman's baby. These were elements of Kari's current fear of which she was unaware.*

*Kari believed, "Being adopted was never an issue for me. I have the best parents." When asked to tell us more about the car that drove past her house, she said, "A woman is driving." When asked who she thought the woman might be, she spontaneously blurted out, "Maybe it's my biological mother." Kari's idea, and sarcastic attempt to make a joke, began our exploration of her rivalry with both her biological mother and adoptive mother. Kari had been able to achieve having biological children, something that her adoptive mother had not, and she was able to achieve something her biological mother had not, to keep her babies. Kari's fears about kidnapping were rooted in both the intergenerational anxiety about the threat of a baby being taken from a mother and her own unacceptable feelings of pride and pleasure in having given birth and keeping her babies, that she viewed as too aggressively competitive with both her biological and adoptive mothers. Kari's fantasy that her biological mother was driving the car represented both Kari's fears of retaliation for her aggressive victories and a repair of disavowed feelings of loss by a reunion with her biological mother. Kari's kidnapping anxiety subsided with these new shared meanings.*

## Separation

Reactions to separation start when a baby develops an attachment and continue throughout life. Mothers' memories about separation and loss have information about the meanings of their current separations from their own children, and their children's reactions. Mothers whose own mothers have died are vulnerable to revived or intensified grief reactions that may have an impact on current mother-baby and mother-toddler interactions. Vignettes describing mothers' revived grief reactions are discussed in Chapter 4.

Children use play to adapt to separation. For example, *after mastering peek-a-boo, 10-month-old Harper created a new game. She repeatedly threw a small ball that fit perfectly in her hand across the floor and scooted to the other side of the room to retrieve it. If it rolled under the sofa, it was particularly pleasurable. Harper's game reinforced her learning that the ball existed even when she could not see it. It also gave control to Harper of separating from the ball and reuniting with it, unlike when separated from her mother which she could not control. Original play created by a child to master a stressful event has enormous learning power. This play was repeated daily for several weeks.*

Another version of this kind of play is children hiding things between sofa cushions or keeping a treasured item in a pocket that can be revealed when the impulse is triggered. Sometimes children hide their most treasured toy, creating an intense grief and panic reaction until it is found: the repetition of which can be painful but also have a happy ending – reunion. Another form of separation play is children hiding themselves, sometimes until their mothers are screaming in desperation to find them, which is reminiscent of children screaming for their mothers when separated. Games of peek-a-boo, tag, and hide and seek confirm and re-confirm that separations are followed by reunions. Mothers' descriptions of their children's play and discussion of the underlying meanings are an important part of the group-process and lessens mothers' distress that some of their children's play causes.

When mothers have experienced traumatic separations or loss, they may have difficulty recognizing, acknowledging, or tolerating their children's or their own feelings about separation. A mother sneaking out of the house without saying good-bye may be her attempt to avoid witnessing her child's painful feelings about separation or to avoid re-experiencing her own. Sneaking into the house may be another kind of enactment of the past. When mothers sneak out of the house without saying good-bye they prevent the child from adaptation to the imminent separation. In addition, the children not knowing when Mommy is going to leave can promote anxious hypervigilance. Mothers sneaking into the apartment can create uncertainty about what is known, I hear Mommy in her room, but Daddy says she is not here. What is real?

A mother's core theme, conflict between work and family life, can have an impact on separations and reunions with her child. Daria's devaluation of her mother as a woman and idealization of her as a mother intensified her conflict. *Daria had a full-time, demanding job with some flexibility in terms of hours. When Declan was 16-months, Daria enrolled him in four play activities to attend with his nanny. Each day, Daria left work, battled NYC traffic, gobbled down her lunch on the way to meet the nanny and Declan at music, story time, baby massage, or gym, and in addition two-times-a-week at the playground. Daria was frazzled, and separations after these joyful 40-minute reunions were becoming increasingly difficult for Declan. Identifying and linking childhood memories with Daria's simultaneous idealization and devaluation of her own mother, her current conflicts about family life and work, and the stress she had created with separations from and reunions with Declan, enabled her to find better solutions to her conflicts.*

A frequent reunion experience of mothers with babies is, *"I walked into the apartment after being away for the weekend and Axl looked totally confused. He did not recognize me."* Another explanation is, during mother-baby separations babies are imagining Mommy, envisioning her. The image of Mommy they imagine is a composite of Mommy that is based on their many experiences with her. When babies are reunited with their mothers after a separation, they are trying to reconcile their mental image of Mommy with the actual Mommy in the moment with whom they are reunited.

Reunions may also be related to childhood memories. *Peggy described that Bonnie, 20-months, did not want to play with Daddy when he came home from work. She explained, "Bonnie and I are happy playing in her room, and my husband comes in. He has not seen her all day and wants to play with her. I think the transition is hard for Bonnie." When asked about establishing a reunion routine that might make the transition easier and more joyful for them all, Peggy asked, "What might that be? I have no idea. My mother was always so angry that my father was working all the time. I remember one night he came home so late she would not let me play with him." Interpreting a connection between her memory, her current interactions with her husband, and her inability to envision a happy reunion, paved the way for advice, "It sounds like your memories of your mother's anger at your father are awakened when your husband comes home from work and make it difficult to imagine a happy reunion. A transition activity when you hear your husband at the front door could be, 'Daddy's home! Let's run to the door and say hi.'"*

Another aspect of mother-baby separation is the discovery and confirmation of separateness of minds. For example, *it's story time and the baby points to the bookcase and indicates a book choice. Mommy gets the book, and the baby rejects it and points again. Mommy gets the book she believes the baby is pointing at now, and the baby rejects this book. This interaction is repeated several times until the baby accepts a book.* This frequent mother-baby interaction is often experienced by mothers as the baby's deliberate attempt to annoy them or their own inability to understand their baby. Another explanation is that the baby is practicing having something in mind that Mommy cannot know until the baby let's her know. The baby has created a substantiation of separate minds.

## Play

Like dreams and memories for adults, play provides a glimpse into the inner world of babies and toddlers: their wishes, fears, conflicts, and trial solutions. Babies and toddlers play for pleasure, to learn, for social interaction, to master trauma, and to adapt to everyday stresses. Understanding the meaning of their play enables us to understand more about what is on their minds.

*Savannah was 24-months. While ice-skating with her family, her mother accidently stepped on her finger. Savannah's nail was ripped off, devasting both her mother and Savannah. After a dash to the emergency room, several painful injections to numb her fingers, and an x-ray, a bandage was applied that covered her entire hand. There was uncertainty as to whether her nail would grow back.*

*A week later, after the bandage was removed, her finger was healing, and the nail was growing back, Savannah's main play activity for several weeks was shredding pieces of paper, crumpling the pieces together into a ball the same size that her bandaged hand had been, and binding the clumps together with scotch tape. This activity was repeated many times a day. The corners of the living room floor were piled high with these put-together body repair constructions. Savannah's play represented the accident, the medical treatment, and most importantly the healing. The play had been entirely created by Savannah to cope with the damage to her body. When her feeling of body integrity was restored, the play was no longer needed.*

Doctor play enables children, even very young children, to gain feelings of control and mastery of stressful experiences, or as in the following example for both Mommy and baby to feel close when stressful things are happening or are going to happen.

*Wesley was scheduled for surgery. He was 14-months and needed an appendectomy. Parker, his mother, asked if he was too young to be told about the surgery and if doctor play before and after, could help him. Parker, who also had an older child, was familiar with doctor play. She described what she imagined, "I will buy a stethoscope, masks, syringes, a blood pressure-cuff, gauze, and band-aids. We can play with these together, with a doll, and with Wesley's older brother. We can take turns being the doctor and being the patient. I will tell Wesley that the doctor said that to get all better he needs something called surgery, and we will be going to a special place for the surgery called a hospital. I will emphasize that I will be with him. I will also tell him that he is very strong, and he can do this."*

*Even though Wesley was only 14-months, familiarity with the medical devices, the play with Mommy and his brother, and the importance to his mother of doing something to help him to cope were worthwhile. Wesley may not understand all the words, but he will get the feeling of being close to his mother, being taken care of, and being safe.*

*Wesley had his surgery and recovered well. His doctor play evolved and transitioned from hospital play to the details of well-baby-care doctor visits. For a while his teddy bear had a small band-aid on its tummy. One day Wesley took the band-aid off and threw it in the garbage, "All better, no more shugary!" Perhaps Wesley had added a bit of sugar to his surgery.*

Wrestling, throwing babies in the air and catching them, and deep tickling that evokes intense laughter are typical between parents and children, and increase in vigor during their first three years. The intense body sensations may obscure the meaning and the accompanying fantasies of the play. The warning, "This will end in tears" is often heard from bystanders and captures the fragility of the pleasure in high arousal play. Mothers' related childhood memories may be vivid and contain elements of the ambivalence. A frequent name remembered is "tickle-torture."

The exact form this play takes is specific to each parent and child. The intimacy, excitement, and conflicts about rough and tumble play are evidenced in mother-baby-toddler group discussions. Aspects of the play that are overwhelming to a child, that trigger biting, hitting, or tears are identified. Different thresholds for and signs of over-stimulation are discussed.

A baby's and toddler's attachment to a treasured toy or blanket creates a special category of play. A child's attachment to the object and its endowed ability to comfort are created by the child and are achievements of the child's developing mind. A child's experience with the treasured toy promotes the development of the child's capacities to perform the mental functions that had been attributed to the toy including emotion regulation and self-constancy. When this occurs at around 3 or 4 years of age the toy is given up by the child because it is no longer required. When the toy or blanket is retained, sometimes into adulthood, it serves a different function. Children who do not create a treasured toy attachment may have created other experiences that serve the same functions.

Mothers often have conflicted feelings about their children's attachments to treasured toys and restrict access to them. Mothers may have concerns about their children becoming "too attached," the treasured toy being lost, and the child's grief being overwhelming. They may worry about the toy getting too dirty; mother-child conflicts about washing the toy may emerge. To the child, the familiar scent is precious and the washing machine may seem dangerous; to the mother, its cleanliness may be prized. Mothers' responses to their children's treasured toys are often related to their own childhood memories.

## *Aggression*

Aggressive thoughts, angry feelings, and hostile behavior trigger strong reactions in babies, toddlers, and adults. Children biting, kicking, and hitting occur early; angry, hurtful words appear later. There are innate and acquired differences in both mothers and children in terms of the intensity of their aggression and their reactions to the aggression of others. Self-assertiveness to protect oneself and to keep and to get what is needed or wanted emerges early. Sometimes a baby's or toddler's assertiveness or self-protective aggression is merged with or confused in the mother's mind with destructive aggression. Clarification can be useful.

Mothers feel angry at their babies and toddlers, and like their children are adapting to these feelings in the context of a loving mother-child relationship. Sometimes aggressive impulses are triggered, for example when mothers roughly grab their toddlers by the arm and squeeze, and the children, outraged, shout, "Mommy, you hurt me!" or simply look stunned. A mother's frustration and aggression may be revealed when rather than protect her child, she says, "If you don't listen to me, you will get hurt, then you will learn." The intensity of mothers' angry feelings, loss of control, and hurtful fantasies may surprise and frighten them. *Speaking for all the mothers in a group, one mother confessed, "I now understand why some mothers hit or even beat their children. I never could understand it before. I never imagined how angry, helpless, and frightened I could feel with my baby."*

Another form that aggression may take is teasing, mocking, or laughing at a baby or toddler. These types of aggression may be unrecognized or denied by mothers and may need to be identified.

Kicking a ball, punching a blow-up clown, dueling with soft swords, and a variety of water toys that squirt are forms of aggressive play. Mothers have different thresholds for aggressive play. When children's aggressive play makes mothers feel uncomfortable, they may prohibit play that would benefit their children. *In response to a series of group questions including, "When would you like your child to be more assertive?" Bethany explained, "Other children are always taking toys from Otis. He's a very sweet boy. He shares his toys all the time. He's generous and nice. I think he takes after me. He's not rough like my brother was when we were little. When Otis is playing with something and another child approaches him, he just hands over the toy. I used to think that was good. I don't know how to help him stand up for himself." Interpreting aroused affect broadened the discussion, "It sounds like you and Otis are angry when children take toys away from him and maybe frightened." Bethany looked curious, but uncomfortable. I continued, "You want Otis to be more assertive, but you don't want him to be an aggressive, angry bully like you remember your brother. Maybe the first step is to identify angry feelings. Playing a kicking game or a dueling game together with toy swords may also help Otis to be more assertive. Children need to feel entitled to defend themselves and empowered to assert themselves: these are healthy forms of aggression." Bethany responded, "My father spanked my brother because he was a boy, but he never spanked me. My brother hit me." In Bethany's family male aggression was dangerous. The meaning of Bethany's memories expanded to include that her brother's aggression towards her was connected to her father's aggression towards her brother, rather than a frightening male trait. Bethany's inhibition of healthy aggression was related to her fear of male aggression that had been awakened by having a son.*

*The following week Bethany and Otis arrived with two long rubber swords. Bethany told us with delight that she and Otis were having fun dueling and that he had started asserting him*self *with other* children. *They were taking the swords everywhere with them. With his mother's support, Otis was holding on to toys and telling children who tried to take things away from him, "Stop. It's my turn." Bethany added, "I had* wanted Otis to be a nice boy not a bully, but I was afraid to help him stand up for himself. Even that seemed too aggressive. We are both having fun with the swords."

Pretend play scenarios can also have aggressive themes and at times may overwhelm children. For example, *when Tabetha was 2.5 years old, she and her mother Elenore had a vast repertoire of pretend play with action figures and wild animals. Elenore led the play, as her brother had, and always included growling attacks and fighting. Tabetha began to hit playmates. When it was suggested to Elenore that Tabetha's hitting might be related to the aggressive play scenarios she was introducing that might frighten her, she decided to take Tabetha's lead. The play themes shifted to events of everyday life and Tabetha's hitting stopped.*

Aggression between parents also gets talked about. *Penny told the group that she and her husband had a "huge fight."* Penny elaborated, "We were screaming at each other and said some very mean things. I always said I would never fight in front of my children like my parents did; for the moment Kelly was completely out of my mind." Characterizing this as "a good example of reliving the past" promoted group discussion. We talked about the content of the fight that Penny had with her husband, how 22-month-old Kelly reacted, what was said to Kelly after the fight, and what Penny's parents' fights were like for her when she was a little girl. She remembered clearly, "I needed to take sides between my parents, it was terrible. I wonder if Kelly felt she needed to take sides."

A related group question explored was, what do others think about fighting in front of the children? Malinda responded, "I never saw my parents fight, then one day they said they were getting divorced. I'm not sure what I think." Malinda's comment triggered a discussion about the rupture and repair cycles in all love relationships: the fighting and the making up, and the ruptures that do not get repaired. We also talked about the different ways couples fight: yelling, mocking, criticizing, and physical aggression. The content of couple fights related to disagreements about the children were also discussed.

Generalized questions raised for group discussion in response to Penny's comments included, what are other situations in addition to parents fighting when children are put in a position to "take sides"? When is choosing between Mommy and Daddy useful, when not? When does asking a child "who do you want to carry you" mean "who do you love more"? When parents ask "who do you want to read to you" they may wish to communicate that we both want to read to you, but sometimes the children feel "neither Mommy nor Daddy want to read to me."

## *Body awareness*

Body pleasure, body pain, being touched, and self-touching are part of body awareness. Babies react to their body sensations: they smile and grimace. They cry when they feel pain. When they feel the urge, they poop, pee-pee, sneeze, hiccup, burp, and spit-up. They shiver and startle. Babies suck their fingers, kick their feet with exuberance, and laugh a belly-laugh that delights parents. They move their hands in front of their eyes and make them appear and disappear from view. They touch their feet, genitals, tummies, ears, and hair: they squeal with excitement. Early body awareness and experiences of vitality are part of the emerging sense of self.

Mother-baby and mother-toddler body games highlight attention to parts of the body and include labeling them. Body functions are identified. Some body parts are touched, kissed, and tickled: others not. Some body parts can be seen, and others are internal: both are part of mother-child play. The heartbeat rhythm is often introduced by mothers as part of their play: listening to it, feeling it, and imitating its beat. Perhaps the meaning of this play is its reference to the conscious awareness of being alive, and in the moment a denial of mortality.

Babies and toddlers develop in the context of enormous attention to their bodies: motor development, body-care, gentle caresses, medical procedures, bumps and bruises, and mother-child body-play. Babies and toddlers explore their bodies and all they can do and feel. Mothers have thoughts and feelings about their children's bodies, the parts they like and the parts they do not like: the parts that are ok to touch and to talk about, and the parts that are not, including birth marks, scars, and other anomalies. Mothers' thoughts and feelings about their children's bodies are communicated to them both explicitly and implicitly. Both have an impact on their children's developing sense of self.

Toddlers experience exhilaration exercising their developing body capacities: walking, running, jumping, and snapping fingers. Toddler boys are intrigued by their erections and scrotum and may ask their mothers about them. Toddler girls may discover their labia, clitoris, and vagina and ask their mothers about them. Some girls discover and like the scent of their vaginal secretions. Both boys and girls may be curious about their anus, touch it, and try to look at it. They may pursue genital pleasure. Children's body exploration and pleasure trigger strong reactions in their mothers: some exciting, some shameful. Sometimes mothers' curiosity is aroused. For example, *A little girl 33-months-old pointed to her labia and asked her mother, "What is this?" The mother had been referring to her daughter's genitals as "private parts" and "down there." The mother was embarrassed to not be able to answer her daughter's question and was determined to learn words for the parts of her own genitals that she had never wanted to learn but did want to teach her daughter. She did not want her daughter to have the same sexual inhibitions that she had.*

In many families, bellybuttons get a great deal of attention. Not incidental to bellybutton interest is that both males and females have them. An aspect of attention to the bellybutton is the fun of designating it either an innie or an outie, perhaps a genital gender reference. It is noteworthy that in many situations the word bellybutton rather than navel continues to be used by adults. This may be related to the power of childhood experiences, meanings, and memories of the bellybutton.

Toddlers may be captivated by their pleasurable genital sensations. Mothers have intimate contact with their children's bodies arousing their own early fantasies and body experiences that may be enacted with their children. For example, *A mother told the group about a nighttime ritual of gently fingertip tickling her daughter's arm, back, and tummy before sleep, as she had been tickled as a little girl. One night, pointing to her genitals, her 2-year-old daughter said, "Mommy, tickle me down there." The mother was startled. She had not remembered or realized that the tickling was arousing, "in that way."*

Families establish different patterns of nudity. *Elaine had strong beliefs about the value of family nudity. Bathing, walking around the apartment, cuddling, and story time were family naked times. There were some indications that Gary, 22-months, was overstimulated by the amount of nudity, but Elaine insisted, "It's natural, it's good."*

*When Gary was 4-years, his sister was born. Gary helped to change her diaper and especially enjoyed putting the cream on her bottom. Family nudity continued. Gary began to fondle his penis more frequently: during meals, walking around the apartment, while showering with his parents, while watching videos, and in day-care: a possible indication of over-stimulation and maybe anxiety. With encouragement, Elaine decided to limit some of the family nudity. She stopped bathing with Gary and walking around the apartment naked. Gary was no longer allowed to put cream on his sister's bottom. In a few weeks, Gary primarily touched his penis when urinating, during bath-time, and occasionally while watching a video.*

Things that are pleasurable during one phase of development may be overstimulating at another and disgusting at another. Behavior that is pleasurable to do with one person, may not be with someone else. *Jannette, like many mothers, to determine if her daughter's diaper needed to be changed, put her face next to Judi's bottom and inhaled the scent deeply. This routine body interaction on the surface seemed un-noticed by them both. Janette's husband thought it was "weird." On the other hand, Judi picked her nose which her mother thought was "disgusting."*

*Judi was 3 years old and picked her nose frequently with great pleasure and enthusiasm. Jannette did everything that she could think of to get Judi to stop. Jannette was also doing everything she could to teach Judi to use the potty. Judi refused to do both. Janette explained Judi's position, "My poop stinks, yucky, I won't do it." Mother's disgust with nose-picking and child's disgust with poop seemed to be connected. The following question was a way to understand it, "I wonder what the connection might be between Judi picking her nose, something you think is disgusting, and Judi thinking that her poop stinks and it is disgusting." Jannette was intrigued. The following child development information included an allusion to Janette's pleasure with Judi's poop of which she was unaware, "Judi may need to know that her poop smells just the way it is supposed to smell. In some ways children need to know that they are giving a wonderful gift to Mommy when they poop in the potty, and that the gift from their body is pleasurably received." Jannette smiled, seeming pleased, excited, and a little self-conscious with the idea that Judi's poop would be given to her as a special gift. Perhaps it resonated with her pleasure in smelling Judi's poop when it was in her diaper. Adding the following was important: "While poop is valued, it is also discarded. It is applauded, but not touched. Both attitudes about poop are simultaneously held by mothers and communicated to the children in equal measure: not overly valued, not disparaged."*

The following week Jannette reported to the group, *"I told Judi that her poop smells just right. I also told her that it is ok to pick her nose in private. I realized that it was pleasurable to her, and she was asserting her autonomy and control over her body. She now tells me when she needs to poop, and she poops in the potty. I leave it there a few minutes before I flush it. It seems important to her just to know it's there."*

The change in Judi's behavior may have been coincidental to the changes in her mother's interactions with her, but Jannette thought that the changes she had made helped Judi to poop in the potty and to stop picking her nose. Perhaps Judi's frequent impulse to pick her nose and the pleasure she derived from it abated as she was able, for a short while, to see and to smell her precious body product with her mother. Perhaps for Janette, the intimate pleasure of smelling Judi's poop in her diaper shifted to the shared pleasure of Judi's poop in the potty.

Mothers often ask, "When should I start toilet training?" It is useful to highlight that learning about using the toilet has already started. In fact, learning about pee-pee and poop starts when babies are very young. Body sensations of urinating and defecating are pleasurable, frequent, and become familiar. Toddlers may practice starting and stopping their urine stream, and sometimes exercise controlling their bowel movements. For example, when babies crawl behind a chair to have a bowel movement they are inhibiting the impulse long enough to get behind the chair. The ways in which mothers respond to their children's awareness of bowel and bladder functioning, body exploration, and body experiences influence the process of learning to use the potty.

Whether naked or in a diaper, pooping gets their mothers' attention from the beginning of the children's lives. Babies learn that their mothers are interested in their poop, and it is something that can be talked about together. When naked, urinating also gets mothers' attention. Mothers introduce specific words for the body parts involved, body sounds, and body products. Children are interested in the things their parents are interested in. Urinating and defecating are pleasurable body self-experiences that trigger interaction with Mommy – a joint focus of attention, a word, and care-taking body-interactions.

Some toddlers go to a chosen place to focus on the experience of having a bowel movement and to enjoy it without interruption or competing stimulation. Other toddlers continue their play as if nothing is happening. Both have meaning and both have a different impact on learning to use the potty. Life events, including mothers' pregnancy, injuries, and the regularity of bowel movements influence mother-child interactions related to learning to use the potty. Experiences of diarrhea, constipation, and vomiting may also have an impact. The details are talked about during groups.

In some families the bathroom and toilet have been established as a safe place for babies and toddlers. In some families they are dangerous, scary, and off limits. The question, *"When should I start toilet training?"* can be reframed into, *"Let's think about where you and your child are in the process now and what the next steps might be to peeing and pooping in the potty."*

## Children's interactions with other children

Babies' and toddlers are interested in other children: looking at them, touching them, and imitating them. They are interested in the toys other children are holding, and items they wear, for example eyeglasses and barrettes. It appears that their interest is beyond the intrinsic properties of the items; it is connected to their interest in the people. Motivation for social interaction is pre-wired and highly adaptive.

Babies vocalize with each other in turn-taking rhythms, as if they are having a conversation. They imitate the sounds of each other. When they begin to crawl and then to walk, they approach each other and touch: sometimes gently, sometimes not. Toddlers begin to play together. They may pass a toy back and forth to each other. With adult scaffolding, they can build a tower together, and join group activities. Mothers attend to peer interactions. They are eager for their children to have friends.

The group-leader identifies interactions among the babies and toddlers and attributes social motivation to them. For example, *"Suzanna crawled next to Tatianna. It may look as if her primary interest is in the toy Tatianna is playing with, but another possibility is that her interest is in being next to Tatianna."* Or *"I wonder if Adrian's interest in the toy was triggered by watching Cal play with it. It had been on the shelf, untouched for the last half hour."* Mothers welcome the evidence for their babies' and toddlers' social interests.

Mothers are reactive to interactions between children when they view their child as too aggressive or too passive. At times they romanticize or sexualize boy-girl, or same-sex interactions, *"Bart, give your girlfriend a kiss. She wants to marry you."* For some children, in some situations this might be a useful comment, in many situations it may seem to pass by the children, and in others it may raise concerns for the children. Bart reassured himself when he told his mother, *"Mommy that's silly. We are too young to get married."*

Sometimes toddlers imitate something they see another child do that they are curious about; sometimes the imitations horrify mothers who fear their child will adopt the behavior permanently. *Avery told the group about Misa's playdate with Arielle. Both girls were almost 3-years. While they were playing, Arielle put a lock of her hair into her mouth and began to suck it. Avery went on, "This is a nervous habit Arielle has, she does it frequently. Arielle's mother firmly tells her to stop. Arielle spits her hair out of her mouth when her mother tells her, but in a few moments her hair is back in her mouth and the interaction with her mother gets repeated. I think it's pretty disgusting, her hair is always wet."*

*Avery was concerned that Misa would learn this "nervous habit" from her friend and was wondering if she should continue the playdates. Another possibility expanded the group discussion: "Sometimes when children see another child do a self-soothing behavior like suck their hair or bite their nails, they may be curious and try it out to see what it feels like. Part of the motivation may be to imagine their friend's experience. Misa may also have had a reaction to the angry interaction between Arielle and her mother."* The following week, Avery reported that she had told Misa, *"I think you have seen Arielle suck her hair, I guess it feels good to her. It does not feel good to most people. Maybe she does it when she has a feeling she does not like. Her mother is trying to help her to stop. I think you are curious about what it feels like, so you tried it."* Misa and Arielle continued to have playdates, Arielle continued to suck her hair, Misa did not. Misa may have been influenced by what her mother had said. Alternatively, a self-soothing behavior that is imitated may not have the same pleasure as one that has been originally created.

Opportunities for apologizing and accepting apologies arise when children interact. Distinctions are useful between apologies as social convention or as expressions of remorse and forgiveness. Promoting the development of a child's capacity for remorse may require processing the complexity of the interaction rather than a precipitous apology. For example, *"You were so angry when Patti grabbed your car. You hit her so hard, she cried. You got scared when she cried. I think you felt sorry that you hit her, you did not want to hurt her."* On the other hand, the social rituals of apologizing and accepting apologies can contribute to the development of remorse.

### *Emotion regulation*

The ability to regulate emotions is innate, maturational, interpersonal, and learned. A frequent mother-baby affect regulation play interaction occurs when a mother initiates and repeats a predominately pleasurable high arousal interaction and her baby's intense laughter repeatedly erupts in response to the novel yet expected elements. For example, while maintaining mutual gaze, a mother puts her 5-month-old baby's pacifier in her own mouth and as the baby reaches for it, the mother spits it out beyond the baby's reach, with a playful popping sound. The baby laughs uproariously. The playful interaction is repeated many times. The baby's complex response includes familiarity with pacifier sucking, surprise perhaps mixed with some displeasure to see his pacifier in Mommy's mouth, further surprise mixed with displeasure as he attempts to grab it and Mommy spits it out with a playful noise that gently startles, and the pacifier flies out of her mouth and beyond the baby's reach, a frustrating and novel event in a playful context. The rising and falling intensity of affect, movement, and sounds during the interaction with each other, the well-synchronized timing and rhythm of their turn taking, and their loving playfulness are essential elements of the experience of mutual regulation traversing the threshold between pleasure and unpleasure. When unpleasure predominates the interaction, the baby's laughter sounds more like crying.

Babies express their emotions. When responded to, a baby's expression of distress develops into a communication. The ways in which babies' and toddlers' feelings are both expressed and communicated are influenced by mother-child interactions. Mothers help their children to regulate disturbing emotions by acknowledging feelings and labeling them. *During a group discussion about labeling feelings, Darlene had an insight, "I just realized that I often tell Kitty that she is sad, when I really know that she is angry."*

Babies and toddlers need help to process overwhelming feelings. *Tammy was 17-months and frequently pinched and hit herself creating red blotches on her arms. While this was happening, her mother Linda froze. Tammy had no way to process her feelings or to regulate her state without her mother's help. Linda asked, "Why does she do that? What's wrong with her? She looks crazy." The following was an attempt to identify with Linda what she thought triggered Tammy's behavior, "What happens before Tammy pinches herself? What do you think Tammy is feeling? Maybe we can understand how you can help her at these times." Linda had no idea. At a loss I added, "Tammy might need to know that you want her to be touched gently by others and when she touches herself. I wonder how you might communicate that to her."*

*As Linda approached Tammy in response to my implied and perhaps useless suggestion that was triggered by my shared helplessness with Linda, Linda's facial expression was alarming. For a fleeting moment she looked vicious. Her lips were pursed and curled exposing her clenched teeth, her eyes were glaring. It was a frightening expression. In response to being asked if she was aware of how she felt as she approached Tammy, Linda said, "I'm furious with her." The following intervention highlighted both Linda and Tammy's fear, "I think when you feel so angry at Tammy, you look at her in a way that frightens her. I wonder if you are afraid also. It may be easier for you to feel angry than scared." Linda became aware that when her anxiety was triggered by Tammy's behavior that seemed "crazy" to her, it was easier for her to feel angry than to feel scared, helpless, and overwhelmed with anxiety. This insight helped Linda to temper her own rage at Tammy, which helped Tammy to feel safer in general. The frightening threat that her mother posed lessened.*

*After identifying both Linda and Tammy's fear, it became apparent that Tammy's hitting and pinching herself was triggered by the approach of another child. Tammy seemed afraid that she would be hit or that a toy would be taken from her, or afraid that she would grab a toy from the other child or hit the approaching child. In response to her fear, and to control these impulses Tammy pinched herself. With this new shared meaning of Tammy's hitting and pinching herself, Linda began to protect Tammy from both. For example, "I am not going to let Sammy take the truck, I'm going to help you to keep it." Linda also helped Tammy to wait her turn for a toy she wanted or to trade toys with a child who had a toy that she wanted. In these ways she mitigated Tammy's impulse to grab from another child or to hit, and thereby protected Tammy from her own aggressive impulses which also frightened her. Tammy's feelings of safety when other children approached increased. The pinching herself and hitting herself abated and then stopped.*

A variation of a mother's reaction to her child's pain occurred with Marla and Zeke. *Marla believed mothers over-react to their children's slightest pain and promote their over-reaction and crying. She thought it best when your child gets hurt to, "Stay calm, reassure children, and tell them 'you're ok.'"* When her son Zeke was 19-months and was beginning to cry louder and for longer periods of time after typical toddler bumps and bruises, Marla's response continued, "It's nothing, you're ok." Noting that Marla's intended approach included "stay calm" suggested that she might not feel calm herself and "reassure the children" may have suggested that it was she who wanted reassurance to cope with her own anxiety when Zeke got hurt.

The following intervention highlighted these meanings: "Children have a range of severity of injuries and pain, from significant requiring a visit to the emergency room to very minor, and everything in between. Marla, it sounds like for you there are only two categories of harm: catastrophic and nothing." Marla quietly responded, "My parents were holocaust survivors; everything that ever happened to me was nothing, even when I broke my leg. I just don't know what to say to Zeke." The following interpretation combined with child development information addressed Marla's core theme and linked her childhood memory to her interactions with Zeke, "It sounds like the pain your parents suffered and their reactions to your pain interfered with you getting their understanding and soothing, and now influences your interactions with Zeke. Sometimes children want to know that Mommy saw what happened and that Mommy knows how they feel. For example, if it is a slight bump, 'I saw you bumped your head on the table. It must have surprised you.' If it is a more severe bump, we can acknowledge that it looked like a hard bump. 'Does it still hurt? Let me know when it starts to feel better.' The soothing words and the kiss that a mother gives to her child can become the child's self-soothing." Marla experienced this intervention as a recognition of the memory of her own childhood pain that was not acknowledged, still hurt, but could feel better.

Marla's life-long experiences related to her parents' time in a concentration camp, and her associated childhood memories about what she was told and what she imagined, continued to re-emerge in interactions with Zeke. A core theme for Marla, rooted in her childhood memories and influencing her interactions with Zeke, was her conflict between protecting her parents from her pain and being taken care of and soothed by them. As new shared meanings of her childhood memories and interactions with Zeke emerged, Marla's interactions with Zeke evolved to include a range of pain acknowledgments, maternal soothing, and a process of healing. Zeke's crying in response to injuries became more modulated and specifically reactive.

## *Gender*

Throughout history, ideas and attitudes about gender have gradually changed in some ways for both adults and children. Sexual harassment, same-sex marriage, and anti-discrimination laws have been passed. Some personality traits and behavior that had been gender-linked in the past are now viewed as desirable for both boys and girls, or undesirable for both. Some picture books for 3-year-old children include having two mommies, two daddies, a mommy and a daddy, or one parent. Story-line plots reflect societal changes. Seeing the gendered world through the eyes of a young child can be illuminating. As 34-month-old Natalie and her mother walked through the park and past a basketball court Natalie asked, "Why are only the boys playing and the girls watching?" Her mother had not noticed.

Many years ago, at the Sackler Lefcourt Center, a survey was conducted about parents' views about their children's developing gender identity. There was an interesting response to the following question, "How does your son know that he is a boy?" "How does your daughter know that she is a girl?" Many mothers answered, "Because I tell him." "Because I tell her." In contrast, in recent years mothers have expressed uncertainty as to whether it is ok to tell their son that he is a boy or their daughter that she is a girl, "What if they are gay or trans, I want to be supportive?" *A question for group discussion is, "What gender-related thoughts about or interactions with your children do you have now? What are the opportunities to support your child's developing gender identity?"*

Children's behavior that reflects an aspect of the gender identity process and their own gender-related thoughts and feelings might include little girls trying to urinate standing up, and little boys pretending to breastfeed, or boys shaving like Daddy and girls wearing nail polish like Mommy. These are typically gender-linked behaviors observed by the children. Children may be influenced by their parents' conscious and unconscious attitudes and implicit and explicit communications about gender. Children are discovering ways to feel close to the parent of the opposite sex without being like them in gender-specific ways. Women have vivid childhood memories of their own gender-related behavior. For example, "I was a tomboy" is frequently recalled with multiple meanings. The mother of a 2-year-old girl remembered, "When I was little, I insisted that my clitoris was my little penis."

A consistent, non-conforming gender-related behavior in a toddler may require attention. For example, *a boy 30-months cried to wear his "smock-dress" during his repeated pretend-play driving the mommy-car fast, screeching and crashing it into the family figures, and knocking them down. This little boy experienced his mother as dangerous and seemed to believe he would be safer if he were a girl.*

Discovery of the male-female genital difference and observations of gender role differences capture children's attention. While adult attitudes about gender are evolving, and some attitudes about gender difference are dissolving, young children often highlight gender differences. *When Brody was just over 22-months, his mother gave him a bath with his cousin Autumn. They splashed, blew bubbles, and washed each-others' backs. The excitement and pleasure aroused during the bath for the children and the mothers was evidenced in the telling. The fun stopped when Autumn tried to touch Brody's penis and both mothers said, "No!"*

*For the next several days Brody played a new game. Each evening after his bath, he sat on the edge of his bed and opened and closed his legs slowly exposing and hiding his penis between his thighs.* Brody's mother was curious about the meaning of his play until she remembered his bath with Autumn. She believed that he had created this game in reaction to his discovery of, or confrontation with, the boy-girl genital difference. In addition, she thought that his play was in reaction to Autumn trying to touch his penis and both mothers saying, "No!" Brody's play repeatedly confirmed his penis was always there. Brody also began to identify who was a boy and who was a girl, and boy-girl differences such as long hair and short hair.

Brody's mother decided not to share her interpretation of the meaning of Brody's play with him, but to let him use his play to reassure himself without her words. She did talk to him about his discovery, "I think you are interested in the differences between boys and girls. You have discovered a body difference. Boys have a penis and girls have a vagina."

Danny was 34-months. He was bright and inquisitive. He had become interested in designating who was a boy and who was a girl. He emphasized that his toys were "boy-toys." Danny had been told by his mother that he was a boy like Daddy and had a penis, and Mommy was a girl and had a vagina. His mother, Darleen, was 7 months pregnant and had explained to Danny what she thought was an age-appropriate description of pregnancy and childbirth. Danny had appeared not too interested in any of these details.

Seeming to Darleen to be completely disconnected, she told the group that last night she had taken Danny to the emergency room because he had put a small toy in his nose, and she was not able to remove it. Also seeming to Darleen to be disconnected was Danny's nose-picking and sometimes eating what he removed from his nose. In contrast to Danny's apparent body interest as demonstrated by his explorations of his nose, we were told, "Danny never touches his penis." Danny's body explorations, and thoughts about what is inside and what is outside, how things get into the body, out of the body, and back into the body were focused on his nose. He did not ask questions and was not interested in what his mother said about bodies, including her pregnancy, and boy-girl differences. Learning to use the potty, another inside-outside body experience had gone easily without much discussion. When Danny was 28-months, he was wearing underpants. Danny was an avid eater. He had slept through the night since he was 7-months. Danny's body regulations worked smoothly.

The challenges of helping Danny with his quest for answers to the big questions he was grappling with when he was not yet 3-years, and his mother's motivation to give a great deal of information to Danny, were addressed with the following child development information: "Sometimes children, rather than needing more knowledge, need help to adapt to what they cannot know or to things that cannot be known. Danny has so many important questions about his body and other bodies, what goes in and what comes out. It takes a long time to learn all about the body. Play with a pastry decorating tool that includes filling the pastry bag with sweet icing, squeezing it out to decorate a cookie, and the pleasure of eating it, might be a useful substitute for some of Danny's body experiments with his nose."

Mothers have complex reactions to their children's gender. Some of their thoughts and feelings are easy for them to talk about, some are difficult, and others are acted out. For example, *Nan, with great excitement, brought a photo to show the group of her 17-month-old son wearing a dress. This provided the opportunity to explore her pleasures in his wearing girls' clothes and her related fantasies about him being a girl. After showing us the photo and carefully returning it to her wallet indicating her wish to preserve the image, she said, "He would make such a pretty girl."* We were able to begin to talk about Nan's grieving for the daughter that she would never have. We talked about her pleasure in the photo as a realization of her fantasies and she became able to differentiate her fantasies about having a daughter from her son's developing male gender identity that she wanted to support and enjoy.

It is interesting to note that in most of the examples in this section, the children are male. Whether it is statistically valid that boys have more gender-related behavior reported by their mothers is not known.

## Underlying meanings of behavior

All behavior, including actions, thoughts, feelings, and memories, the children's and the mothers', have multiple meanings. The meanings are developmental, conscious, unconscious, wish fulfilling, and defensive. They may be contradictory and paradoxical. Exploring and understanding underlying meanings are a central part of the mother-baby-toddler group-process. Babies' and toddlers' behavior without consideration of its complex underlying meanings can be experienced by mothers as irrational, provocative, manipulative, or mean.

A mother communicating her understanding of the developmental meaning of her baby's or toddler's behavior to her child can promote a process of the child's self-reflection, frustration tolerance, ability to tolerate ambivalence, emotion regulation, and growing self-awareness and interest in the inner world of others. This developmental process of self-reflection in a young child is entwined with the mother's understanding of her child's developing mind: what has been described as reflective functioning.

Mothers value truth-telling. They teach their children the importance of telling the truth and are disapproving when their children appear to have lied. Sometimes what appears to be a child's lie can be understood as the expression of a wish. A question mothers know the answer to may be a perfect set-up for such a "lie." For example, *Greta walked into the kitchen and saw a big puddle on the floor. She asked Lance, "Did you make pee-pee on the floor?" Lance said, "No, Mommy." Greta said, "You are lying? There is no lying allowed."* Another way to understand Lance's answer to the disapproving accusation is that he wished he had not made pee-pee on the floor because he wanted his mother's approval.

A distinction between narrative truth and historical truth may be useful in this situation. *It was easy to verify that Lance had urinated on the floor, but his wish that was revealed in his "lie" may have been more important to focus on to achieve the goal of learning to use the potty, "I know you are learning to make pee-pee in the potty.*

*Sometimes people make mistakes." Or another scenario, "I know you are learning to make pee-pee in the potty, but I think you were angry that I did not let you play with the water, so you made pee-pee on the floor. Pee-pee goes in the potty, even when you are angry."* Mothers' disapproval of the behavior is important. Acknowledging and supporting the child's motivation to do what Mommy wants, promotes both the behavior and feelings of self-worth.

## *Internal conflict*

As babies and toddlers develop, their sense of self evolves and internal conflict gradually emerges. Attachment needs and needs for autonomy sometimes clash. Wishes to please Mommy conflicted with autonomous wishes take root. Often interpersonal mother-child conflicts reflect internal conflict – the mother's, the child's, or both.

Babies and toddlers' need to feel loved and safe, and at the same time they strive to feel autonomous and self-reliant. "Do it myself" is a frequent refrain, as is "Mommy, Mommy, Mommy!" In one moment they push their mothers away and in the next seemingly cannot get close enough. *When Martine was 23-months and her mother began to talk to another mother during a group, Martine stopped her play, climbed onto her mother's lap, held her mother's cheeks lovingly in her hands, and rotated her mother's face seeking her gaze. This familiar sight communicating, "I want all your attention, all the time" alternates with asserting autonomy. As soon as Martine captured her mother's gaze, she slid off her lap and said, "Go away, Mommy."*

Whining is sometimes a child's compromise between pleasing Mommy by renouncing a wish and demanding something to please oneself. For example, *a mother said to her 26-month-old daughter, "No more cookies, don't ask me again" and the child whined for more cookies. The child's internal conflict between pleasing herself by demanding a cookie and pleasing her mother by not asking for another cookie was revealed in her whining, was being negotiated interpersonally, and was acknowledged by her mother, "I know you really want another cookie, and I've told you, don't ask me again, so you are asking in your squeaky voice instead of your strong voice. Tomorrow, you can have another cookie."* This may seem like a subtle and complex distinction for a 2-year-old but having it in the mother's mind was useful to resolve both the conflict between them and address the whining. Throughout the *MBTG Guide* the importance of children knowing their own minds – what they think, want, like, do not like, and do not want – while they learn to accept behavioral limits and directions is emphasized.

As a child experiences the mother's expectations as the child's own, and the mother's prohibitions become the child's self-prohibitions, internal conflict between satisfying wishes and self-disapproval emerges. Increasingly for children, interpersonal conflicts become internal conflicts.

## Mother-child differences

Mother-child differences in terms of physical traits and personality characteristics are sometimes gratifying and sometimes disturbing to mothers: traits and characteristics different from what the mother had imagined or wished for. When a mother experiences aspects of her child as alien, or her child has characteristics reminiscent of those she tries to conceal in herself or those she envies, the impact on their relationship may create difficulties. On the other hand, what appear to others to be extreme mother-child differences may be barely noticed by the mother. Some mothers want to do everything possible to remove a birthmark; the blemish seems large and overpowers other characteristics. For other mothers, a birthmark, scar, or disability may seem to disappear, or its presence may enhance their relationship. Family constellation differences also have an impact on mothers; differences include families with a mother and a father, two mothers, or a single mother, only children, or siblings. Single father or two-father families are not discussed in the *MBTG Guide*.

Group questions in Chapters 3 through 7 explore the ways in which mothers view their children. The meanings of a mother's description of her child are enriched by understanding the ways in which the mother views her child as similar to and different from herself and others important to her. Exploration of the meaning to a mother of the differences and similarities is a way to learn more about mother-baby and mother-toddler interactions.

For example, *Bianca joined a mother-toddler group with Marty, her first born son. She had a 9-year-old daughter from a prior marriage. Marty was a 14-month-old, active, bright little boy. He had been walking since he was 11-months. While Marty busily played, he and his mother remained distant from each other both physically and emotionally. They rarely interacted. There was no touching, mutual gaze, or shared smiles. A core theme for Bianca was her conflict between how close to and how distant from Marty she wanted to be. Marty's babysitter was described as his primary caretaker.*

*Identifying aspects of Marty's play that were well developed for his age, his attention span, and the multi-piece puzzles with which he was competent and enjoyed, was a first step to increase his mother's attention to him. For example, "Marty is very capable for his age to do the complicated puzzles he does. He's very curious, he sits and looks at a book for a long time." Bianca began to look at Marty, and self-consciously smile with pride. In response to his mother's increased affectionate gaze, on occasion Marty began to approach his mother and at times to play next to her for brief moments. Highlighting Marty's responses to his mother's pride and interest in him promoted this process, "Marty looked delighted when you told him he did that hard puzzle so well." As the weeks passed, there were increasing opportunities to identify Marty's proximity-seeking to his mother, and Bianca's reserved delight and attention to him. For example, when Marty walked in the direction of his mother, highlighting it as Marty's intention* to be closer, "I think Marty came closer to you because he wanted you to see what he was doing with that puzzle." Or attributing other attachment motivations, "I think Marty was startled when he heard that loud noise and wanted to be close to you to feel safe." Interventions also included highlighting Marty's responses to his mother, "It looks like Marty was so reassured by you."

Marty began to hand toys to his mother, and then at times to sit on her lap for a few minutes. At first, Bianca appeared mildly uncomfortable but delighted. She changed her work schedule and began to spend more time with Marty. She began to derive more pleasure from their interactions, which became more physically affectionate and appeared more intersubjectively nuanced. Marty's attachment behavior, including seeking physical proximity and contact with his mother, increased. Social referencing when at a distance during groups began to appear. When Marty had a cold and could not come to the group, Bianca came herself. While she chose to leave Marty at home with the babysitter, coming to the group and missing him was a valuable first experience, "This is the first time I missed Marty."

When Marty was 18-months, Bianca told the group, "I was not able to breast-feed Marty because when he was a baby, he looked just like my brother." Bianca was able to tell us this now, because as she explained, "Marty no longer looks just like my brother, he looks like my husband." Bianca had now claimed Marty as her and her husband's baby. She continued, "It was weird. I never thought my baby would look like my brother." Bianca's phrase, "I never thought..." seemed to have important meaning related to conscious and unconscious thoughts that she did have about her brother and was warding off. Bianca explained, "When Marty was born, I had not seen my brother for a few years. He has started to visit Marty. I watch them play; they have a close relationship. They have fun together." I asked Bianca several times, "How often do you and your brother see each other now?" Bianca did not answer. Her conflict between how close to and how distant she wanted to be from her brother may have made it difficult to answer.

Bianca's retrospective story about not breastfeeding Marty and her relationship with her brother was accompanied by another memory. She had seen her best friend having a drink with her brother at a neighborhood hotel bar and had the fantasy that they were having an affair. The two memories, not breastfeeding Marty who looked like her brother, she thought, and seeing her brother with her friend and thinking they might be having an affair were connected. Both memories were related to her core conflict about how close to and how distant from Marty she wanted to be and had interfered with breastfeeding. Bianca's two memories shared unconscious sexual fantasies about her brother. The following interpretation linked them, "It sounds like your two memories about your brother are connected." Her sexual fantasies about her brother were not explored further, but perhaps for them to have risen to the surface of her mind as she had linked the two memories in the telling, changed something for her.

Bianca's new solution to her conflict about how close to and how distant from Marty and from her brother she wanted to be evolved into supporting her brother's closeness to Marty while they played, and she retreated into the background and watched. This solution helped Bianca to both spend time with her brother and be closer to Marty. She *assumed more of Marty's care, became more attuned to him, and derived more pleasure with him. Marty's secure attachment behavior increased.*

A mother-child gender difference can provide vicarious pleasure in having a son, or trigger feelings of rivalry, envy, or anxiety that sometimes is expressed as being alien, "I just don't know what to do with a boy. It's so foreign to me, I only have sisters." Mothers can also feel too gender different from their daughters. *Carla described herself as a woman who rejected female gender stereotypes and found her daughter's exclusive choice of sparkling party-dresses and dolls disturbing. She did not want her daughter to be a "girly-girl." Carla and her almost 3-year-old daughter had repeated fights about what to wear and what to play with until Carla recognized that her own mother wanted her to be a different kind of girl than she wanted to be. Carla remembered that when she was a little girl her mother had wanted her to wear bows in her hair and uncomfortable dresses with tights. Now her mother wanted her to wear make-up, "My mom always says things like, get a hairstyle, dress more elegantly, you still look like a ragamuffin tomboy." With this awareness of the connection between her interactions with her own mother and with her daughter, Carla was able to allow her little girl to wear dresses; to be the kind of girl she wanted to be. In addition, she was able to enjoy her daughter's pleasure in being a girl even though the gender symbols her daughter chose were not the same as her own.*

Sometimes a mother's rivalry with her own sibling is triggered by mother-child differences. *Joyce characterized herself as shy and reserved. She described her 2-year-old daughter Jill: "She's such a showoff. She's always trying to be the center of attention. I don't like it. I'm not like that." Joyce's general reserved demeanor was different from her exuberant outgoing daughter's. In addition, her revived memories of her own older sister who she believed, "...did everything better, she was always in the spotlight" had triggered a ferocious rivalry with her daughter that she felt she was losing. As she began to recognize that she had displaced feelings that she had toward her sister onto her daughter, she became able to differentiate her painful childhood memories and continued rivalry with her sister from the normal needs of a 2-year-old to be admired.*

Being bilingual or multi-lingual in many families, communities, and careers is valuable. The inclusion, exclusion, and exclusivity dynamics organized around language may be alluded to during groups. Sometimes a mother's first language is the primary language she speaks to her baby, sometimes it is abandoned. One language may predominate loving interactions and the other angry ones. Parents may speak one language to each other and a different language to the children. When the primary language spoken at home is different from the community language, tensions around when to speak each may occur. Understanding the meaning of a chosen language spoken in a particular context can be useful.

*Camille spoke exclusively French to her 2.5-year-old daughter Antoinette. When in English-speaking social situations with other children and adults, this created a bubble around Antoinette and Camille that interfered with Antoinette's developing social interactions with other children and adults. Camille recognized this but was unable to integrate English into their interactions until she became aware of her sad feelings when she spoke English to Antoinette.*

*Camille's mother lived in France and did not speak any English. When Camille spoke English to Antoinette, she felt not only far away from her mother, but also that she was excluding her mother. Painful accusations of abandoning her mother had surrounded her move to the United States five years earlier. Speaking exclusively French to Antoinette had helped her to feel close to Antoinette and to her mother. This new shared meaning helped Camille to expand Antoinette's social interactions.*

## *Learning*

The goal of most early learning is the development of internal mental structures in addition to learning a task, or a way to behave. Mothers' attention to both the external behavior and the child's inner world results in complementary behavioral learning and emotional development. For example, in addition to learning a task from trial and error, a child learns I can do it myself, it was hard and took a long time, but I did it. With instructional teaching and learning, the task is learned, and the child also learns, I can learn from others. Learning from observation and imitation, a child not only learns the behavior, for example please and thank you, but also learns, I admire Mommy and can learn to be like her. Some teaching-learning approaches are more suitable for certain tasks, specific children, at particular ages.

Most learning requires multiple teaching-learning interactions, and while consistency is often emphasized, inconsistency is also important. Inconsistencies help children to adapt to change and to be responsive to variations and nuance. It is as though the baby and toddler are learning this is the way we do it on rainy days, sunny days, and snowy days. This is the rule all the time except when Mommy is on the phone. Some things are not ok when Daddy comes home. I can eat French fries with my hands, but not spaghetti. These are some examples of inconsistencies that are of value. In addition, there are few non-negotiable, non-flexible limits or ways of being. It takes many slightly varied repetitions to learn all the permutations and respond accordingly. The totally non-negotiable limits are the dangerous ones like running into the street, or a personal non-negotiable priority of a parent.

Mobilizing excessive amounts of anxiety, shame, or anger in a baby or toddler with disapproval or threats may interfere with learning, or the learning may be rigid. A baby's or young child's startle in response to a mother's prohibition may indicate that processing the limit and its flexible parameters will be compromised. An example of this occurred when an 18-month-old, unable to check back with Mommy, pointed at the toys, said, "No touch, no touch" and froze. Limits need to be learned in a way that they can be appropriately applied, and when there is uncertainty the child can check back to Mommy with social referencing.

Part of the long-range goal when teaching babies and toddlers the dos and don'ts of their everyday lives is allowing some space for mistakes and for the inconsistencies, complexities, and nuances of the things that they are being taught. This complexity starts in the mother's mind and will be evidenced in her child's growing adaptation to the changing demands of the environment. Many child development books for parents highlight the importance of consistency. The value of inconsistency also needs to be highlighted. Both are needed.

When mothers complain that their children break the rules, it may be useful to explore when they themselves break rules: drive over the speed limit, jay-walk, or lie to protect someone's feelings but break the moral no lying rule. Children are learning which rules are acceptable to break and in what context, and which rules can never be broken. Running into the street is a non-negotiable, non-breakable rule.

Prohibiting words, ideas, and feelings as if they are dangerous or shameful may be problematic. Stating strong feelings in an objectionable way, for example, when the child says, "I hate you," can be reframed, "I think you mean you are very angry at me." In this way feelings are acknowledged and understood, rather than words, thoughts, and feelings being taboo. Words like "shut up" may not be ok around the family dinner table but in some contexts may be of value to be able to say. While this may not apply specifically to children younger than 3-years, the underlying principle does.

Obedience means to be compliant or submissive to authority, or to avoid externally imposed consequences. The goal of most limit-setting with children is that the child becomes disapproving of the behavior, and the consequence becomes self-disapproval. Loving attachments and feelings of self-worth are needed to promote the development of a rich and functioning inner world: the mainstay of behavior.

There are two developmental milestones that are areas of learning that require mention. For decades, learning to use the toilet has been called "toilet training." Up until more recently it was the only developmental achievement that was referred to as training. In recent years, another developmental achievement has been popularly described as training, "sleep training." The designation "training" suggests that the internal world of the child does not matter in these teaching-learning interactions, but of course it does. While many child development books for parents have included the meanings to children and the emotional responses of children to learning to use the toilet, the term "toilet training" has persisted. The emotional experience of infants, babies, toddlers, and their parents to "sleep training" has received less attention.

Babies, toddlers, and parents need sleep and sleep disruptions are stressful. There are maturational, behavioral, physiological, and psychological components to sleep. When there are problems, understanding the details are useful to resolving them. *Ester was 9-months and was waking every three hours throughout the night. Her mother, Adrianna, was unaware that "checking" on Ester throughout the night was waking her. She was also unaware that her anxiety triggering the night "checking" was related to childhood memories of her mother's stillbirth. New shared meanings helped to resolve the sleep problem.*

In conclusion, these themes are central to psychodynamic mother-baby-toddler groups. They are integral to the group-leader's general approach, to specific interventions with an individual mother, and to the suggested child development information and group questions in Chapters 3 through 7.

Defense mechanisms are also important psychodynamics of everyday life and are revealed in mothers' narratives. Recognizing a mother's defensive psychological maneuvers to protect herself from emotional pain helps to promote group-leader empathy, and the formulation of interventions that achieve group goals. Defense mechanisms are summarized below, defined in the glossary, and discussed in vignettes throughout the *MBTG Guide*. Added to the list of familiar defense mechanisms is, the "enactment of childhood memory."

## Defense mechanisms summary

Denial
Dissociation
Disavowal
Displacement
Enactment of Childhood Memory
Identification with the aggressor
Isolation of affect
Projection
Reaction formation
Splitting

Chapter 2

# Mother-child proximity

Chapter 2 discusses the centrality of mother-child proximity during psychodynamic mother-baby-toddler groups. Examples illustrate the power of the mother-child attachment relationship that is activated, and specific interventions that generate mothers' self-reflection and new shared meanings.

During mother-baby groups, the mothers hold their babies or lay them on a blanket close enough to touch. As the babies' motor development progresses, they sit next to their mothers, then begin to crawl around the room, pull themselves up to standing, and then walk. Once the babies begin to crawl and to walk, they play at a slight distance from their mothers, touching base as needed. The mothers also touch base with their children as they need. The babies and toddlers stay emotionally connected with their mothers through a variety of intersubjective, verbal, non-verbal, and physical interactions.

The proximity of mothers and children during groups is conducive to supporting each mother's attachment to her child, and mother-child interactions that promote the children's security of attachment as observed in mother-child secure base interactions. The group-leader's identification of a child's response to attuned maternal sensitivity is a primary intervention that promotes mother-child reciprocal and pleasurable secure base interactions and increases the likelihood of them re-occurring. Pleasurable mother-child interactions and the power of love and attachment infuse and mobilize the mother-baby-toddler group-process. The painful interactions and feelings are modulated. When problems are occurring, mother-child proximity during groups promotes the ability to identify mother-child interaction details. The links between a mother's childhood memories and mother-child interactions are vitalized in the present moment and promote the mother's self-reflection and insight. The babies' and toddlers' proximity to their mothers during groups excites the mothers' deepest longings with glimmerings of the possibility of fulfillment. The group-leader's awareness of this evolving process and the recognition of beginning indications of it lead to interventions that promote it. Emotionally significant new shared meanings emerge.

DOI: 10.4324/b23150-4

Another perspective on mother-child proximity during groups is that it allows for mothers to experience being seen by the group-leader and thereby see themselves through the eyes of the group-leader during mutually pleasurable, attuned, and reciprocal mother-baby and mother-toddler interactions. Elements of this pleasurable and enriching experience of mothers being seen may also occur when mothers look in the mirror holding their babies and watch with pleasure their reflection in the mirror. An especially gratifying experience for mothers is being seen with their babies and toddlers by their own parents and feeling validated as they are reflected in their parents' adoring eyes. This process was highlighted by Alicia Lieberman when she described the origin of her term "Angels in the Nursery." It was inspired by a grandfather's description of watching his son tenderly interacting with his own baby: an intergenerational transfer of love and attachment. Mothers' everyday experiences of being seen by loved ones and strangers was missed during the Covid pandemic when social distancing was being observed. Mothers were aware of this absence.

Mother-child proximity during groups also provides the opportunity for the babies and toddlers to hear and to participate in the discussion. The rationale for this approach is that the children are hearing, or experiencing in other ways, the disturbances that are triggered and the group-leader can intervene in a way to promote mothers' awareness. For example, *While Patricia was describing how angry and embarrassed she was when Lulu –13-months – had her first temper tantrum in the supermarket, Lulu approached her mother, lay on the floor, kicked her feet, and let out a long, loud shriek. The following intervention demonstrated that the children are paying attention and are reactive to the group-process, angry feelings can be talked about together, and memory narratives can be co-constructed: "Lulu, it looks like you want to join our conversation and show us what Mommy is talking about. You and Mommy were angry."*

When a stressful mother-child interaction occurs and the mother-child equilibrium is disturbed, the group-leader's ability to tolerate the mother's and the baby's or toddler's intense feelings and to reflect on them changes the interaction in the moment for both the mother and the child, and leaves room for the mother's self-reflection and new shared meanings. When a mother is interacting with her child in a way that the group-leader views as mis-attuned, negligent, or hostile, interventions to explore what the mother thinks and feels, and what she imagines her baby or toddler thinks and feels, changes the moment for both the mother and the child.

*Sharon sat next to 4-month-old Joey whom she laid on the carpeted floor next to her. Sharon was almost still-face while Joey actively and joyfully seemed to be pursuing his mother with big smiles, gleeful squeals, and animated kicks. Sharon remained motionless, silent, and smiled ever so slightly: seemingly just enough to keep Joey engaged and energized. She placed her hand strategically close enough to Joey's so he could almost reach out and touch her, which he tried but never could do. While Sharon sat in touching distance from Joey, the upper part of her body and head were as far away* as possible; she never touched him. The following intervention promoted exploration of the meaning of their interaction: "Joey likes playing with you. He plays with you so energetically. Your play style is more reserved." Sharon responded, "I like it this way. I want him to be the active one, in a way to pursue me."

Our conversation had expanded to include Sharon's awareness of and preference for the interaction she was having with Joey. We now could begin to explore its meaning. We needed to understand what was motivating Sharon to seek feeling pursued by her baby and what memories were associated with these atypical, avoidant, mother-baby play interactions. While Joey looked like he was adapting to his mother and his mother liked their play the way it was, the meaning that their interaction had to Sharon, "being pursued," and the ways in which this pattern of play also occurred in other interactions between them, were of concern.

Another mother in the group, Evelyn, commented, "I need to work very hard to keep Cramer engaged. Sometimes he just turns away and won't keep playing, he takes a break." The following child development information expanded group discussion, "One way in which babies 4-months, even younger babies than Cramer, regulate the amount of stimulation that is right for them is to avert their gaze. I wonder if that is exactly what Cramer is doing; you described him as 'taking a break.' Babies and adults have different thresholds for stimulation and different preferences. At those moments Cramer may need less stimulation." Evelyn responded, "I feel rejected when he does that." The following interpretation highlighted her intuitive empathy, "You empathically understand that Cramer needs a break; feeling rejected motivates you to try to keep him engaged." This led to a group discussion about over-stimulation and under-stimulation, and individual differences regarding optimal arousal. Our discussion also included the mothers' vulnerabilities to feeling rejected by their babies. Sharon, described above, was unaware of her vulnerability to feeling rejected, being rejecting, or of Joey feeling rejected, and commented, "Joey never rejects me." There was much work to be done with Sharon.

The following example highlights another mother-baby avoidant interaction pattern. *Maxine was in a beginning mother-baby group with Morgan, 9-months. Morgan rarely approached her mother or looked at her. When she did, Maxine often did not respond, maybe did not notice. When Maxine looked at Morgan as she played, Morgan did not look at her mother. Both mother and baby seemed to seek connecting with each other in mutual gaze but missed many opportunities. They rarely connected, but when they did it was intense and seemed mutually pleasurable.*

*Maxine's core theme, her conflict between how close to and how distant from Morgan she wanted to be, was reflected in their interactions and was revealed when she talked about the importance of both her work and family life. Maxine was unaware of how she was enacting her conflict with Morgan. Maxine also indicated her conflict between closeness to and distance from her own mother. She idealized her mother as a mother and devalued her as a woman, "She was a great mother, but she never did anything else with her life." On the other hand, Maxine painfully recalled, "When I was a little girl my mother was always late, and she is still always late. I remember waiting for her at school; she was always the last mother to arrive at pick-up time."* Maxine was unaware of the links between her conflicted relationship with her mother and interactions with her baby, or any connection between her relationship with her mother and her conflicts between work and family life.

For several weeks interventions focused on identifying the few, brief interactions between Maxine and Morgan that seemed to be pleasurable to them both. Moments when Morgan looked at her mother and a pleasurable interaction did not occur were also identified. In other words, Morgan's attachment behavior of which Maxine was unaware, and which delighted her when noticed, was identified. Perhaps in some ways Maxine was "waiting" for Morgan as she remembered waiting for her mother. Over the weeks mother-baby shared smiles, mutual gaze, and tender touching gradually increased.

When Morgan was 3.5-years, the early avoidant patterns that had existed between her and her mother were no longer visible in terms of missed opportunities for pleasurable interaction. Morgan was thriving. During our last group, while saying goodbye, Maxine reflected on her difficulties enjoying her first year of motherhood with Morgan. She quietly wept as she talked about her sadness having distanced herself, *"I was not able to be close to Morgan when she was a baby. I missed out on so much."*

Until this moment, we had not talked about this sadness during the three years the group had been meeting. Maxine's comments about the emotional pain she was describing, and her role in it, were triggered by our impending separation, this being our last group. Maxine was now aware that she had played a role in her distance from Morgan. Her insight was revealed when she said, "*I was not able to be close to Morgan…*" What was happening between me and Maxine in the moment and between Maxine and the other women in the group, paralleled what she was describing between herself and Morgan: closeness and distance. I did not share my thoughts that connected her sadness about Morgan to closeness and distance in her relationship with the other women in the group, or with me. This is not part of the group-process. Maxine's experience of missing the pleasures of closeness with Morgan during her first year of life, and her own role in it that she was reflecting on, were primary. The mother-child relationship remains at the center of the mother-baby-toddler group-process.

An exception to the focus on a mother and her child is when a mother's feelings towards the group-leader or towards a member of the group are interfering with focusing on her child. This is sometimes indicated when a mother reports a dream during a group. For example, *Brandi reported the following dream after having missed two groups with 2-year-old Eliana:* "I was sitting on a huge trapeze. My feet could not reach the ground. I could easily have fallen off. You were pushing me high across a large open space. It was scary. But it also felt good." The following interpretation addressed her feelings that were interfering with attending the group and maintaining the focus on her child, "The equilibrium that you had established with Eliana has been disrupted by all the things we are talking about together. And while you are enjoying Eliana more and things are easier between you, *all the changes that you may feel I am pushing are scary." The focus on Eliana was restored; Brandi resumed talking about Eliana.*

The group-leader talking to the mothers about the children, talking directly to the children, and the mothers' attention on the group-leader influence the children's initiation of contact with the group-leader. For example, *when Harold, 26-months, gazed questioningly into my eyes, I said, "Mommy feels sad, she's crying. Sometimes mommies cry." At times a child may stop playing and focus on Mommy talking across the room. A comment like, "Yes, Toni, we talk about important things in our group" acknowledges that the child has had a reaction and includes the child in the group discussion. These kinds of group-leader comments to the children, even if the children do not understand all the words, highlight that the children are reacting and that we can help the children to process their reactions.*

*When Bobbie was 34-months, her mother, Carrie, was telling the group how angry and "fed up" she was with Bobbie. Her words were harsh and conveyed her helplessness. Bobbie approached her mother. Carrie's anger escalated as she continued her diatribe. Focusing her attention on her child was useful: "I wonder what Bobbie is feeling about what is happening right now." Carrie gasped and said, "She looks very scared." This intervention* acknowledged to Bobbie that she was having feelings in the moment that warranted attention and enabled Carrie to recognize that her behavior was having an unintended impact on Bobbie. Carrie became able to identify Bobbie's feelings and modulate her own rage.

The other mothers observing these interactions also reacted. The following intervention promoted the group-process, "Mothers are usually *dual tracking*; they are attending to their children while they are focusing on other things like talking on the phone with a friend or cooking dinner. Sometimes they are not dual tracking; they feel passionate about something and are completely focused on it, as just happened to Carrie. When have you realized that your child is not in the front or the back of your mind, but has fallen off your radar?" The discussion expanded to include the other mothers' shared experiences with Carrie. Group support was mobilized.

Mother-child proximity during groups can intensify for mothers the vividness of differences between their interactions outside the group in contrast to interactions during groups and can help make it possible to talk about them. For example, *a mother described her feelings of helplessness when her daughter, 14-months, hit her at home and her inability to stop the hitting, "She only hits me at home." We were able to understand that these mother-child hitting interactions that only occurred at home were an enactment of the mother's memories of helplessness during childhood spankings that only happened at home. Recognizing her feelings of helplessness with her daughter as a childhood memory enabled her to prevent her toddler from hitting her.*

Exploration of each mother's experiences of how her child and she are the same and in what ways they are different during groups than at home is useful and sometimes is alluded to by mothers. For example, *when a mother talks about something stressful that occurred with her child, and says, "It would never happen here" the mother may be suggesting that she is different here and the details of how she is different can be understood.*

It is believed that children should not hear certain things. However, during groups the babies and toddlers have an opportunity to hear things in a different way than when talked about or when they are occurring outside the group. The following vignette is evocative of the controversy.

## Connie, Timmy, and Pete

**Vignette summary**

**Child's age** – twins 28-months
**Mother-child interaction** – Mother's inhibition of Pete's assertiveness and mother's inhibited responses to Timmy's requests to go to the potty to urinate
**Presenting problem** – Pete being "bullied" and Timmy not urinating in the potty
**Childhood memory** – Being hurt by her mother's fingernail while routinely picking her nose
**Mother's core theme** – Conflicts about aggression organized around penis size
**Primary defense mechanism** – Disavowal
**Organizing Fantasy** – "Pete has a huge penis and Timmy has a very small penis"
**Intervention** – Interpretation of mother's unconscious affect and the impact of her penis fantasies on mother-child interactions
**Resolution** – Mother engaged in appropriate, pleasurable aggressive play with both sons and took Timmy to the potty when he requested. Timmy began urinating in the potty and Connie began to take Pete to the potty; Pete's assertiveness increased

*Connie had twin sons Timmy and Pete. Connie did not like Pete's assertiveness and since he had been 18-months was determined to inhibit him. She prohibited him any aggressive play. When he banged the banging toy, she stopped him and said, "Too rough." When he attempted to hold on to a toy that was being grabbed by another child, she required him to relinquish it, "Be nice." When Pete wanted to play with a toy that another child wanted at the same time, she insisted that Pete wait. Efforts to talk with Connie about her reaction to Pete as "too aggressive" and the ways in which she inhibited his assertiveness had limited success. Connie had a different attitude towards Timmy: "He's such a sweet, gentle boy. He's so cute." During a heated group discussion about aggression, Connie provided a way to begin to understand her different attitudes towards her two sons, "Pete has a huge penis and Timmy has a very small one. Pete never touches his penis, but someday he will discover it and be psyched. It's ok that Timmy has a small penis because it's not how big it is that matters, it's what you do with it that counts." Connie's words became a frequent refrain.*

*The boys were now 28-months. Pete was becoming increasingly passive. Connie explained, "Pete is being bullied in the playground. I'm worried." Connie also described her concern about Timmy, "He poops in the potty all the time; he just won't pee in it.*

*I'm not sure how to help him. Pete won't pee or poop in the potty. But that's ok. He's just not ready."*

Connie had two concerns: Pete being "bullied" and Timmy not urinating in the potty. A related theme was crystalizing, Connie's attitudes about penis size, Pete's "huge" penis and Timmy's "very small" penis. Understanding how Connie's concerns and this theme were connected was important.

After Connie described her concerns, she repeated for emphasis, "Pete has a huge penis and Timmy has a very small penis, but that's ok, it's not how big it is that matters it's what you do with it that counts." At this moment, Timmy approached his mother and said, "Pee-pee, Mommy." Connie responded in slow motion as she asked, "Did you make pee-pee in your diaper, or do you want to make in the potty?" Timmy insisted, "Pee-pee, Mommy." Connie remained seated and reclined, "Do you need to make pee-pee or did you already?" Timmy repeated with more urgency, "Pee-pee, Mommy." Connie continued to resist, "Do you need to be changed or do you want to go to the potty?" Timmy persisted, "Pee-pee, Mommy." Finally, Connie took Timmy to the bathroom to change his diaper which was now wet.

It is not clear what triggered Timmy's approach to his mother. Was his need to urinate coincidental to his mother talking about his "very small" penis and his brother's "huge" penis, or had her words or her feelings attached to the words motivated Timmy? Connie's feelings about both Pete's "huge" penis and her efforts to inhibit his healthy aggression, and her devaluation and disavowal of her devaluation of Timmy's "small" penis were expressed in her repeated phrase. In addition, the ongoing meaning and connection between Connie's frequent comments about penis size and her childhood memory about the pain from her mother's "long, red fingernail" when she picked Connie's nose that she had described during the first group when Pete and Timmy were 9-months was emerging. Connie's atypical, inhibited response to taking Timmy to the potty when he said, "Pee-pee, Mommy" was a mother-child interaction during a group that could be used to explore her core theme. Her devaluation of Timmy's "small" penis and her fear of Pete's "huge" penis had emerged in a mother-child interaction.

Upon Connie's return from the bathroom with Timmy, I commented, "I noticed your timing in response to Timmy saying 'pee-pee, Mommy.'" The other mothers noted the likelihood of not getting Timmy to the potty in time to urinate. The following interpretation addressed Connie's related devaluation of Timmy's penis, "It seems like it's hard for you to imagine that with such a little penis Timmy might need to make a big pee-pee urgently." Wanting to highlight for Connie her son's positive feelings about his penis, in contrast to her disparaging attitude which may have been protecting her from other feelings she may also have had, I added, "While his penis may be little to you, to him it is a big strong penis that feels good, that can make a big pee-pee, and he can be proud of it." Connie responded with her often repeated phrase about penis size and prowess, "It's not how big it is that matters, it's what you do with it that counts." The following intervention confronted her attitudes about both her sons' penises and raised a question about the impact she was having on her children, "What a little boy does with his penis also counts. I wonder what the connection is between your reactions to Pete's big penis and him being bullied, and your reactions to Timmy's little penis and him not peeing in the potty." Connie looked intrigued.

Pete did not attend the next group. As Timmy played next to his mother, Connie wanted to talk more about what the connection might be between being bullied and penises. She said that she was confused and wanted me to tell her what the connection might be. I answered her question in terms of her possible feelings evoked by a "huge" penis that might explain her motivation to inhibit Pete's aggression, as well as his absence from the group in the context of her question. I said, "Sometimes a penis can seem scary and dangerous." This statement was brief and targeted the affective core of her conflicts about aggression and penis size. Her association in response confirmed it. Connie said, "I once had sex with a man with a big penis and it hurt me, but it was so long ago, it was not a big deal, it couldn't be affecting me now." The narrative structure of her response was the same as her repeated phrase about penis size: doing and undoing.

Connie's response confirmed that she thought a penis could be dangerous, expressed her need to minimize the danger, and disavowed her fear and its ongoing impact. I did not mention her childhood memory of her mother's painful fingernail when she picked Connie's nose. I told her that I did not know if her experience with the man whose penis hurt her was affecting her now, and while feeling uncertain at the time, I did say, "When you were a little girl your father's penis must have looked big." Connie responded with her frequently repeated statement about penises, "It's not how big it is that counts, it's what you do with it." This time I was struck by Connie's awe, her belief that it is great to have a big penis, and her need to then undo this idea with, "It's not how big it is, it's what you do with it." Connie's earlier statement about Pete had also reflected her awe: "When Pete discovers his huge penis, he will be psyched." I asked Connie if she was aware of her feelings of pride and pleasure in Pete's big penis. With a glowing smile, but somewhat coyly, maybe revealing her envy and excitement, she said, "He's lucky."

I did not interpret Connie's envy or excitement about Pete's penis, or her childhood memories of her mother's hurtful fingernail. I said nothing further about her father's penis. I had triggered her feelings of pride in Pete's penis. I spoke to Connie in terms of Timmy's feelings, which she may also have had glimmerings of: "While Timmy's penis may seem small to you, to him it is something to be proud of, big and powerful, and feels good." At this moment Timmy approached his mother and said, "Pee-pee, Mommy." This time, Connie took him immediately to the potty and he urinated in it. They returned to the group, both appearing proud, and very pleased.

The following week Connie reported that she had bought Power Ranger action figures for Pete, which she said he had wanted for a long time, and dueling swords that she, Pete, and Timmy were all enjoying. Perhaps Connie had found a way to vicariously enjoy both of her sons' penises as represented in their sword play. Timmy continued to urinate in the potty, and she had started to take Pete to the potty.

It is not clear what had triggered Timmy's approach to his mother while she was talking about her sons' penises and again when I described Timmy's penis as big, powerful, and feeling good, or why Connie took him to the potty immediately this *time. The proximity of mother and child during groups made it possible. It is also unclear what motivated Connie to buy the action figures and swords. This had not been discussed.*

*For 19 months, there had been ongoing shifts in the prominence of Connie's feelings and attitudes about penises: pride, fear, awe, envy, excitement, and devaluation. Whether Connie's unconscious conflicts and fantasies about penises had shifted, or whether she was able to change her behavior with both of her sons while the underlying conflicts and fantasies remained the same, is not known. Either way, mother-child proximity during the groups played a role in the emergence of new shared meanings and changes in mother-child interactions.*

# Section II

# Mother-baby-toddler beginning groups

Section II discusses the enrollment process, group composition, and procedures for beginning groups with children ages 2-months to 2.5-years. Two mother-baby vignettes illustrating contrasting pre-group visits are included. Introductory child development information and group questions to be used during the first three group sessions for all ages are presented.

# Chapter 3

# Beginning groups

## Pre-enrollment visits

Before joining a group, the group-leader schedules a half-hour visit for the mother and her child. The goal of the pre-enrollment visit is to answer the mother's questions and to give a description of the group: what can be expected, and what will depend on the specific women in the group and cannot be predicted. This distinction highlights that each group is unique and that the mothers influence aspects of the group-process. A general description of the group includes *"While the mothers talk, the babies and toddlers play. The play-leader, a psychologist or social worker with a specialty in early childhood, will facilitate the children's play. The few simple age-appropriate toys provided are played with in increasingly complex ways as the children develop. There is an opportunity for both independent play in a group setting and play with others. Toys include baby dolls, pretend play animals and family figures, puzzles, blocks, and a banging toy. When age appropriate, water and sand with scoopers and containers, and a toddler-size table and chairs are added. The bathroom has a changing table, a potty, and diapers. The mothers' discussion focuses on general theories of child development and mothering, and how they apply to the specific mothers and children in the group."* The group-leader's interest in the ways in which mothers' childhood memories influence their interactions with their children is described. Suggested language is, *"Mothers' childhood memories are activated when they have babies and toddlers. The memories help mothers to understand their children."* Noting that in some groups mothers talk a great deal about childhood memories and in other groups less, emphasizes that the mothers determine what they talk about. Mothers may acknowledge verbally or non-verbally that their memories are being triggered. When this occurs, commenting on it may be useful. Opportunities that arise during the pre-enrollment visit for the group-leader to demonstrate the *MBTG Guide* approach helps mothers to evaluate the suitability of the group for themselves or to raise concerns they may have. If a mother-child interaction evokes heightened affect during the pre-enrollment visit, or indicates a possible difficulty, commenting on it illustrates what happens during groups. For example, *"I noticed that it looked as if Jeri was coming to you, you opened your arms to greet*

DOI: 10.4324/b23150-6

*her, but she walked past you. These are the kinds of things we talk about in the group. I wonder what you thought."*

A child development or mothering problem is not required to join a group. However, sometimes a difficulty may be reported during the pre-enrollment visit. When a mother raises a concern, responding in a way that demonstrates what occurs during groups is helpful. For example, *Leigh described Sydney 17-months, "We go to a music and movement class. Sydney will only sit on my lap and watch the other children. If I try to get her to participate, she just cries. Is this normal?" An answer to the frequently asked question "Is this normal?" is, "The same behavior can have different meanings at different ages, and different meanings for each child. We need to understand what it means to Sydney, how it fits with her temperament, and recent events in her life. I wonder what she is thinking and feeling while she is watching. What do you think?"*

Sometimes mothers allude to a specific concern they have about their child by asking a general question. For example, *"What happens if a child hits or bites another child?"* Responding to general questions in a way that highlights the importance of specific details to be able to answer the question can elicit the personal meaning of the mother's general question.

Before the session ends, mothers are asked if they have any additional questions or anything else they would like the group-leader to know. If the group-leader takes notes during the pre-enrollment visit, assurance is given that all notes and conversations are kept completely confidential. An enrollment form and group schedule calendar for the 30 sessions is provided.

When the description of the program and the pre-enrollment visit are consistent with the group-process, mothers' assessment of the suitability of a psychodynamic mother-baby-toddler group for themselves is excellent. After enrolling, a pre-group mother-child visit is scheduled.

A formal evaluation to determine a child's or a mother's suitability to participate and benefit from a psychodynamic mother-baby-toddler group is not part of the *MBTG Guide*. If the group-leader thinks a mother is inappropriate, the mother needs to be told and seen individually with her child, or a referral made. If the group-leader experiences a mother as unpleasant, defiant, incoherent, frightening, or under the influence of alcohol or drugs, she may be inappropriate. In some settings a formal assessment procedure may be indicated and will need to be developed.

## Group composition and group schedules

Groups are organized according to the children's ages. It is recommended that within a group, there be a maximum of a 6-month age-range. There are six mothers and their children in each group, with equal numbers of boys and girls when possible. One child being the only boy or girl in the group is not recommended. A mother having the only boy or girl in the group may increase attributions related to gender when they do not apply or might not otherwise occur, and deprives the mother of shared gender-related pleasures and concerns with other mothers. Having same-sex peers with whom to identify and to play is part of the group experience for the children. It is also recommended, if a group is composed of mothers with both first and later born children, that there be at least two mothers different from the majority.

Mothers' current work also contributes to group composition considerations. Many women experience career differences among mothers to be significant and believe that the lives and perspectives of mothers who are employed are completely different from those who are not. It is recommended that one working mother not be in a group where all the others are not employed, or the reverse.

Both diversity and homogeneity vary within groups. Some differences among the mothers include age, race, religion, country of origin, family constellation, and child-care help. Past and current psychotherapy experience, mothers' trauma histories, and adaptations vary. The shared experience of motherhood generates supportive interactions among the mothers and has the most influence on group-process.

Groups begin at different ages and continue until the children are around 3 years of age. Those that begin in the first year of life meet for approximately three years for 30 weeks each year. If a group begins when the children are older, a minimum of nine months' duration of a group is recommended. Groups meet for one hour a week; enrollment is for 30 weeks. In addition to national holidays, all groups have a two-week winter holiday, two-week spring holiday, and two-month vacation during the summer. Vacations provide an opportunity for the assimilation of what has occurred during groups and support the autonomy of the mothers. Optimal scheduling for specific populations may differ.

## Pre-group mother-child visits

An individual half-hour mother-child session is scheduled after enrolling and before the first group. The purpose of this pre-group session is for the child to become familiar with the setting and to begin to build a relationship with the play-leader, and for the mother to ask any questions she may have. The visit is explained, *"Having this time before the first group, remaining close to each other while we are talking and (child's name) plays with (play-leader's name), will help (child's name) to feel secure and comfortable when the group begins and to know that you will be together here."* The mother is asked, *"As we get to know you and (child's name), what would you like us to know now?"* The question is phrased this way because it acknowledges that the mother will make a choice about what she will talk about and implies that at another time she will describe other things.

During the visit, the group-leader comments on mother-child secure base interactions and explains that they are an ongoing part of the mother-baby-toddler group. For example, *"While Jane sits on your lap, she is secure and curious to look around the room and shake the rattle."* Or, *"I can see that in a new place, with new people, Dominique knows how to stay close to you, to feel secure and play."* Or, *"Mariel is comfortable exploring the room, knowing that you are watching her, showing you what she is doing, and coming back to you when she wants."*

It is suggested that the mothers and children arrive 10 to 15 minutes before group starting time. This creates a transitional time and space for a mother and child to be together between home, the street, and the group. The waiting area has only children's picture story books, inviting the mothers and children to read together. Water, coffee, and tea are available. All groups start at the designated time; a quorum is not required.

After the pre-group visit a Group-Notes Outline is filled out by the play-leader and by the group-leader and provides an outline for them to discuss the group. Mother-child interactions including social referencing, mutual gaze and smiles, verbal interactions, and physical contact are described. Mothers' responses to children's attachment behavior are described in terms of affect, sensitivity, attunement, and empathy. Mother's attributions to her child are included. Children's play is described. The core themes in the mother's narrative, mother-child interactions, and child's play are identified. These themes often are the same. The Group-Notes Outline is below.

What is observed in the pre-group visit may prove to be representative of the mother and child or may have been specific to that day, the context, etc. Additional individual visits may be needed if a question about suitability arises or if in preparation for beginning groups a child would benefit from another visit. For example, when it appears that a toddler needs a second warming up visit to begin to play.

### *Group-notes outline*

Date
Mother's name
Child's name Date of birth
Mother's narrative theme
Mother-child interactions
Mother's attributions to child
Child's play
Child's interactions with other children

### Vignettes

The following two pre-group visits occurred after enrollment, before the first group session. The differences between them in terms of mothers' core themes, organizing fantasies, defense mechanisms, and the mothers' responses to interventions are striking. In the first vignette Cora and Lizzie, 5-months, embraced with shared smiles and mutual gaze for the first time. The mother experienced it as "beginning to bond." In the second vignette, Tracey and Dora, 6-months, the mother stated her intention to never talk about her childhood memories.

## Cora and Lizzie

> **Vignette Summary**
>
> **Child's age** – 5-months
> **Mother-child interaction** – Minimal touching, no smiling, no mutual gaze
> **Presenting problem** – "Lizzie won't make eye-contact, she's angry at me."
> **Childhood memory** – "When I woke my mom was still sleeping and when I came home from school she wasn't there."
> **Mother's core theme** – Conflict between maintaining attachment to her own mother and attachment with her baby
> **Primary defense mechanism** – Enactment of childhood memory, isolation of affect
> **Organizing fantasy** – "I'm just like my mom."
> **Intervention** – Interpretation of links between mother's childhood memory, present relationship with her own mother, and current mother-baby interactions
> **Resolution** – Mother-baby embrace, shared smiles, and mutual gaze, "We are just beginning to bond."

*Cora entered carrying 5-month-old Lizzie on her hip. Lizzie's lower body was wedged in the crook of her mother's arm, her upper body at a distance. Cora, dressed for work, adjusted her light beige gabardine suit, hiked up her skirt, kicked off her heels, and joined me on the carpeted floor. Lizzie was dressed in coordinated colors and wore a delicate baby-barrette to keep wisps of blond hair off her face.*

*As Cora and I chatted breezily, she propped Lizzie on the edge of her lap facing towards me. Lizzie remained completely still, her rosy face unexpressive, and her gaze riveted on me. There was a distinct disconnect between Cora and Lizzie in terms of their body movement rhythms, and an absence of any sense of being emotionally connected with each other. Lizzie was on her mother's lap, but it was as if they were barely touching. There were no mother-baby tender caresses and no moments of shared smiles or mutual gaze between them. Cora was lively and engaging with me, Lizzie was quiet and still with an intense seeking of sustained eye-contact with me. The unusual pull from Lizzie for mutual gaze was so strong that I struggled to maintain social eye-contact with Cora. Both the disconnect between mother and baby and Lizzie's intense seeking of mutual gaze with me were atypical.*

*Our light conversation ended when Cora told me that she had returned to full-time work when Lizzie was 10 days old. Cora explained, "I'm different from most mothers. I'm like my mom, I work all the time. Sometimes I don't see Lizzie for four or five days." Underlying Cora's surface indifference to what she was describing seemed to be a suffering that was too painful to be acknowledged but was revealed in her next sentence,* "When I do see her, she won't make eye-contact. No matter what I do, she won't look at me." *Cora's focus was on the absence of eye-contact and not being seen. The emotional underpinnings were omitted; what it feels like to Cora was absent from her description.*

*As we spoke, Lizzie's gaze remained focused on me. I was surprised by Cora's description and wanted to learn more,* "How does it happen that you don't see Lizzie for four or five days?" *Cora replied,* "If I leave for work before she wakes up and return after she's asleep, I don't see her for days. When I get home and she's already asleep I think, why did I make my last appointment so late?" *I probed further,* "Why do you think she won't make eye-contact with you?" *Cora confided,* "She's angry at me."

Cora's explanation for returning to work 10 days postpartum and sometimes not seeing Lizzie for several days were her similarities to her mother, "I'm like my mom, I work all the time." *Her core theme, a conflict between maintaining her attachment to her own mother and having an attachment to Lizzie, was emerging. Cora's preferred focus as we spoke was on the similarities between herself and her mother in terms of work: a way of feeling close to her mother. Our focus together was shifting to Cora's wish to be closer to Lizzie*

*Cora's self-questioning about why she came home too late to see Lizzie was important, though spoken almost in passing. The self-blame in questioning why she came home too late to see Lizzie may have been a remnant of blaming herself for her own mother's absences. It also reflected her new perspective as a mother which included that it is the mother's wish to be with her baby and the mother who can arrange it.*

*Cora was convinced that Lizzie was angry and that this was the reason Lizzie would not look at her, but she was not aware of the possible meanings of her belief. Cora's anger towards Lizzie for not looking at her was secondary. More important was Cora's dawning self-awareness, or readiness to become aware, that she was not only like her mother whom she had described as working all the time, but also that she was like she imagined Lizzie and had angry feelings towards her own mother. Her conviction that Lizzie was angry may have also reflected her feelings of closeness to Lizzie. Cora's self-questioning about why she had been coming home too late to see Lizzie indicated her beginning self-reflection in addition to self-blame: a potential opening for exploration.*

*Seeking an answer to her rhetorical self-questioning, I asked about Cora's childhood memories,* "Who took care of you when you were a child?" *Cora began,* "Not my mother, other people. I remember when I woke up in the morning my mom was still asleep, and when I came home from school she wasn't there."

*Cora's statement confirmed a connection between her childhood memories and her interactions with Lizzie. Although they occurred at different ages, the way in which Cora remembered the lack of contact with her own mother was almost identical to the way in which she described her lack of contact with Lizzie,* "If I leave for work before Lizzie wakes up and return after she's asleep, I don't see her for days..." *and when describing her childhood memories,* "...when I woke up in the morning my mom was still asleep and when I came home from school, she wasn't there." *The narrative similarities, the lyrics and the music sounded as though they emanated directly from her unconscious. Cora was unaware of the similarities and what they might mean. Cora was convinced that Lizzie was angry because she was away at work, but omitted her feelings connected to her memories about her own mother's absences. Cora's wish for more eye-contact reflected her emerging wish to have a different kind of relationship with Lizzie than the one she had with her own mother.*

*As Cora and I spoke, the absence of any emotional connectedness between mother and baby persisted. Lizzie remained on the edge of Cora's lap facing away from her mother. Cora went on to describe the physical distance combined with emotional closeness between her own mother and herself who had lived in different cities at opposite ends of the country since Cora was 16 years old. Cora explained, "I moved to New York with my dad, my mom stayed in Oregon to work." While Cora was describing the extensive physical distance between herself and her mother since she was a teenager, she emphasized, "We are very close. We have a very intimate relationship. We talk on the phone every day."*

*Cora's description of current interactions with her mother mirrored aspects of her description of separations from Lizzie and Lizzie's avoidance of eye-contact. Her belief that Lizzie was angry because they did not see each other encapsulated her childhood memories and her current feelings of anger and disconnectedness from her own mother which she struggled with and was disavowing. At the same time, Cora's desire for emotional connectedness with Lizzie was apparent.*

*The links between the absence of eye-contact between Cora and her mother, the lack of eye-contact between Cora and Lizzie, and yearnings for emotional connectedness were captured in the following interpretation: "You describe a very close, intimate relationship with your mother that takes place mostly on the phone. There is no eye-contact possible on the phone. (This occurred before facetime.) When you and your mother are talking, you don't see each other. You also tell me about coming home too late to see Lizzie and wondering why, and moments with Lizzie when you want her to look at you and she won't." Cora looked surprised and invited me to continue; Lizzie was intensely focused on me. "It sounds like you want Lizzie to look at you and you want to look at her, but something interferes." I said to Lizzie, another way of speaking to Cora, "Mommy wants to look at you and Mommy wants you to look at her."*

*At this moment, Lizzie twisted her entire body around to face her mother. It is not known whether their heart rates, body temperatures, or breathing rhythms changed first. It is unclear whether Lizzie rotated towards her mother and then Cora's arms embraced her, or Cora's arms embraced Lizzie first, and then Lizzie rotated towards her mother. Either way, Cora and Lizzie, cradled close in her mother's arms, now faced each other and smiled in mutual gaze. They lingered for many moments in this shared pleasurable interaction of emotional connectedness. I talked to Lizzie again. Earlier these words had expressed wishes, now they were an affirmation, "Mommy wants to look at you and you want to look at Mommy." I said to Cora, "You have two important relationships without eye-contact; we don't know what the connection might be between them. Maybe we can understand more about this." Cora's core theme,* a conflict between maintaining an attachment to her own mother by being like her and working all the time, and an attachment to Lizzie, had crystalized. The intervention had targeted Cora's core theme.

The following week during the first mother-baby group Cora told us, "Lizzie and I are just beginning to bond." The experience the week before of smiling in mutual gaze, a moment of intimate intersubjectivity, had kindled their falling-in-love: the kind of love that includes feeling emotionally connected. Cora experienced it as "…beginning to bond." Thoughts of "I am your Mommy, and you are my baby; I love you and you love me" emerged and began to consolidate.

It is not clear what exactly had prompted the close body contact, intense mutual gaze, and shared smiles between Cora and Lizzie, or the feeling of bonding that Cora described. My comments had interpreted a connection between Cora's interactions with Lizzie and with her own mother, had been encouraging, and gave permission, but the mechanism of change was imperceptible. Perhaps Cora felt seen by me in a way that she was only dimly aware herself. I saw her as a mother who wanted to and could connect with her baby. What had not been included in our conversation were Cora's feelings about an emotional connection to Lizzie. She had only talked about eye-contact with Lizzie but had emphasized how "close and intimate" she was with her own mother. The omission of her feelings about what she was missing emotionally in her relationship with Lizzie and her longings, too painful to speak, were activated and then expressed in her description of "beginning to bond." Perhaps my comment to Lizzie that stated what Cora wished, "Mommy wants to look at you and Mommy wants you to look at her," connected to Cora's longings for closeness and intimacy with Lizzie and some possibility of fulfillment.

As Cora participated in the mother-baby group, her childhood memories began to include feelings. She became aware of her conflict between being either like her mother as she described her, which helped her to feel closer to her mother, or different, which helped her to feel closer to Lizzie. She began to feel increasingly gratified by her relationship with Lizzie, but sad and angry about the distance from her own mother. Her impulses to escape from Lizzie faded. Cora found a new job with shorter hours. She never again mentioned avoidance of eye-contact with Lizzie. The meaning of her childhood memories had changed, and new feelings emerged.

Typically, between adults and between adults and babies, patterns of gaze and gaze averting fluctuate and are comfortable. When the gazers are in synch, there is a rhythm that is seamlessly smooth and goes unnoticed. When the rhythm or intensity is amiss, if there is too much avoidance of eye-contact as there had been for Cora with Lizzie, or long stares as there had been for Lizzie with me, it is disconcerting. As part of their growing attachment and falling-in-love, mothers and babies engage in pleasurable mutual gaze interactions. After Cora recognized how she was reliving her past with Lizzie, as she became aware of aspects of her current relationship with her own mother which she had disavowed, and new shared meanings were created, loving moments of mutual gaze with Lizzie became possible. Feeling bonded emerged.

## Tracey and Dora

> **Vignette Summary**
>
> **Child's age** – 6-months
> **Mother-child interaction** – Mother held baby as she slept
> **Presenting problem** – none reported, none observed
> **Childhood memory** – Left home at 15-years
> **Mother's core theme** – Needs to separate from her own mother conflicted with intensified activation of memories
> **Primary defense mechanism** – Suppression and sublimation
> **Organizing fantasy** – "My mother has nothing to do with what I do or what I don't do."
> **Intervention** – Support: accept mother's wish to not talk about her mother, enabling her to reject her mother and to feel in control of our interactions
> **Resolution** – The establishment and maintenance of an ongoing relationship between the group-leader and mother that supported mother-child interactions to promote the child's development, security of attachment, and mother's well-being

*Tenderly embraced in her mother's arms, Dora, 6-months, slept during the pre-group individual session. In response to my statement "Mothers want to do some things the same as their mothers, and some things differently" Tracey objected strongly. She insisted, "My mother has nothing to do with what I do; she has nothing to do with the kind of mother I am. I don't do the same as she did, and I don't do different than she did. What I do has nothing to do with my mother. I don't want to talk about her."*

*During groups, as the weeks and months went on, activated by interactions with Dora and group discussion, Tracey said things that implicitly referenced her mother. In response, I frequently commented, "I remember you said that you do not want to talk about your mother, but what you are saying makes me wonder about her and wonder what you are thinking about her." Tracey always replied, "Even though the other women talk about their mothers, I still don't want to talk about her. She has nothing to do with me." After many repetitions of this interaction between us, when Dora was almost 1.5-years and I said to Tracey again, "I know you said you do not want to talk about your mother, but I am wondering..." Tracey began to laugh, and my laughter was triggered. Our shared laughter was a turning point. It signaled our agreement that Tracey could maintain not talking about and attempting to not think about her mother, and I could maintain thinking about her mother and referencing her. At this moment of shared laughter, Tracey and I had a simultaneous meeting of minds and separateness of minds. Tracey said, "I left home when I was 15 with my older brother and sister."*

*Our shared laugh was a mutual acknowledgment that the horrors of her past had existed, they were recalled in interactions with Dora, and in moments as we talked. They triggered painful feelings and memories. The dangers of her past threatened to intrude but could be kept far away; Tracey was safe now. For Tracey, keeping the past a private memory helped her to feel safe and in control. Separating from her mother as a teenager seemed to have been needed for survival. Not telling me any childhood memories helped her to keep the past in the past. Not talking about her mother, a symbolic killing her off, was Tracey's way of maintaining feelings of safety. In other words, not talking about her mother may have been an adaptive sublimated murder that helped to establish and maintain an ongoing supportive relationship with me.*

*Mothers not talking about childhood memories is the opposite of a main thesis of the* MBTG Guide *and of many mother-child clinical approaches. This vignette demonstrates that a guide is only useful if it remains in the background of psychodynamic mother-baby-toddler groups. Tracey also joined groups with her second and third born children. They all thrived.*

*The meaning of the mother-baby-toddler group experience for each mother is unique. For some, the support component of the group is primary, for some the educational elements are important, and for others the new shared meanings of childhood memories and their impact on mother-child interactions are central. In a mother's words, "For moms whose lives are like drinking from a firehose, a mothers' group is life-saving."*

## First three group sessions

The child development information and group questions in this chapter apply to the first three sessions of all groups that may begin at different ages, 2-months to 2.5-years. After each group the Group-Notes Outline (page 72) is completed by the group-leader and play-leader.

During the first group session, the mothers and children are welcomed, and after each mother has introduced herself and her child, the group-process and procedures are described by the group-leader. The goal is to create a comfortable atmosphere and introduce some interesting ideas. Suggested language follows.

*"We will be talking about many aspects of child development and mothering this year. We will talk about how general theories apply to you and your child. While we are talking, we will also be watching the children play. We know that when mothers watch their children, in moments they are imagining their child's experience and at other times they are focused on their own thoughts and feelings. There is a moment to moment shifting of focus. This is something we can talk about while it is happening.*

*"We also know that mothers' childhood memories are awakened when they have babies and toddlers. Memories may be triggered when they watch their children and when they interact with them. Mothers' childhood memories influence how they think about their babies and toddlers. The memories also influence mothers' interactions with their children. Mothers think about the things they want to do the same as their parents and the things they want to do differently. Other memories also come to mind. These are some of the things we will be talking about this year.*

*"What we talk about together may be exciting, controversial, disturbing, or reassuring. What mothers talk about is personal. You might talk with others about what occurs here. When you do, it is essential that the identities of the mothers you talk about be kept confidential.*

*"When a mother or child is ill, we rely on each mother, if needed in consultation with your child's pediatrician or with your own physician, to determine if your child or you are contagious, are too sick to attend a group, or have been exposed. If anyone comes to a group who appears too sick in our opinion to be here, we will ask them to leave. In line with these concerns, the toys are washed after each group. If you are unable to attend a group, your child can come with Daddy or other parent. Friends, relatives, and child-care professionals do not attend groups. If you plan to miss a group, we would like to know."* Depending on Covid outbreaks or other similar conditions, special procedures may needed.

### Mothers are asked to describe their babies and toddlers

Each mother's description of her child and follow-up discussion occurs during the first three group sessions. Before asking the mothers to describe their babies and toddlers, some version of the following introductory child development information is suggested to be presented by the group-leader.

"This year we will talk about many aspects of child development. An important part of child development is what babies and toddlers are thinking and feeling. Theories, research, and what we imagine help us to understand babies and toddlers. We will talk a great deal about what we imagine. There is so much that is unknown about child development or is not agreed upon, and every child is unique. What mothers imagine is important.

"Babies and toddlers have physical and personality traits, some innate and some acquired. The traits they have may be different than those of their parents, different than siblings, and maybe different than you had imagined. Mothers and fathers may view their children differently. Children achieve developmental milestones at different ages. Some traits may create greater challenges than others. We can talk about what the children's beginning awareness is of the traits that you describe and what they have been told about these traits. 'You are so shy.' 'You are so smart.' Some elements of your description of your child may be phase specific, others may be lifelong. These are some of the things we can think about as you describe your child"

Each mother is then asked to describe her child. The following questions can be used to convey further interest and to understand more about each mother's description of her baby or toddler. The questions also begin a conversation with each mother and generate group discussion.

1. When did you first observe this trait?
2. Who do you know who has the same trait? Yourself? Child's father, siblings? Others?
3. Which of the traits you described did you know or imagine your baby had before birth? How did you know?
4. Which of the traits that you described do you think are innate? Acquired?
5. Which of the traits that you described do you think are phase specific? Lifelong?
6. What impact does a trait you described have on your interactions with your child?
7. In what ways are your husband or partner's views of your child the same and in what ways different from your description?
8. What would be your child's description of a mommy?
9. What traits that you described are you trying to influence or change? Which traits are you encouraging? How?
10. Which of the traits that you described surprised you?

After all the mothers have described their children, and their descriptions have been discussed, they are asked about how their babies' names were chosen. The following introduction and questions about names can be raised for group discussion.

Mothers have different experiences choosing their baby's name and reasons for the name. Some name choices may have required mutual agreement with your baby's father. One of you may have had a louder voice during the process.

*Mothers have feelings about their child's name and about their own name. Sometimes their feelings change.*

*Name choices are determined by personal, familial, and cultural meanings and traditions. You may have lingering feelings about the process and choice of your baby's name. The following questions may trigger pleasurable or disturbing memories. You may remember your feelings and decisions about your own name at different phases of life.*

1. How was your child's name chosen?
2. Are any nicknames used? How did they emerge? What name would you like me to call your child?
3. How did your parents choose your name?
4. What nicknames have you had?
5. Has your name changed? How?
6. How does your baby's name that you chose when a new-born fit now?
7. What would you like your child to call you? What would you like your child to call Daddy? Grandparents? Others?
8. What do you call your mother?
9. How does your child react when you say your child's name?
10. Have any of the children's names been changed? Are any changes planned?

## Child development information and group questions

Chapters 4 through 7 include the child development information and group questions categorized by age and psychodynamic theme. Their primary purpose is to generate group discussion, group support, self-reflection, and insight – new shared meanings. Some of the content is specifically relevant for each age-range in which it appears. Other content may apply to all groups 2-months to 36-months. Questions that have not been asked within the age-range in which they appear can be asked at different ages. Some of the information and questions will be repeated. The group-leader chooses from among the questions and themes. A precise sequence is not what is intended, inclusion of all information and questions is not required. Additional questions may be added. The group-leader's familiarity with the information and questions across ages and psychodynamic themes is useful.

Mothers' questions and comments take priority. The *MBTG Guide* child development information and questions are to be used by the group-leader to elaborate, normalize, and generalize themes raised by or alluded to by a mother, to address an observed mother-child interaction, and to initiate group discussion. There will be fluctuations within each group and variations among groups in terms of resistance to exploration and self-reflection. An important variable to consider when group-leaders choose questions is an evaluation of the current group-process in terms of anticipated resistance and anxiety the question or information might arouse. In other words, the timelier the question and information the more group discussion and self-reflection will be promoted.

The longer a group has been meeting, the more the mothers raise the topics. In part this is because there is greater comfort and safety in the group and the mothers have become intrigued by the process; in part because the mothers have learned what is of interest to the group-leader.

Re-emerging topics for group discussion are each mother's experiences before and during the birth of her baby: miscarriages, stillbirths, and IVF; pregnancy, labor, and delivery; surrogacy and adoption; prematurity; alcohol and drug use. Unresolved aspects of each mother's experiences related to these topics may continue to influence her interactions with her baby and toddler.

At the beginning of a group session, if a question or comment is not raised by a mother, the group-leader begins by asking if anyone has any further thoughts about the prior group, or anything else they want to raise. If not, the group-leader can begin either by adding to the prior week's discussion, or by describing an observation that elaborates on the prior discussion, or that is related to the child development information and group question theme the group-leader had planned for the session because of an observed problem or age-specific developmental task. Whenever possible, linking the information and questions to an observation of a child, a mother-child interaction, or a comment by a mother is useful.

The child development information and group questions are chosen by the group-leader to generate interest and excitement as the mothers discover new aspects of their children's developing minds and their own. Topics related to pleasurable mother-child interactions are balanced with discussion about stressful interactions. The balance is weighted more towards pleasurable to provide security and comfort to address the painful. The information and questions raised by the group-leader communicate to the mothers what the group-leader finds important or interesting and sparks their interest. The mothers come to appreciate the complexity of conscious and unconscious motivation, fantasies, conflicts between wishes, and the relationship between their own childhood memories and current mother-child interactions.

During the first several groups, many topics may arise and be touched upon briefly. Suggested language when a topic is dropped because there are many competing topics is: *"There are so many important topics for us to discuss and each one connects to others. At the beginning we touch on many topics and then talk about each in greater detail."* This statement affirms that the mothers and the group-leader have a future together until the children are 3 or 3.5-years when the group ends. In addition, this statement means we have not said everything there is to say about this topic and can talk more about it. The expectation of a future with a termination date contributes to the group-process and the process with each mother. When the motivation for shifting topics is in response to the disturbing feelings the topic evokes, it is useful to comment on the stress that has been triggered, and when possible to relate the stress to something known about a mother or child in the group. For example, *"It seems that it is difficult to talk about accidents; it may remind everybody of Cody's accident."*

The following four chapters include child development information and group questions categorized by age and psychodynamic theme. Mother-child vignettes at the various ages illustrate group-process and interventions with an individual mother-child dyad during groups.

# Section III

# Child development information and group questions

Chapters 4 through 7 are organized by children's ages and psychodynamic theme. Suggested child development information for group-leaders to present provides a context for raising the group questions. The purpose of the information and questions is to generate group discussion and mothers' self-reflection. The MBTG Guide provides a flexible model to be adapted as needed. The exact sequence of information and questions across psychodynamic themes and ages is determined by the group-leader. Each chapter also includes mother-child vignettes to illustrate the guidelines at different ages.

# Chapter 4

# 2 to 10-months

Beginning groups with children 2 to 10-months, including suggested language for welcoming the mothers, describing group procedures, child development information, and group questions for the first three sessions were discussed in Chapter 3. Following are suggested information and questions, categorized by psychodynamic theme, for subsequent sessions. The purpose of the information and questions is to generate group discussion, group support, and mothers' self-reflection. They are also used to expand or generalize a mother's comment or question, to initiate group discussion, or to address an observed mother-child interaction. The brief child development information provides a context for the questions. Preceding a question with a brief relevant child development idea can promote mothers' reflection about the question. The order in which questions are raised varies from group to group. Questions can be added or omitted as useful.

## Child development information and group questions

### Mother-child interaction

*As you get to know your babies, as they develop, and as your relationship evolves, you will discover more and more about your baby and more about yourself as a mother. The babies are learning more about themselves and about you. Your baby may have strong likes and dislikes. Some of their likes and dislikes will be related to age, some to temperament, and some to life experiences they have already had. Rolling over, sitting, crawling, and then walking will influence their likes and dislikes. Their likes and dislikes will influence your interactions with each other. Some of your interactions will be pleasurable to you and to your baby, some not. Some of their likes and dislikes may create challenges.*

1. What are some of your baby's likes? Likes related to sleep? Feeding? Being held? Bath? What are some of your baby's dislikes?
2. How does your baby react to transitions? Sleep to wake? Wake to Sleep? Out of the bath, into the bath? Dressed to naked? Into the car, out of the car?

DOI: 10.4324/b23150-8

3. What are some of the things your baby likes that you do not like? What are some of the things your baby does not like that you are trying to help your baby adapt to?
4. What are feedings like with your baby? Bottle, breast, other? What does your baby like about feedings? Not like? What do you like about feedings? Not like? Have you introduced a cup, solids? Where does your baby eat? When does your baby eat? What parts of feedings does your baby control? What parts do you control? What are your ideas about weaning? Introducing solids? A cup?
5. What are going to sleep routines like with your baby? What happens in the middle of the night?
6. While your baby is dependent on you for so many things, in what ways is your baby independent? What does your baby control? In what ways do you want your baby to be more independent? Less independent?
7. What are some of the most pleasurable interactions with your baby? Most difficult or stressful?
8. What interactions are you having with your baby that you did not expect to be having? What interactions are you not having with your baby that you expected to have?
9. When do you talk to your baby? What do you talk about? How does your baby respond? What do you think your baby understands?
10. When are you and your baby focused on the same thing? Pointing? Playing? Picture books? Shared emotions? Smiling? Laughing? Scared? Angry? Sad, crying? What are these interactions like for you? For your baby? While setting limits, in what ways is the focus of attention on what you want and in what ways is the focus on what your baby wants?

### *Mother-child attachment*

*There has been a great deal of research about mother-baby attachment and many related published books for parents. Attachment is one way to describe the mother-baby and mother-toddler relationship. Mother-baby attachment evolves and looks different at each phase of development. A main feature of an attachment relationship is that it confers a sense of well-being, self-worth, safety, and shared pleasure.*

*We are going to focus on what your attachment relationship with your baby feels like to you, what you imagine it feels like to your baby, and how it influences your interactions with each other.*

1. How do you know that your baby recognizes you?
2. How would you describe your baby's attachment to you? How would you describe your attachment to your baby?
3. When is your baby soothed by you? When does your baby want your attention? Want to be close to you?

4. How does your baby react to separations from you? How do you react to separations from your baby?
5. What stresses for your baby are eased by being held by you? Doctor visits? Strangers? Loud noises? Hungry? Tired?
6. When does your baby reject you? Ignore you? How do you react?
7. After you and your baby have been separated, what happens when you reunite?
8. How does your baby respond to others? Father, siblings, grandparents, caretakers?
9. What other attachments does your baby have? A treasured toy? Family pet?
10. What impact has your baby's attachment to you had on you? On your husband or partner, and on your relationship with your husband or partner?

## Mother-child communication

*Babies express what they are feeling. As their expressions get responded to, their expressions become communications. For example, when babies cry because they feel hungry and you come to them and feed them, their cry becomes a communication: "I am hungry, feed me." As their communications are responded to, they develop expectancies. Their expectation to be responded to helps them to feel secure and to wait. For example, expecting gratification helps your baby to keep sucking until your milk lets down, or to wait while you are preparing the bottle.*

*When babies feel understood during mother-baby communications, they learn to understand themselves. We will talk a great deal about the ways in which babies feel understood.*

1. When does your baby communicate by crying? Smiling? Vocalizing? Laughing? Turning away? Pointing? What does your baby communicate in each of these ways?
2. How does your baby communicate the need to be close to you? Crying? Gesture? When does your baby need to be close to you?
3. What does your baby communicate by gesture? Pick me up? Look at that? No? Yes? How does your baby communicate feelings?
4. How does your baby know if you understand? How does your baby feel understood when you do not gratify the wish or need that is being communicated?
5. When do you talk to your baby? What do you talk about? What does your baby understand when you talk? When does your baby understand you, but not do what you want?
6. When does your baby need to wait? How does your baby react when needing to wait? What communications from you help your baby to wait? For example, when your baby is crying for you, or calling you, when

does hearing your voice trigger the expectation of seeing you and promote waiting?
7. How do you differentiate whether your baby is communicating a need or a wish? What are the differences between needs and wishes? Which wishes do you gratify, which do you frustrate? When? What happens?
8. When have you noticed that your feelings have been communicated to your baby, even when you did not intend to communicate your feelings? How did your baby react?
9. How does your baby communicate over-stimulation? Or needs more stimulation?
10. When is it difficult to understand your baby's communication? How do you lay a foundation for future communicating with words? For example, spitting out food to communicate, "I don't like this." Or, hitting to communicate, "I am angry or scared." How do you help your baby to feel understood in these moments? What words is your baby learning?

## *Mothers' childhood memories*

*Mothers' childhood memories are activated. Sometimes a specific memory may be triggered while interacting with your baby. Some childhood memories are cherished others are haunting. Mothers' childhood memories help them to think about interactions with their babies: the things they want to do the same as their mothers and the things they want to do different. Memories about your pregnancy and delivery may also come to mind, and other memories.*

*Babies are creating memories: not with words yet, but as expectations, feelings, and body memories. For example, "When I smile at Mommy, she smiles at me, it feels good." "When I am scared, Mommy holds me, and soothes me." "When I get a shot, it hurts." Some memories you are creating together.*

1. How have your childhood memories influenced you with your baby? When are specific childhood memories triggered?
2. What are the things you want to do the same as your parents, what things do you want to do differently?
3. What memories of your pregnancy and delivery come to mind?
4. What childhood memories are you aware are being repeated with your baby? Which ones do you want repeated? Which ones do you not want repeated?
5. When do memories come to mind about IVF, surrogacy, adoption, miscarriage, NICU?
6. What painful or frightening experiences has your baby had that will have a long or permanent impact?
7. What experiences do you help your baby to remember?
8. In what ways are your mothers' memories of your childhood the same as yours, in what ways different? Siblings' memories the same and different?

9. What experiences has your baby had that will become childhood memories? How are you helping your baby to remember in an adaptive way?
10. What do you wish your baby would not remember?

## *Separation*

*Mothers have different patterns of being with their babies and being separated from them. Babies are learning about separations. They are learning that you still exist when they cannot see you and that separations are followed by reunions. They are developing a stable reliable memory of you caring for them and loving them. This internal sense of you, in time, will comfort them when separated from you. It will become part of their sense of self: I am safe, I am loved. Some of you may have returned to work, some may be planning to return to work, some may be uncertain. Childcare arrangements and anticipatory feelings about this separation may be complex.*

1. When are you separated from your baby? Sleep? Work? Social activities? Vacations? Exercise? Bathroom? Which separations do you control? Which separations are influenced by or controlled by others?
2. What are good-byes like?
3. What are these different separations like for you? For your baby?
4. What separations from your baby are you expecting in the future? When?
5. Who cares for your baby when separated from you? What instructions are they given? What contact do you have with caregivers while separated from your baby? What information do you want from them when you return?
6. What contact do you have with your baby when separated? Phone? FaceTime?
7. After separations, what are reunions like?
8. What were separations like for you when you were a child?
9. Who in addition to you does childcare? What do they do?
10. What kinds of play related to separation do you do with your baby? Peek-a-boo? Hiding objects? Pretend with dolls?

## *Play*

*Play is an important way in which babies learn about themselves, others, and ways of being with others. During moments of face-to-face play with you, including mutual gaze, shared smiles, gentle touching, and melodic sounds or phrases, babies experience the shared pleasures of intimate, attuned interactions. These kinds of evolving pleasurable play interactions may provide a foundation for intimate interactions throughout life.*

*Beginning play with toys provides the opportunity to learn about how things work and promotes a sense of self that can make things happen: shake a rattle and make it jingle, press a button and make a clown pop up.*

*Pretend play to practice and control everyday life experiences and to master stressful experiences like separation from Mommy and visits to the doctor begins to emerge. Babies may have a special treasured toy that they have endowed with the ability to soothe. Repeated play has the additional pleasure of knowing what to expect.*

1. How do you and your baby play? Face-to-face play? Play with toys?
2. What is playing with your baby like for you? What kind of play do you like? Not like? What kind of play does your baby like? Not like?
3. When does your baby play alone? How does your baby play alone? When does your baby play alone in your presence; you are together, but each focused on different things?
4. What happens during tummy-time play?
5. How do you and your baby play peek-a-boo?
6. What pretend play does your baby do? Pretend play together?
7. Does your baby have a treasured toy? Does your baby sleep with it? Take it out of the crib, out of the apartment? How does your baby play with it?
8. What happens when your baby is struggling to achieve a task with a toy, for example with a puzzle? How and when do you help? When do you not help? How do you decide?
9. What items of yours or Daddy's does your baby play with? Siblings' toys?
10. When does your baby look in the mirror? What happens?

## Aggression

*There are different ideas about aggression. Some see aggression as innate, others as reactive. Some see aggression on a continuum between healthy assertiveness and destructive hostility. Some behaviors have a different meaning when a baby does them or when a toddler does them; for example, kicking or pulling someone's hair. They can be motivated by anger or curiosity. Babies may bite when they are overstimulated, angry, or frightened.*

1. When is your baby aggressive? What do you do?
2. When is assertiveness aggressive? Grabbing a toy from another baby? Grabbing the spoon? Curious exploration? Demands to breastfeed? When does a kiss turn into a bite, or a hug turn into a tackle?
3. When have you seen healthy assertiveness in your baby?
4. When have you seen aggression in your baby's play? Banging a banging toy? Knocking down a block tower?
5. When does your baby hit? Bite? Pull hair?
6. When is someone aggressive with your baby?
7. When does your baby feel angry? Frustrated?
8. What does your baby do when feeling angry? Frustrated?
9. When do you get angry at your baby?
10. What do you do when you feel angry at your baby?

## Body awareness

*Part of a baby's sense of self is an emerging body sense of self. Babies experience whole body sensations, for example what it feels like to be held or rocked, and skin sensations, being caressed and washed. Some are gentle and some less gentle. Babies experience internal sensations: pooping, hiccups, swallowing, sneezing, etc. Babies also discover different body parts: mouth, hands, feet. They are having body pleasure and body pain. Part of your baby's sense of you is your body: how it feels, smells, moves, and looks. Babies have different sleep, feeding, and bowel rhythms. Some are regular, some more irregular.*

1. Which parts of your baby's body do you think your baby has discovered? How were they discovered? Which have you named? Does your baby have any birth marks, scars?
2. Which body parts does your baby touch, look at, or move purposely? Eyes, hands, head, feet, tongue, lips, genitals? When?
3. What body pleasures does your baby enjoy? Thumb sucking? Rocking? Massage? What body pain has your baby had? Teething, diaper rash, injections? Accidents? Surgery? What have your baby's reactions been to vomiting, diarrhea, constipation, choking? Your reactions?
4. Which parts of the body does your baby like touched or kissed by you? By others? How are they touched? Tickled? Which parts of the body does your baby not like to be touched? By you? By strangers? What happens?
5. What happens when your baby gets an injection? What is it like for you? If your baby was circumcised what was that like for him? For you? What medical procedures has your baby had? Accidents? Illnesses? Allergies? Surgeries? NICU?
6. What body parts do you talk to your baby about? What body functions do you talk to your baby about? What do you say? What words do you use?
7. Are your baby's body rhythms more regular or irregular? Sleep? Eating? Bowel movements?
8. What are your baby's responses to sensory stimulation? Touch? Sound? Smell? Texture? Music?
9. What is your baby's awareness of his or her genitals?
10. What body activities is your baby practicing? Rolling over? Sitting? Crawling? Standing? Walking? Climbing?

## Children's interactions with other children

*Babies are interested in other babies and older children. Babies look at other babies and sometimes vocalize in interaction with each other, or cry in unison. Babies touch each other and sometimes imitate each other.*

1. When does your baby see other children? Siblings? Cousins? Others?
2. How does your baby interact with other babies? Toddlers? Observe? Imitate? Seek proximity? Touch? Smile?
3. How does your baby interact with older children? Siblings?
4. What kind of help does your baby need with other babies?
5. When do the adults help the babies play together? How?
6. How is your baby like other babies? In what ways different?
7. In what ways is your baby the same with boys and girls? In what ways different?
8. What does your baby learn being with other babies?
9. What is it like for you when your baby is with other babies?
10. When do you agree/disagree with other mothers about intervening during the babies' interactions?

## *Emotion regulation*

*Babies have different thresholds for stimulation, over arousal, and under arousal. Some babies can fall asleep or nurse in a noisy room, some need quiet. Some startle easily. Some re-regulate quickly when their equilibrium is disrupted, others more slowly. Some babies scream loud, others are quieter. Some babies acquire self-soothing behaviors very young; others require mother-baby mutual-regulation interactions, including being held, until they are older. Identifying feelings with words helps children to regulate their emotions. A mother's ability to tolerate her baby's emotions evolves.*

1. What does your baby find soothing: being held, rocked, hearing your voice? What does your baby find stressful? When is it difficult to soothe your baby? What is it like for you?
2. Does your baby use a pacifier? When is a pacifier used to satisfy the sucking need, when is it used for something other? What do you think about pacifiers, swaddling, rocking?
3. What self-soothing does your baby do?
4. How does your baby react to transitions? Wake to sleep? Dressed to naked? Out of the bath, into the bath?
5. How much and what kinds of arousal are optimal for your baby? What is over-stimulating, what is under-stimulating for your baby? Tickling? Rough and tumble? How do you know?
6. When does your baby get overwhelmed? What helps your baby re-regulate?
7. What feelings does your baby have?
8. What feelings that your baby has do you identify with a word? Happy? Surprise? Fear? Anger? Sad? Excited?
9. When is your baby happy? Angry? Frustrated? Scared? Sad? Excited? Content?
10. When does your baby laugh?

## Gender

*Ideas about gender in our culture are always evolving. Laws, customs, and attitudes change. Ideas about gender may be different today than when you were a little girl. You may have observed the reactions of others to your baby being a boy or a girl.*

1. Did you know the sex of your baby before birth? How did you know? How did you decide whether to know? What was your reaction?
2. Does your baby know that he is a boy? Or she is a girl? How do they or will they know?
3. What traits, physical and personality, does your baby have that are masculine? Feminine?
4. Do people think your baby is a boy or a girl? Why do they think it?
5. What information does your baby get from you, from others, about whether he is a boy, or she is a girl?
6. What about gender is important to you? What about gender is not important to you?
7. How are your ideas about gender the same as your husband or partner? How are they different?
8. How do the books that you read to your baby reflect ideas about gender? How are your child's clothes, toys, hair, related to gender?
9. How are the toys that your baby likes related to gender?
10. What is your husband's or partner's reaction to having a son or daughter?

## Underlying meanings of behavior

*Behavior is motivated and surface behavior may have underlying meanings. A baby's smile can have different meanings, as can a baby's cry. Sometimes babies cry when they are scared, sometimes they laugh when they are scared. We cannot always know what a baby's behavior means to the baby, but what we imagine is important.*

*We can also imagine what a baby's developing sense of self is. Expectations are a part of the developing sense of self. For example, "When I call Mommy, she comes to me, I am effective."*

*Understanding what a baby's behavior means and what motivates it helps us to communicate to the baby that we understand. For example, "I think you felt scared when the dog barked, so you want me to hold you." Feeling understood is at the core of feeling loved.*

1. What are the different situations and feelings that trigger your baby crying? What is it like for you when your baby cries?
2. What do you imagine your baby's inner experience is when you respond to the crying?
3. When does your baby laugh?

4. What do you think is your baby's emerging sense of self? For example, "I am loveable, Mommy delights when she sees me." "I am safe." "My hand is part of me, I can see it when I want to." "I can do it." "Mommy is proud of me."
5. What behaviors of your baby have an underlying meaning that is related to developing expectations? "I cry, Mommy appears." "I am hungry, Mommy feeds me." "I throw my food on the floor, Mommy gets angry." "I smile at Mommy, Mommy smiles at me."
6. What experiences does your baby have that are contributing to a developing sense of self? Crawling? Walking? How does your baby react to looking in the mirror? What does your baby do that evokes feelings of pride?
7. When does curiosity motivate your baby's behavior?
8. When does asserting autonomy motivate your baby's behavior?
9. When does attachment motivate your baby's behavior?
10. When does anger or fear motivate your baby's behavior?

## *Internal conflict*

*Internal conflict refers to contradictory feelings and opposing wishes. For example, a 3-month-old baby may need to suck more but may be too full to eat more. A 3-month-old probably does not experience this as a conflict of wishes. But you may wonder what to do in this kind of situation. An 8-month-old may be frightened by the noise the blender makes but may also be curious about turning it on and off. Internal conflict develops with age and increases with development. 10-month-old babies may have a conflict between pleasing themselves and pleasing Mommy. They may crawl towards an electric socket, get your attention, smile, communicate their intention, and then dash towards the socket. Internal conflicts for women may intensify when they have a baby. Mother-baby conflict sometimes reflects internal conflict.*

1. What conflicts does your baby have? Conflict between the wish to explore and fear?
2. What conflicts do you have with your baby? What internal conflicts are related?
3. What conflicts do you have between gratifying or frustrating your baby? For example, conflict about picking your baby up when crying? going to your baby?
4. What conflicts do you or did you have about bottle feeding, breastfeeding, pumping? Pacifier?
5. What conflicts do you have about tummy time? Sleep? Food?
6. What conflicts do you have about separations from your baby?
7. What advice have you been given that you disagree with? Did you follow it or not?

8. When does your baby seem in conflict about pleasing you? For example, crawls towards the socket, stops and smiles to get your attention, then speeds towards the socket? Throws food on the floor? Other examples?
9. When are you in conflict about letting your baby struggle to achieve something, fail, or get your help? When does your baby seem in conflict about getting help or doing it alone?
10. When are you in conflict about letting your baby self-feed or make a mess? Do something dangerous?

## *Mother-child differences*

*Mothers have reactions to the differences from and similarities to their children. One of the first known similarities or differences is the sex of a baby. Facial features may seem familiar or foreign. Hair color and texture, eye color, and skin color may be different from you. Personality traits may be identified early and be more like one parent or the other.*

1. How is your baby the same as you, how is your baby different: physically, personality, birth order?
2. Who is your baby like? Physically? Personality? Intelligence?
3. What impact do the differences between you and your baby have on you? On your interactions?
4. What impact do the similarities between you and your baby have on you? On your interactions?
5. What have other people noticed about the similarities and differences between you and your baby?
6. In what ways do differences between you and your husband affect your baby?
7. What differences between you and your partner do you think your baby is aware of?
8. How do the differences between you and your husband benefit your baby and not benefit your baby? Personality? Race? Language? Religion? Child rearing ideas?
9. How is your baby the same, and in what ways different than you imagined?
10. Which differences and similarities have been talked about? Which not? Which do you plan to talk about with your baby? Which not?

## *Learning*

*Maturational readiness is required to learn. Mothers teach their babies a great deal. Babies also learn by themselves. Some things are learned quickly and some slowly. Some learning requires many repetitions or practice. There are different kinds of teaching-learning interactions: imitation, instruction, physical. Different approaches may be more suitable for different tasks, at different ages, for different children. Mothers may favor one approach or another.*

*Babies are learning about the pleasures of social interactions. They are also learning about interpersonal conflicts and the ways in which they get resolved. They are learning about feelings. The babies are beginning to learn limits and to inhibit their impulses. They are learning what to expect.*

1. What kinds of things are you teaching your baby now? How are you teaching? What is your baby learning?
2. What is your baby beginning to learn to expect? Mommy tells me when she is going away. When I am hungry, I get fed. When I throw my food on the floor, Mommy says, "No" and stops me. After I poop, Mommy changes my diaper.
3. What things are you teaching your baby now that help build a foundation for future learning? For example, words for poop. Words for feelings. The pleasure of reading.
4. What is your baby learning by imitation? What is your baby learning by verbal communication? Gesture? What is your baby learning by trial and error? What has your baby learned by a leap in maturation?
5. What is your baby practicing with your help? Alone? Rolling over, sitting, standing, walking?
6. What words is your baby learning to say? No? Yes? Mama? Dada? This or that? What words does your baby understand? Words for feelings? Wishes? What languages are spoken to your baby?
7. What behavior is your baby learning to inhibit, for example the impulse to throw toys on the sidewalk from the stroller? How?
8. When is your baby learning to accept a substitute when frustrated? How is your baby helped to shift attention to a substitute? When does your baby not accept a substitute? What happens?
9. When and how is your baby learning to wait? What helps your baby to wait?
10. How is your baby using play to learn? Cognitively, emotionally, physically?

## Vignettes

The following three vignettes about mother-baby attachment illustrate interventions with an individual mother-child dyad during groups. Each mother-baby dyad was in a different group.

The first vignette is about Blair whose childhood traumatic loss of her own mother was being enacted, without awareness, with her 2-month-old baby, Kyra. The vignette illustrates interventions that link childhood memories to current mother-baby interactions, the emergence of new shared meanings, and the mother's resolution of reactivated grieving.

The second vignette is about Doris and 9-month-old Mackenzie. Doris was being treated for depression with medication by a psychiatrist. The depression was triggered three months earlier by the discovery of her husband's two-year affair and his request for a divorce. Interventions during the mother-baby group focused on the mother's anger, feelings of rejection, being unlovable, and the baby's attachment behavior.

The third vignette is about Marlene and 10-month-old George. Marlene was unaware that her belief that George did not think she was his mother and her subsequent relinquishing his care was motivated by her own fears about being a mother. Interventions leading to the mother's self-reflection and mother-baby attachment are described.

100  Child development information and group questions

## Blair and Kyra

**Vignette summary**

**Child's age** – 5-months
**Mother-child interaction** – Baby remains asleep on mother during groups: an enactment of mother's childhood memory
**Presenting problem** – Baby's birth triggered mother's grieving her own mother's death
**Childhood memory** – Lying on mother's body after mother's stroke
**Mother's core theme** – Reactivated feelings of childhood loss and intensified grief reactions to mother's death
**Primary defense mechanism** – Pleasurable childhood memory enacted
**Organizing fantasy** – "My mother is missing so much"
**Intervention** – Linking childhood memories to mother-baby interaction
**Resolution** – Baby remains awake during groups; mother's awareness of disavowed childhood loss; reactivated grief resolved

*Pleasurable memories are sometimes enacted to substitute for or to ward off associated painful feelings, memories, and thoughts. The security and support in the mother-baby group, and exploration of the meaning of her interactions with her baby, enabled Blair to tell her story and to mourn.*

*Kyra was 2-months when she and Blair joined a new mother-baby group with six mothers and their babies 2 to 5-months. The mothers and I sat in a circle on the carpeted floor. While the babies sat on their mothers' laps or lay on blankets next to them, their babbling and cooing could be heard through the din of our voices. It was a lively group with bubbling discussions about the amazement and delights of infant development, and the stresses for mothers during this phase. Blair was an active participant.*

*The mothers were close observers of the week-to-week changes in their babies. Each woman was discovering the uniqueness of her baby and of herself as a mother. The babies were thriving. As the weeks passed, the mothers were feeling less stressed and more competent. Sleep routines were becoming more stable and predictable. Smiles were being enjoyed. Mother-baby play was flourishing. As the babies approached 4 to 7-months they were alert, could roll-over, some were beginning to sit and starting to crawl. The babies watched each other, played with the toys, and sometimes had turn-taking vocal interactions. Mother-baby interactions were joyful. Blair and Kyra were different.*

*Week after week, throughout each group Kyra slept nestled under a soft, pink cloud of cashmere against her mother's body, tenderly held in her mother's arms. Both Blair and Kyra seemed completely content with this cozy arrangement. It is unusual for babies* to sleep throughout every mother-baby group. In general mothers prefer that their babies be awake. They either arrange their sleep schedules or stimulate the babies to keep them awake during groups. Mothers enjoy an intensified pleasurable way of being with their babies during groups. Because Kyra's sleep pattern was unusual, I wondered about its meaning to Blair. When asked about Kyra sleeping, Blair had always noted, "This is a good time for Kyra to sleep." Blair had not been ready to talk about the meaning of Kyra sleeping throughout every group.

When Kyra was approaching 5-months and was still sleeping throughout every group, I asked Blair again whether our group met at a time when Kyra usually slept. This time Blair had a different answer indicating her readiness for exploration, self-reflection, and insight. She was calmly reflective, "No, this is not her nap-time, but I like Kyra sleeping on me like this during the mother-baby group. It feels just right." More details were needed to understand the meaning of this sleep pattern. I asked Blair what she liked about it. She thoughtfully identified the details of her experience, "I like the way her body feels. I like the feeling of her weight on me, warm and still. I can feel the rhythm of her breathing – the gentle bursts of her breath on my neck, her heartbeat. It feels good." Blair seemed to be capturing in the slow tempo of her carefully chosen words, the specifics of an experience from long ago: fragments of a distinct body sensation memory. Because the details were so specific, I asked Blair if what she was describing reminded her of anything. She thought for a moment and then said, "When I was 3 years old my mother had a stroke and became paralyzed."

Blair remembered being cared for by her grandmother after her mother's stroke. She did not talk about the loss that she experienced but described her pleasurable daily visits with her mother. Blair fondly remembered being placed on top of her mother's reclined immobilized body. She painted a vivid picture, "I remember walking into my mother's room holding my grandmother's cold hand. My mother's bed was high. My grandmother lifted me and laid me down on my mother. She felt warm. I don't remember how long I lay there or when we stopped having these visits." Blair's words alluded to loss; perhaps her childhood pain of loss was contained in the memory of her grandmother's "cold hand." The following interpretation connected her pleasurable childhood memory to current interactions with Kyra, and included her disavowed feelings of loss, "It sounds like your memory of lying on your mother's body and Kyra sleeping on you during our group are connected. It seems as if Kyra sleeping on you is a way for you to remember the pleasure of being with your mother, without remembering the pain of what you lost."

Blair's mother had died three years before Kyra was born and since her birth Blair was missing her mother in a way that she had not before. Blair mused, "My mother will never know Kyra; she is missing so much. It's so sad. I especially miss my mother during the mother-baby group." Blair's awareness of missing her mother "especially" during the group referred to reactivated feelings of childhood loss and associated memories of loss that had compounded Blair's grief about her mother not knowing Kyra.

Kyra sleeping on Blair throughout the group and Blair feeling her breath and heartbeat were ways to feel close to her own mother rather than remember or re-experience her painful childhood losses. At the same time, this sleep pattern was interfering with Kyra's age-appropriate alertness, interactions with the other babies, and play during the mother-baby group. It was also preventing Blair from experiencing these kinds of pleasures with Kyra and sharing them with the other mothers, as her own mother had also missed similar experiences when Blair was a little girl.

After interpreting a connection between Blair's pleasurable memories about lying on her own mother's body as a child and Kyra sleeping on Blair during the group, and her own disavowed loss, there was a change. The specifics of how this change occurred are not known; nor is it known how the sleeping pattern between mother and baby had been created or sustained. The next time the mother-baby group met, Kyra awoke for the last 15 minutes. During the following group she was awake for the last 25 minutes, and at the next group Kyra remained awake throughout the entire group. Kyra continued to stay awake during groups. The mother-baby interaction details that brought about these changes could not be seen.

Now, rather than sleeping, Kyra began to manipulate toys, squeal, kick with delight, and observe the other babies. She had a glowing smile and was beginning to sit. Blair and Kyra maintained emotional connectedness when at a slight distance through mutual gaze, shared smiles, and gentle caresses. At times Kyra sat on her mother's lap, observing, or interacting with the other babies. At other times, she lay on her pink blanket excitedly kicking and rolling over. It is true that Kyra was now older and needed less sleep. However, something else also seemed to have happened. More details emerged.

Blair was a doctor and had a busy work schedule before maternity leave. She believed that she had decided to become a doctor because of her mother's stroke and the disabilities her mother had suffered. Being a doctor had always helped Blair to feel close to her mother. Blair recalled, "After my mother died I was ok. I buried myself in work. But since Kyra's birth, I miss my mother more." Blair described her intensified grief with each developmental step Kyra took, "My mother is missing so much, each new thing Kyra does." When Blair talked about her current sadness about what her mother was missing now, it was as though she was also re-living her own childhood pain about all her mother had missed during her childhood, for example a school play when Blair was 10. Blair became aware of feelings related to childhood loss that were reactivated. In addition, her sadness about her mother not seeing her as a mother emerged. Blair also became aware that while Kyra had been sleeping during groups, she was missing Kyra's participation in the group as her mother had missed parts of her life: another re-living of the past.

Blair's renewed grieving with each of Kyra's emerging maturational milestones was signaled by a subtle gesture from Blair that presented a slight impediment to Kyra and a communication to stay close. For example, when Kyra was beginning to crawl, Blair placed Kyra in the center of her encircling legs creating an obstacle to crawling. Blair and I became able to recognize this pattern together. On the threshold of each developmental step, we began to recognize her revived feelings of loss that triggered the impulse to create an impediment. We could talk about the painful feelings of past and present losses instead of Blair acting them out with Kyra. Group mothers provided additional support and shared with Blair the pleasure in Kyra's development.

*Ever-present in my work with Blair were my observations of her sensitive mothering, and Kyra and Blair's attuned mother-baby interactions. Together we had enjoyed the pleasures of Kyra's early developmental achievements and navigated Blair's associated grief. Many years later, Blair called to tell me that Kyra had graduated college and had been accepted to medical school. We were both moved by this shared moment.*

# Doris and Mackenzie

> **Vignette summary**
>
> **Child's age** – 9-months
>
> **Mother-child interaction** – No physical or emotional mother-baby interactions during groups, baby's proximity seeking attachment behavior ignored or rejected by mother
>
> **Presenting problem** – Ruptured mother-baby attachment interactions. Onset of maternal depression three months prior to joining the group when she discovered husband's affair, and he wanted a divorce
>
> **Childhood memory** – Idealized childhood, no specific memories
>
> **Mother's core theme** – Rage at her husband; unable to feel loved by her baby or love towards her baby
>
> **Primary defense mechanism** – Mother's depression interfered with effective defenses
>
> **Organizing fantasy** – Emerging fantasy of concrete mother-baby attachment
>
> **Intervention** – Identified baby's attachment proximity seeking, and interpreted mother's difficulty feeling loved by her baby because she felt so hurt, rejected, and angry at her husband.
>
> **Resolution** – Mother-baby attachment interactions emerged.

*Doris entered the mother-baby room, placed 9-month-old Mackenzie in front of a toy-shelf, and walked away. Three months earlier, Doris had learned that her husband had been having an affair for almost two years and wanted a divorce. A psychiatrist was treating Doris's acute depression with medication.*

*Doris and Mackenzie were new to the mother-baby group that had been meeting for several months. As Doris sat alone at a distance from Mackenzie, she ignored Mackenzie's attempts to approach her and rejected any suggestions that Mackenzie wanted to be close to her. Doris disagreed with my idea that Mackenzie might be reacting to a new setting with strangers and that she wanted to be close to her mother for security and comfort. Doris looked vacant. Mackenzie looked lost.*

*Two months earlier, Doris had stopped making entries in Mackenzie's photo album. She had delegated most of Mackenzie's care to a babysitter and no longer played with her. With all the painful and humiliating rejection and rage Doris was experiencing with her husband, it was impossible for her to feel that Mackenzie wanted to be close to her or that she wanted to be close to Mackenzie. A significant rupture in their mother-baby attachment, and all its pleasures, had occurred. Doris continued to shun Mackenzie's efforts to be held or even to touch. Much of Doris's behavior could be explained globally in terms of the extent of her depression and maybe an attempt to protect Mackenzie from her rage. Interventions focused on the potential power of mother-baby attachment interaction details.*

*For the next three weeks during the mothers' group, at every possible opportunity, I drew attention to the behavior of the babies that indicated their growing love, feelings of safety when close to Mommy, and emotional attachment to their mothers. Glances from across the room, climbing onto mothers' laps for cuddles, seeking comfort when needed and being soothed, bringing toys to their mothers, shared smiles, and mutual gaze: mother-baby interactions that accompany feelings of pleasure and emotional connectedness. There were many opportunities to identify and describe these mother-baby interactions during the group. In addition, whenever Mackenzie looked at her mother, even if only a fleeting glance, or made any attempt to get close to her, I highlighted it: "I think when Mackenzie looks at you while she is playing, she wants you to see what she is doing." Or, "I think Mackenzie got startled and wants to be close to you to feel safe." There were many opportunities for this kind of intervention.*

*Doris continued to criticize and ridicule Mackenzie's typical attachment behaviors, "It's weird when she hangs on me, or tries to climb on me. It's strange when Mackenzie clings to me. I hate it when she touches my hair." While Doris was insistent, I persisted: "You've been so hurt and rejected by your husband, it's hard for you to feel that Mackenzie wants to be close to you or that Mackenzie loves you." At other times I noted, "Maybe Mackenzie reminds you of your husband, how angry you are at him, and how much you want to hurt him."*

*Four weeks after joining the group, Doris entered the mother-baby room with a slight smile and for the first time sat close to Mackenzie who reached out and touched her mother several times. In striking contrast to the past, Doris did not recoil. When Mackenzie settled on her mother's lap for the first time, Doris tentatively asked me a question that revealed her emerging fantasy that corresponded to the changes in their interactions. Doris hesitantly said, "Mackenzie has discovered her bellybutton. She plays with it all the time. Do you think she remembers when she was attached to me by the umbilical cord before she was born?" I responded, "It sounds like you feel that Mackenzie loves you and wants to be close to you."*

*Doris's fantasy of actual mother-fetus attachment via the umbilical cord was her concrete vision of my identifying mother-baby secure attachment interactions and my descriptions of mother-baby psychological attachment and love. I did not validate the idea proposed by Doris that Mackenzie remembered being attached by the umbilical cord, nor did I deny it. I affirmed the underlying meaning of her question: "Mackenzie loves you and wants to be close physically, and to feel emotionally connected to you."*

*Maternal depression and painful current life events can disrupt early mother-baby attachment. It was difficult for Doris to repair the mutually nurturing mother-baby relationship with Mackenzie that had been ruptured a few months earlier. My conviction about Mackenzie's attachment and love helped to lessen Doris's feelings of being unlovable and unloving that had been triggered by her husband's rejection. She was now able to enjoy the rewards of mother-baby love even in the context of the painful, humiliating rejection from and anger towards her husband. Doris resumed caring for Mackenzie, playing with her, and making entries in Mackenzie's photo album.*

*Doris did not describe any childhood memories. Her descriptions of her parents and siblings were completely idealized. Both her idealization and family support during her marital crises and depression was useful. Some combination of the gratifying mother-baby interactions Doris was now having with Mackenzie, the anti-depression medication she had been prescribed by her psychiatrist, and synergies between them had helped to begin to alleviate her acute depression. Attuned mother-baby interactions nurtured Mackenzie's development and Doris's recovery.*

## Marlene and George

> **Vignette summary**
>
> **Child's age** – 10-months
> **Mother-child interaction** – No physical or emotional contact during groups
> **Presenting problem** – "I feel like I am not George's mother."
> **Childhood memory** – Illness and death of mother's mother
> **Mother's core theme** – Fear of being a mother, conflicted with wish
> **Primary defense mechanism** – Projection and disavowal of conflict about being George's mother, enactment of conflict with baby
> **Organizing fantasy** – Being a mother means dying
> **Intervention** – Interpretation of connection between organizing fantasy and childhood memory
> **Resolution** – Attachment interactions developed; mother resumed care of baby

*Marlene was a beautiful and professionally successful woman. She was tall and slim, with long blonde hair cascading down her back. George was a robust 10-month-old. His platinum hair framed his angelic face. Each week Marlene carried George into the mother-baby room, placed him on the floor next to a toy-shelf, and walked to the other side of the room to sit. They never touched and George never looked at his mother. From a distance, Marlene gazed longingly at George. I wondered about the meaning of these atypical mother-baby interactions.*

*George was a competent crawler and was able to pull himself to standing. He was physically capable, though he barely moved from where his mother had placed him. It was as though if he moved from where he had last been with his mother, he would completely lose the ability to find her again. George drooled excessively; his chin and cheeks were always smeared with saliva that dribbled down and soaked his shirt. He explored the toys in a muted quiet manner and appeared uninterested in the other babies. Marlene seemed sad; George was low-key.*

*During the third time the mother-baby group met, Marlene confided, "I feel like I'm not George's mother. He thinks his nanny is his mother; I've turned his care almost completely over to her. She's with him more than I am. He laughs with her in a way that he never laughs with me." In some ways Marlene took responsibility for George thinking the nanny was his mother. She had turned his care over to the nanny and she acknowledged that she did not feel like George's mother. Marlene implied that she was being reactive to George. She was unaware that she was distancing herself from George, and unaware of her motivation. For Marlene, joining a mothers' group with George meant that she qualified as his mother, even if she did not feel like his mother.*

*Marlene quickly became an active member of the group. She was eager to recount memories of her own childhood. She was the youngest of three children whose two older brothers lived in California. Their mother had died when Marlene was 15 years old after a long, painful, and disfiguring illness. While Marlene spoke about her memories of her mother and events after her death, I began to wonder whether for Marlene becoming a mother herself meant becoming sick, ugly, and then dying as had her mother. I shared this idea with Marlene: "I wonder if you have mixed feelings about being a mother. You love George and want to be his mother but being a mother may frighten you. Being a mother may also mean getting sick and dying like your mother." My words seemed to hover quietly over the mothers and babies, and to resonate with the tear that floated down Marlene's cheek.*

*Over the next several months, as the mothers in the group talked about their own mothers, Marlene told us about the sad, horrifying details of her mother's illness and death, and how much more she missed her since George was born. In some ways feeling that she was like her mother and would get ill and die had helped her to feel close to her mother, even though it also frightened her and distanced her from George. Happy pleasurable memories began to emerge. Glowing smiles lit up and animated her face. Mourning was resumed. It included her sad and frightening memories, happy loving memories, and healthy images of her mother. Her tears dried. Becoming a mother became unlinked from dying.*

*Gradually, Marlene assumed more of George's care. She frequently bathed him. She ate breakfast with him every morning before going to work, and frequently dinner. Marlene and George began to play together. Marlene also began to tuck him into his crib at bedtime. Perhaps most meaningful, she made-up what became their special bedtime song. Psychologically, Marlene became George's mother. George thrived. The drooling that had drenched his face and shirt no longer flowed. Of course, George was older, but something else that had changed between George and his mother may have had an impact on his drooling.*

# Chapter 5

# 11 to 19-months

Beginning groups with children 11 to 19-months, including suggested language for welcoming the mothers, describing group procedures, child development information, and group questions for the first three sessions were discussed in Chapter 3. Following are suggested information and questions, categorized by psychodynamic theme, for subsequent sessions to initiate group discussion, to expand and generalize a mother's comment or question, or to address a mother-child interaction. The children in this age-range are transitioning from baby to toddler. It is helpful for the group-leader to acknowledge this transition and reflect it in referring to the children as either babies, toddlers, or children depending on their age. Questions should be chosen from among different psychodynamic themes based on the timeliness for the group. A question raised for group discussion can be preceded by a brief related child development idea to promote mothers' reflection about the question.

## Child development information and group questions

### Mother-child interactions

*Your children are transitioning from being babies to being toddlers. Some things remain the same, many things change. We can think about what this transition is like for you and for your children. Walking and beginning language are major developmental steps with new experiences of autonomy. Mother-child loving interactions and angry interactions both occur. Their intensity may be surprising. Intersubjective interactions, that is, a sense of knowing what each other are thinking and feeling, emerge during mutual gaze and pointing. Intersubjectivity can also occur during limit-setting.*

*During some interactions, you may have a sense of knowing what your baby or toddler is thinking or feeling, and a sense of being on the same wavelength. During other interactions, it may be unclear. As your child develops, your interactions are becoming more complex.*

DOI: 10.4324/b23150-9

1. What are some of the changes in your interactions as your baby transitions to being a toddler or has become a toddler? Changes related to walking? Talking? Breastfeeding? Taking bottles? Pacifier? During diaper changes? Stroller? Car seat? Sleep routines? Eating?
2. What are the most pleasurable interactions for you? Most difficult or stressful? For your baby/toddler?
3. How are interactions during our group the same and how are they different from at home? Why do you think?
4. What kinds of joint focus of attention interactions do you and your child have? Pointing, reading a book, toys, laughing? What are these interactions like for you? For your baby/toddler? What are joint focus of attention interactions like during limit-setting? In what ways is the focus of attention on what your child wants, in what ways on what you want?
5. What are feedings like? Bottle, breast, other? What does your baby/toddler like about feedings, not like? Have you introduced a cup? Solids? Are there feeding times? Do feedings occur in a regular place? What parts of feeding does your baby/toddler control? What parts do you control? What plans do you have for weaning? Solids? Finger foods? Utensils? When does your baby/toddler choke, gag? Have allergic reactions? What happens?
6. What interactions are you having with your baby/toddler that you did not expect to be having? What interactions are you not having that you had expected to have?
7. When do you talk to your baby/toddler? What do you talk about? What do you think your baby/toddler understands when you talk to him or her? What talking is your child beginning to do?
8. What items that you don't want your baby/toddler to touch are out of sight, reach? What items are available that you interact with each other about touching, how to touch, and not touching? What is the value of both kinds of experiences?
9. What are your baby/toddler's interactions like with others? Daddy? Siblings? Grandparents? Others?
10. What age does your child seem to you? What age do you imagine your child in your mind? When do you think about your child at a future age?

## *Mother-child attachment*

*Attachment is one way to describe the mother-baby and mother-toddler relationship. It highlights that the children are learning that they can rely on you to keep them safe, though at times they get hurt; to teach them what they need to know, though at times they protest; to share their pleasures, and to soothe their pain. They are learning that you delight in them and that they are of value, though at times you disapprove of their behavior. Their sense of self is emerging in the context of their complicated relationship with you, "I am loved, I am safe, sometimes we are angry, then we are loving again."*

1. How does your baby/toddler show love for you? Wanting your attention, protesting separations, wanting to be close, seeking your approval?
2. How would you describe your growing attachment to your baby/toddler?
3. How has having a baby/toddler influenced your relationships with others? Husband? Parents? Friends? Relationships with your other children?
4. What stresses for your baby/toddler are eased by being held by you? Being close to you? Doctor visits, strangers, loud noises, hungry, tired?
5. When does your baby/toddler reject you? Get angry at you?
6. Who in addition to you does childcare? Daddy? Other relatives? Paid employees? What do they do? How would you describe the relationship they have with your child? What is your relationship like with the other caregivers? How is their care the same as yours, how is it different?
7. What do you want your baby/toddler to call you? Daddy? Others? What do you call your mother?
8. How does your baby/toddler respond to separations? What are reunions like?
9. How is your relationship with your baby/toddler the same as you expected? How is it different?
10. In what ways have you changed since your baby was born? In what ways has your baby/toddler had a positive impact on you, in what ways negative?

## Mother-child communication

*Feelings, ideas, intentions, wishes, and empathy can be communicated verbally and non-verbally by babies, toddlers, and mothers. Newborns have needs, babies and toddlers have wishes and needs. Understanding each other's communications and feeling understood are central to relationships. Misunderstandings occur and get repaired. Mothers have ideas about what their babies and toddlers understand, but sometimes are uncertain. Communicating "I understand you" can be challenging. Feeling understood is vital.*

1. How does your baby/toddler communicate needs? Crying? Gestures? Words? When and how do you intuit what your baby/toddler needs? When are you uncertain?
2. How do you differentiate whether your baby/toddler is communicating a need or a wish? In what ways is this a useful distinction? Which wishes do you gratify, which do you frustrate? How does your baby/toddler respond when wishes are frustrated?
3. How do you communicate that you understand your baby/toddler when you do not gratify a request? How does your baby/toddler respond when frustrated but feeling understood?
4. When have you noticed that your feelings have been communicated to your baby/toddler, even when you did not intend to communicate the feeling? Sad, angry, loving, impatient, how did your baby/toddler react?

112  Child development information and group questions

5. What feelings do you communicate with words, I love you, I am angry, I am sad? What feelings does your child communicate with words?
6. How and when do you communicate approval? Disapproval?
7. When does your baby/toddler understand you, but not do what you want?
8. When do you apologize to your baby/toddler? What does the apology mean? Remorse? Don't be angry at me?
9. What limits do you communicate verbally? Which verbal communications are accompanied by a physical interaction in addition to the words? For example, while restraining your baby/toddler, "You remember, no touching the socket. I am going to help you stop."
10. When do limit-setting communications frighten your baby/toddler? When does your baby/toddler laugh when you set a limit? Cry? Startle? Ignore you?

### Mothers' childhood memories

*Mothers' childhood memories are activated: some pleasurable, some disturbing. Some memories are vivid and may rush to the front of your mind, others may hover ever-present, but the details are hazy. Childhood memories help mothers to think about interactions with their own babies and toddlers and help them to understand their babies and toddlers. Memories about your baby's conception, your pregnancy, and delivery may also get triggered. Your children's experiences are being remembered and are creating what will become their childhood memories.*

1. In what ways have your childhood memories influenced you as a mother? Other memories?
2. In what ways do you want to be the same as your mother, in what ways different?
3. When are your childhood memories triggered? Cherished memories? Disturbing memories?
4. What childhood memories are you aware are being repeated with your baby or toddler?
5. When do your memories about IVF, surrogacy, adoption, miscarriage, pregnancy, labor, delivery, NICU come to mind? How do they influence you?
6. What other memories have influenced you? When do they come to mind?
7. What childhood memories of yours have you told to your baby/toddler?
8. What memories do you never want your child to know? What is the difference between a secret and privacy and their different impact on children?
9. In what ways will significant experiences that your baby/toddler has had be remembered? What experiences are talked about together? Captured in photographs? Video?

10. What experiences that your baby/toddler has had are you helping to be remembered? How? What experiences do you want to be forgotten?

## Separation

*Mothers have different patterns of being with their children and being separated from them. The babies and toddlers are learning about separations and reunions. Their memories of you loving them and keeping them safe are gradually increasing reliable even when they are separated from you or angry at you. The children's attachment to you is also increasingly powerful. Reactions to separation may be stressful. Families have different saying good-bye routines and reunion routines.*

1. When are you with your baby/toddler, when are you separated? Sleep? Work? Social activities? Vacations? Exercise? Manicure and pedicure? Haircuts? Doctor visits? How does your baby/toddler react when with you during these activities? How were these decisions made?
2. How does your baby/toddler react to separations? Bedtime separations and bedtime routines? Daily separations, for example work or exercise? Brief separations, while showering or on the phone? Long separations?
3. Who is with your baby/toddler when you are separated from each other? When does your baby/toddler know the person well, a little, not at all?
4. What are good-byes like? What separation routines do you have?
5. What are reunions like? Reunion routines?
6. What are separations from Daddy like for your baby/toddler? From others?
7. What are separations from your baby/toddler like for you?
8. What contact do you have with your baby/toddler during separations? Phone? Facetime? What information do you get about your baby/toddler when separated? How are your child's other caregivers the same as you, how are they different?
9. What helps your baby/toddler adapt to separation? Treasured toy? Pretend play? Knowing what to expect?
10. What were separations from your mother like?

## Play

*Play can be quiet with focused attention or loud with high arousal excitement. Play can be cognitive, physical, or symbolic. Play is an important way in which children learn about themselves and others. They explore the world around them with fascination. A special pleasure is play with items that Mommy and Daddy use. Pretend play is a way in which toddlers learn to cope and to master stressful situations like visits to the doctor. Peek-a-boo and hide and seek are games of separation: the separations are brief and the reunions joyful. A child can have control during the play. Reading to toddlers is a kind of parent-child joint focus of attention mental play.*

114    Child development information and group questions

1. What are your baby/toddler's primary play activities? With you, alone, with others? With toys, without toys? With other items? Books? What play does your child reject? When does your child control the play, when do you?
2. What kind of pretend play does your baby/toddler do? With you, alone? What is your baby/toddler able to control in play that you control at other times? Eating, cooking, bathing, haircuts? Pretend play with dolls and figures? Cars and trucks? Animals? What are some of the pretend themes or scenarios?
3. When is play with your baby/toddler pleasurable, when is it boring, or stressful? When is the play soothing? Frightening? When does your child reject play that you initiate?
4. What is your baby/toddler learning through play? Manipulative toys? Pretend play? Self-initiated? Other-initiated? Mastery of past stressful or frightening experiences? In anticipation of stressful events?
5. If you look in the mirror with your baby/toddler, what is it like for you? For your baby/toddler?
6. How do you and your baby/toddler play peek-a-boo? Hide and seek? Games of control: start and stop, loud and quiet?
7. What items of yours and Daddy's does your baby/toddler play with? Jewelry? Glasses? Cell phone? TV remote? Computer? Siblings' toys?
8. Does your baby/toddler have a treasured toy? How does your child play with it? Sleep with it? Take it out of the apartment? What do you do with your child's treasured toy? Did/do you have a treasured toy?
9. What kind of high arousal play does your baby/toddler do? Alone? With you? With others? What happens? Wrestling, tickling, spinning, rocking?
10. What videos, movies does your toddler watch? Alone? With you? What kinds of music? Singing? When is adult TV on? How does your child respond?

## Aggression

*Aggression may be stimulated when babies and toddlers feel angry, frightened, over-stimulated, or frustrated. Aggressive behavior may be triggered when they have witnessed the aggression of others or been the recipient of aggression. When babies and toddlers want something, they may be assertive and grab it. When they are frightened they may hit. When they are over-stimulated they may bite. Babies and toddlers are learning about what to do when they have these feelings and impulses. Babies and toddlers are also learning about coping with the aggression of others.*

1. When is your baby/toddler aggressive? With you? With others? What happens?
2. When is your child assertive? With you? With others? What happens?

3. When are your child's efforts to be self-protective aggressive? What are the differences between being aggressive and being assertive?
4. What impulses are you teaching your baby/toddler to inhibit or redirect? Hitting? Biting? Throwing things? Pulling hair? Others? How?
5. When are you so angry at your baby/toddler that you have the impulse to squeeze, hit, shake, or throw your child? What do you do? What is your thinking about spanking?
6. When is your baby/toddler frightened by you? Daddy? Others? When are you frightened?
7. When does your toddler have frightening dreams? What have you told your child about dreams?
8. What kinds of aggressive play does your child do? With you? With others?
9. When is your baby/toddler rough with parts of the body? Head bang? Pull hair? Pinch skin?
10. When does your toddler's attempt to kiss or hug another child become a bite or a push?

## Body awareness

*The babies and toddlers are learning about their bodies. They are beginning to learn the names of body parts. They may have acquired self-soothing body activities: thumb or finger sucking, pulling their hair or stroking it, rocking. Body routines are developing. The children may participate in bathing parts of their bodies and brushing teeth. They may have developed strong food preferences and self-feeding. They may show awareness and interest when they are having a bowel movement: change their activity, gaze, or go to a special place. They may be curious about your body. Some interactions you are having with your baby/toddler may be laying the foundation for the future. For example: weaning, learning to use the potty, self-feeding. Some body experiences they are having are high arousal, some are soothing. The children have acquired new body skills.*

1. What body parts do you talk to your baby/toddler about? Touch? Kiss? Tickle? Birth marks? Scars? What new body skills has your child acquired? When does your child want to be looked at and admired by you?
2. What kind of accidents has your baby/toddler had? Allergic reactions? Medical procedures? Medications?
3. What body self-stimulation or soothing does your baby/toddler do? Rocking? Spinning? Thumb sucking? Flapping? Genital? When does your child use part of your body for soothing? Your hair, ear lobe, breast?
4. What are your baby/toddler's sleep patterns? Routines? Sleep alone, with others?
5. What are eating routines? Times? Places? Food preferences? Aversions? Allergies? Choking? Gagging? Self-feeding?

6. What awareness does your baby/toddler indicate or communicate when having a poop or pee-pee? What kinds of things do you say when your baby/toddler is pooping or peeing? In what ways are these interactions laying a foundation for future learning to use the potty?
7. What is your son's awareness of his genitals? Penis, erections, scrotum, testicles? What is your daughter's awareness of her vulva, vagina, clitoris, vaginal secretions? Have you told your baby/toddler the words for these body parts? What is your thinking about that?
8. What is your baby/toddler practicing? Crawling? Standing? Walking? Climbing? Riding a scooter?
9. How does your baby/toddler react to tickling? Massage? Shampoos? Nail cutting? Haircuts? Vomiting? Diarrhea? Constipation? Rectal temperature? Suppositories?
10. What things related to their bodies do the children control, what things do you control? When they protest being touched, what happens?

## Children's interactions with other children

*Babies and toddlers are interested in other children: looking at them, touching them, and interacting with them. Babies may pass a toy to each other. Toddlers begin to play together and with adult help can build a tower. Toddlers may be affiliative and seek proximity with other children or prefer more separateness. They may imitate each other. They may be more interested in a toy when another child is playing with it which may reflect their interest in the child.*

1. When does your baby/toddler see other children? In groups? Individually? Siblings?
2. What does your baby/toddler do with other babies/toddlers?
3. When does your baby/toddler imitate another child? Imitate behavior that pleases you, that does not?
4. When is your baby/toddler aggressive with other children?
5. When does your baby/toddler show empathy for another child?
6. What kind of help does your baby/toddler need when with another baby or toddler?
7. When do you agree with other mothers about helping the babies and toddlers with each other, when do you disagree? What happens?
8. What have you seen related to a beginning friendship for your baby/toddler?
9. What toys are your baby/toddler required to share? What toys do you protect for your child? Treasured toys? With siblings? Friends? What toys have been designated playdate toys? Non-playdate toys?
10. How does your child play the same and how differently with boys and with girls?

## Emotion regulation

*Identifying feelings with words helps children to regulate their emotions and helps mothers to communicate that they understand their child's feelings. Some babies and toddlers have intense emotions; when they are happy, they are ecstatic and when they are unhappy, they scream. Others are less intense. A mother's ability to tolerate her baby's or toddler's emotions is variable depending on context, intensity, and her own childhood experiences.*

1. What feelings does your baby/toddler have? Happy? Sad? Fear? Surprise? Anger? Guilt? Disgust? Shame? Pride? Other? When are they triggered?
2. Which feelings have you identified with a word? What words?
3. How do you react to your baby/toddler's emotions? What is it like for you when your baby/toddler is angry? Sad? Happy? Frightened? Shy?
4. How do you let your baby/toddler know that you understand? How
5. What soothes your baby/toddler? When does your baby/toddler need soothing?
6. When can your baby/toddler not be soothed? What happens?
7. Does your baby/toddler use a pacifier? When? Does your baby/toddler use a bottle, or breastfeed to regulate emotions? What is your thinking about it?
8. Does your baby have a treasured toy? Does your baby/toddler use it for soothing? When? How? What is your thinking about it?
9. How would you describe your ability to tolerate your baby/toddler's strong feelings? Pleasurable? Painful? Physical? Emotional? What happens when your child gets overwhelmed?
10. When does your baby/toddler laugh? What does the laughter mean? Amused? Startled? Frightened?

## Gender

*There have been many cultural changes in the last 20 years related to gender. Same sex and opposite sex marriage, transgender children, and ideas about gender non-conformity and non-binary are more prevalent. Some of these changes have had a particular impact on parents with babies and toddlers. You may have had thoughts about this. The children are interested in gender differences and similarities.*

1. Do you think your baby/toddler knows that he is a boy, or she is a girl? How?
2. In what ways is your baby/toddler told that he is a boy? Or she is a girl? Words? Clothes? Toys?
3. Do other people think your baby/toddler is a boy or a girl? What are they responding to?

4. What is important to you about gender? What do you want to communicate to your child about gender? What is not important to you about gender?
5. What about your son is feminine, masculine? What about your daughter is masculine, feminine?
6. What ideas related to gender had an impact on you when you were a child?
7. What has your child said or done that indicated thoughts about gender?
8. When does your child imitate someone of the opposite sex? When does your son imitate you? When does your daughter imitate Daddy? Imitate a sibling?
9. When does your child want something or do something that is prototypic of the opposite gender? When does your son want to wear lipstick or nail polish? When does your daughter want to shave her face? What happens?
10. What do you think about some of the current controversies about gender? What impact do they have, or do you expect them to have, on your child?

## *Underlying meanings of behavior*

*Behavior can be described by what is seen and behavior can be understood in terms of its underlying meanings and what motivates it. The same behavior can have different meanings and be motivated by different feelings. For example, a baby/toddler may hit when angry, scared, or over-stimulated. Hitting may have been something recently seen, and is being processed. The meaning of the behavior and what motivates it matters because it will influence how you respond. Mothers' childhood memories may influence the underlying meanings they attribute to their babies' and toddler's behavior.*

1. What was a recent behavior of your baby/toddler when its underlying meaning was central to how you responded? For example, awakened in the middle of the night crying? Hit a child? Screamed the moment you walked into the doctor's office? Gagged on food?
2. What behavior have you observed when the underlying meaning was not clear?
3. When did the underlying meaning of a behavior not matter?
4. When has the underlying meaning of your behavior with your child been related to a childhood memory?
5. How does your baby/toddler react to haircuts? Baths? Band aids? What might the underlying meaning be?
6. How does your baby/toddler react to a mirror? What does the reaction mean?
7. What kinds of things frighten your child? What is the meaning of the things your child finds frightening?

8. When does your baby/toddler wake in the middle of the night? Why do you think your child awakens? When is it related to an experience during the day? A dream? Reaction to separation?
9. What indications are there that your child dreams? What do you think your child dreams about?
10. What has been said to your baby/toddler about dreams?

## *Internal conflict*

*Internal conflict begins to emerge. Babies and toddlers want to please their mommies, but also want to please themselves. Both strong wishes are sometimes in conflict. Babies sometimes signal Mommy about their conflict. For example, a baby may bang the spoon on the highchair tray, get Mommy's attention, and then throw it on the floor. The gravity experiment and the autonomy assertion come into conflict with the wish to please Mommy. Throwing the food on the floor is also an opportunity to trigger and cope with Mommy's anger. An 8-month-old may have a fear reaction to a stranger, and simultaneously be curious. A 15-month-old may be both afraid of the vacuum cleaner and at the same time be curious about it. Mothers', babies', and toddlers' internal conflicts sometimes cause Mommy-baby and Mommy-toddler conflicts with each other. Recognizing emerging internal conflicts can be useful to resolving interpersonal conflict.*

1. What conflicts have you observed that your baby/toddler has between self-pleasing or pleasing you? For example, your baby/toddler signals you the intention to touch the wall socket so you can help? Or your child is both afraid of the blender noise and interested in turning it on and off? How have you responded?
2. How do you decide which side of your baby/toddler's conflict to support? How do you communicate to your baby/toddler that you understand the conflict?
3. What conflicts do you have with your baby/toddler that will become internal conflicts for your baby/toddler? In what ways can you see that your disapproval is becoming your child's own self-disapproval?
4. When have you seen your child start to do something you disapprove of, and then stop? Or signal an intention so you can help?
5. What do you do to help interpersonal conflict become internal conflict for your child? When do you acknowledge the emergence of your child's internal conflict?
6. When do you use approval and understanding to promote your child's resolution of internal conflict? When do you use disapproval? When do you use guilt, fear, or shame to promote your child's resolution of internal conflict? What is the role of each?
7. What conflicts do you have with your baby/toddler that are also internal conflicts for you? Separating? Taking medicine? Eating? Pacifier? Sleep in your bed?

8. What conflicts do you have between work and family time, or personal activities and family time?
9. What conflicts do you have between being with your baby or your husband? Gratifying your baby or your husband?
10. What do you and your husband or partner agree about your child, and disagree about your child? How are these conflicts between you related to internal conflicts you each have?

## Mother-child differences

*Babies and toddlers may be like their mothers in some ways and different in others, for example looks, personality, intelligence. They may be like their fathers in some ways. Mothers have reactions to the similarities and differences, as do the children. Others will also have reactions.*

1. In what ways is your baby/toddler like you? In what ways different? Physically? Personality? Intelligence? Temperament? Gender?
2. Which ways that your baby/toddler is like you do you think were inherited? Learned? How were they were learned?
3. Which traits that are like you and which traits that are different do you want to support? Discourage? How?
4. Which differences and which similarities make it easier, and which make it difficult to be empathic to your child?
5. In what ways is your baby/toddler like Daddy? Do you think these traits were learned or inherited? Do you want to support the similarities or discourage them? How?
6. What are Daddy's reactions to the similarities and differences?
7. What similarities and differences are the children aware of? Physical: hair, skin, eyes? Gender? Personality? Language? Race?
8. Which similarities and differences have been talked about? Which have not been talked about? Which do you plan to talk about? Which do you plan not to talk about?
9. In what ways is your baby/toddler like and different from siblings?
10. How is your baby/toddler like you imagined? How is your baby/toddler different than you imagined?

## Learning

*Learning is exponential at this age: motor, social, cognitive, language, and emotional. Certain things they learn are maturational, some things they learn by observation, and other things their parents teach them. Some things they learn from siblings. Babies and toddlers spend many hours practicing what they are learning. Sometimes practicing in one area captures all their attention.*

1. What is your baby/toddler practicing? Standing? Walking? Talking? Practicing with you? Without you?
2. What are you teaching your baby/toddler to do? When do you use approval? When do you use disapproval? Punishment? Shame? Fear? Play?
3. What are you teaching your baby/toddler by modeling? Instruction? Values? Manners? Household routines?
4. What are some of the things that you used to do for your baby/toddler that your baby is beginning to participate in? Self-feeding solids? Putting toys away? Using a cup? Some children this age hold their bottles, some mothers continue to hold them. What do you do? What is your thinking about it? When do you carry your child, when does your child crawl or walk? How is it decided?
5. What things are you teaching your baby/toddler not to do? How are you teaching it? How does your baby/toddler respond?
6. What is your baby/toddler learning now that will provide a foundation for future learning? Weaning? Learning to use the potty? Reading? Swimming?
7. What do you do that you do not want your baby/toddler to learn?
8. What words are your baby/toddler learning to say? To understand?
9. What things did you think your baby/toddler would have learned by now but has not?
10. What has your baby/toddler learned that you would prefer had not been learned?

## Vignettes

Two vignettes follow. The mother-toddler dyads were in different groups. Taylor's childhood memories of terror prevented her from providing 15-month-old April with the secure base she needed. Exploration of the meaning of April dropping a doll on her mother's lap stimulated her mother's empathy, enabled her to talk about her frightening childhood memories, and promoted mother-toddler attachment interactions.

In the second vignette, Naomi's childhood memories were linked to her conflict between continuing to breastfeed 17-month-old Wally or to wean him. Interventions that revealed the meanings of breastfeeding of which Naomi had been unaware enabled her to resolve her conflict.

## Taylor and April

> **Vignette summary**
>
> **Child's age** – 15-months
> **Mother-child interaction** – No social referencing, no physical contact
> **Presenting problem** – Child whimpered and wandered aimlessly
> **Childhood memory** – Father's terrorizing rages, mother's helplessness, and her own fear
> **Mother's core theme** – Empathy for her child, conflicted with reactivated feelings of childhood terror interfering with providing a secure base
> **Primary defense mechanism** – Enactment of childhood memory of terror and aloneness; dissociation
> **Organizing fantasy** –Mother-child closeness is dangerous
> **Intervention** – Interpretation of the meaning of child dropping a doll on mother's lap; promoting "doll-play" as a symbol of mother-child attachment
> **Resolution** – Mother-child "doll-play" a symbolic bridge to social referencing, physical affection, and child's increased secure attachment behavior

*April was 15-months. Her hair was neatly held in two short ponytails with yellow ribbons. In her plaid skirt and stylish boots, she ran stumbling forward to catch up with her mother who was entering the mother-toddler room. This was the second time the group was meeting. Taylor, April's, mother quickly joined the other mothers huddled together on red cushions. The mothers were eager for the pleasures of adult female companionship in the sea of toddler dirty diapers and temper tantrums. April, alone as she crossed the threshold, looked adrift.*

*While the mothers were commiserating about the difficulties navigating the city with little children and warding off the advice and criticisms of strangers, perhaps also a concern about the group, the children played. Some children stayed close to their mothers, one remained on her mother's lap, and others played at a distance, periodically touching base. Either a glance across the room, a quick hug, or a shared play activity with Mommy enabled the children to resume their independent play, or to join a group activity.*

*April and Taylor were different; April did not play. She whimpered as she wandered aimlessly around the room. Taylor appeared not to notice April's distress. April did not have the needed sense of self with her mother, an internal image, which could enable her to feel emotionally connected when at a slight distance. In addition, she was unable to initiate physical contact or intersubjective interactions with her mother, who did not provide a needed secure base; there was no social referencing. When on a few occasions*

April approached her mother and dropped a doll next to her, an indirect way of giving the doll to her mother, Taylor seemed not to notice. When April dropped the doll on her mother's lap, Taylor removed it from her lap and placed it on the floor; April walked away.

After observing this pattern several times, the following child development information helped to interest Taylor in the possible meanings of April's behavior, "Children use play to learn and to communicate. When a child gives something to Mommy, it means something." I asked Taylor, "What might April mean when she gives the doll to you, or drops it next to you, or on your lap?" Taylor was interested and asked, "What could April mean?" I continued, "I wonder if April wants to watch you with the doll so she can feel something about what it's like to be close to you: to feel secure. As April explores the toys and interacts with the other children, she may need to be reminded what it feels like to be held by you, and to feel safe." In response to my implicit suggestion, Taylor grabbed the doll, though roughly and held it awkwardly.

Taylor's curiosity was piqued. Taylor's empathy for April's feelings of aloneness and needs to feel safe were revealed by the quickness of her response to my explanation of the possible meanings of April giving the doll to her. Taylor's childhood memories were also awakened. During the next group, while sitting close to me and holding the doll more gently and protectively, Taylor talked about her frightening memories of her father's alcoholic rages, and her mother's fear and helplessness. In both memories Taylor is ignored and alone. The image she painted was reminiscent of the doll she ignored or had cast aside. Taylor described one night when her father threw a lamp at a window. Her mother screamed. Splintered glass scattered the floor. Taylor was not sure if the light bulb or the window had broken, but she remembered feeling terrified.

Taylor's childhood memory, which included her ability to reflect on her feelings of terror, her mother's feelings of helplessness and fear, and her attempt to understand her father's rages – "My father had an alcohol problem, it doesn't excuse his behavior, but it makes it understandable" – enabled her to respond to April intuitively and empathically.

Taylor continued to sit next to me during each group, perhaps feeling in some ways held and protected by me. April increasingly handed the doll to her mother and watched as her mother increasingly held the doll gently, embraced it tenderly, and protected it from the other children who wanted to take it. April began to sit on her mother's lap. Her mother cuddled and caressed her. Social referencing when April was at a distance began to include mutual glances and smiles. The mother-child "doll-play" had provided a symbolic bridge to mother-child secure base attachment interactions.

The parallels between my interactions with Taylor, the evolving ways in which Taylor tenderly embraced the doll, and the intersubjective social referencing and physical interactions between Taylor and April were striking. April and Taylor's "doll-play," qualitatively and functionally, was like my interactions with Taylor. As Taylor sat close to me, I listened to the details of her childhood memories of terror which she now felt safe enough to describe. When I spoke to the other mothers and Taylor lost my direct attention, she continued to hold the doll and to feel safe. When across the room from her mother, April was no longer distressed. She felt held and safe watching her mother *tenderly hold the doll. April's independent play had become more organized and focused. She was now able to both initiate physical contact with her mother and to connect with her emotionally from a distance. They shared an intersubjective experience of: I see you, you see me, you are thinking about me, I am thinking about you, we are safe, we are emotionally connected. In time, the doll remained on the shelf.*

*Social referencing and proximity seeking are typical toddler attachment behaviors. For Taylor, frightening feelings and memories had been triggered by April's needs for closeness and protection during the group and had interfered with needed mother-toddler attachment interactions. It was as though Taylor could not hold April either physically or emotionally in mind during the mother-toddler group because feelings of being un-held and all alone herself had been activated. Taylor's mild social anxiety about a beginning mother-toddler group may have been enough to trigger childhood feelings of fear. Taylor understood that April needed to feel held, emotionally connected, and safe. She wanted to provide a secure base for her child, but her aroused feelings had interfered. Taylor was now able to remember feelings of aloneness and fear, without re-living them with April.*

## Naomi and Wally

> **Vignette summary**
>
> **Child's age** – 19-months
> **Mother-child interaction** – Child nestled next to mother's breast
> **Presenting problem** – Mother's conflict between weaning and continuing to breastfeed
> **Childhood memory** – Scalding coffee accident, mother's rages, and painful loneliness
> **Mother's core theme** – Wishes to maintain an idealized mother-toddler relationship fantasy conflicted with the actuality
> **Primary defense mechanism** – Enactment of an idealized repair of childhood trauma and loneliness; disavowal of negative feelings towards child
> **Organizing fantasy** – Magical safety and idealized fulfillment of breastfeeding
> **Intervention** – Interpretation of unconscious meaning of breastfeeding
> **Resolution** – Mother decided to wean child

*When Naomi was 10 years old, as she sat eating breakfast, her mother jumped up from the table to answer the phone, tripped, and spilled a cup of scalding coffee. The coffee blistered Naomi's face, shoulders, and thighs. The accident was horrendous and the treatments painful.*

*By the time Naomi was 12-years, her face was completely healed. One small scar remained on her thigh. For Naomi, worse than the accident and the treatments was her mother's persistent hostile fury. In some ways for Naomi the two experiences, the blistering hot coffee and her mother's anger were merged. Throughout her teen years, following her mother's "explosive rages" and her father's absence, Naomi lay on her bed soothing herself by counting the years remaining till she would grow up, leave home, marry, and have a baby. The idealized mother-baby relationship she envisioned was the remedy for her emotional pain, aloneness, and rejection. Naomi had told this story to me during her pre-group visit with 17-month-old Wally.*

*It was the fifth time the group was meeting. The mothers and I were beginning to know each other. We had talked about their pregnancies, labor, and deliveries, and how each child's name was chosen. A feeling of safety had been created. We had begun to talk about the ways in which each mother wanted to be like her own mother and the ways she wanted to be different. We had started to talk about how specific childhood memories were related to current interactions with their children.*

*The children were exploring the playroom, occasionally touching base with their mothers. Wally sat on his mother's lap; his face nuzzled into her breasts. Brimming with conflict Naomi told us, "I'm still breastfeeding, but not sure if I want to continue.*

Many people think Wally's too old to nurse. He's now 19-months, but I think I'm giving him all the attention, love, and security he needs. He's completely safe. I'm giving him all the things I never had when I was a child." Naomi's childhood memories about her accident, loneliness, and unhappiness had been triggered and spilled out. She also described her current feelings of anxiety and insecurity.

Weaning from breastfeeding occurs at different ages, for different reasons. Pediatricians, infant mental health professionals, and breastfeeding advocacy organizations have strong opinions. Mothers also have opinions and often strong feelings about weaning. For Naomi to resolve her conflict between continuing to breastfeed or not, she needed to understand more about the meaning of her conflict.

Naomi went on to describe her relationship with Wally as "blissfully happy." In addition to her authentic statements of deep love for Wally, her profound pleasures and rewards being a mother – specifically her satisfactions with breastfeeding, were intermittent brief asides that conveyed her underlying frustration, resentment, and anxiety. She gingerly alluded to the unrelenting demands of caring for a toddler: "My husband doesn't do any childcare. He never changed a diaper. I feel like a single mom. I do it all. At 8:00, I fall into bed exhausted."

Naomi's description of her husband's absence was reminiscent of her earlier description of her father's absence when she was a child and her mother screamed at her. She had needed her father's help but did not get it. This was now being repeated with her husband. "I fall into bed exhausted..." was her current experience in contrast to her childhood memory of lying on her bed envisioning an idealized reparative version of becoming a mother.

Naomi emphasized her exclusive care of Wally, "I never use a babysitter. My parents don't help at all, and I wouldn't want them to. I'm with Wally all the time. I never do anything else. I never see my friends or even talk to them on the phone. I even sleep with Wally. Wally nurses all day and all night. I love breastfeeding. We are very close." Naomi added, "I'm quick to get angry at other people, but I never get angry at Wally. The other day I was so angry yelling at the super in my building. I worry about how my anger at other people will affect Wally."

Naomi had talked about how close she and Wally were, all the love, comfort, and security she was providing for him, and how gratified she was by their relationship. Simultaneously, she had conveyed that she was stressed, resentful, and angry. She denied being angry with Wally, but worried about the impact on Wally of her anger at others. She had described some elements that were preventing her from deciding about continuing to breastfeed or to wean but remained stuck in her conflict. There was more to understand.

To understand more, I asked Naomi what she thought about while she was nursing. Naomi described breastfeeding as a pleasurable time to think about things other than Wally. "I think about things I need to do, friends to call, sometimes I read, I send emails, things like that. I know he's safe and happy, I can think about other things." I summarized what Naomi had been saying: "It sounds like breastfeeding is very satisfying for you. While breastfeeding you can feel close to Wally, feel like you are giving him all the love and security he needs, and at the same time you can think about other things."

Naomi nodded and I continued, "You don't need to talk to him, look at him, worry about him, or play with him." Naomi cautiously smiled in agreement with my slight twist on her words. Feeling encouraged that new meanings were emerging, I went on, "It sounds like the only time you get away from Wally is while you are breastfeeding." Without skipping a beat, Naomi responded, "The only break I get is when I'm breastfeeding. I'm with him all the time. I never leave him with anyone. Breastfeeding is my only escape." A new meaning of breastfeeding crystalized for Naomi.

The following week, Naomi told us that she had begun to wean Wally. She stated, "I realized that nursing is my way of getting away from Wally." My comment to Naomi the prior week, "It sounds like the only time you get away from Wally is while you are breastfeeding," hit a nerve that could have been painful, but instead felt true in a way that enabled Naomi to face an aspect of her internal conflict between continuing to nurse or stopping of which she had been unaware.

During the next several weeks we talked in the mothers' group about the different ways in which children experience love and security at each phase of development. We also talked about ways, other than nursing, in which the mother-baby relationship is unique. In addition, we talked about the typical anxieties mothers feel about their toddlers' safety.

Naomi and Wally began to discover multiple pleasurable ways of being together. Naomi began to recognize the unique aspects of her relationship with Wally in addition to breastfeeding. Gradually, she arranged for a babysitter a few hours a week and helped Wally to sleep in his crib. Wally and his father began to spend more time together. Gradually and easily for both Wally and Naomi, by the time Wally was 20-months he was no longer nursing.

Naomi's painful childhood memories about her accident, her mother's hostile and disapproving angry rages, her father's absence, and her feelings of anger, loneliness, and insecurity that were eased by breastfeeding, in addition to her teenage fantasies of getting away from her parents, had all been activated and had influenced her interactions with Wally and her conflicts about breastfeeding. Naomi now recognized that her childhood memories had been motivating many of her interactions, not only with Wally but also with her husband.

Naomi realized that any separation from Wally had felt like she was abandoning him, and he would feel abandoned; any childcare help had felt like she was neglecting him, and he would feel neglected; any time Wally was with his father had felt like she was ignoring him, and he would feel ignored; and weaning had seemed like she was rejecting him, and he would feel rejected. The feelings she had been attributing to Wally were her own unacceptable feelings. In addition, breastfeeding had retained a magical meaning of protection that would keep Wally safe. Elements of Naomi's childhood memories had invaded her interactions with Wally. New shared meanings and the emotional shifts they encompassed enabled Naomi to better meet Wally's changing developmental needs and her own.

# Chapter 6

# 20 to 28-months

Beginning groups with children 20 to 28-months, including suggested language for welcoming the mothers, describing group procedures, child development information, and group questions for the first three group sessions, were discussed in Chapter 3. Following are suggested information and questions, categorized by psychodynamic theme, for subsequent sessions. Their purpose is for the group-leader to expand or generalize a mother's comment or question for group discussion, to address a mother-child interaction, or to initiate group discussion. It is useful for the group-leader to have the full age-range of information, questions, and psychodynamic themes in mind and to choose among them when most timely.

## Child development information and group questions

### Mother-child interactions

*Emerging language and pretend play are developmental achievements that reveal the complexity of a young child's evolving inner world of thoughts, feelings, and intentions. A strong sense of self is emerging. Attachment needs and autonomy strivings are both strong, and sometimes clash. Mothers' feelings about their children and about themselves as a mother have become more complex.*

*The children are beginning to grapple with some of life's big questions about birth and death; they are beginning to be talked about. Mother-child interactions are influenced by a mother's view of the developmental process.*

1. How would you describe what this phase of development, around 2 years old, is like for you? For your child? In what ways are your interactions the same as they were before? In what ways different?
2. What impact does developing language and pretend play have on your child? On you? On your interactions? When do you want your child to talk more? When less?

DOI: 10.4324/b23150-10

3. What are the most pleasurable interactions for you with your child? For your child? What are the most stressful interactions for you? For your child?
4. What happens during meals?
5. What are sleep routine interactions like? Middle of the night interactions? What have you and your child said about dreaming?
6. How are your interactions with your child the same during our group as at home, how are they different?
7. What joint focus of attention interactions do you and your toddler have? Pointing? Playing? Picture books? Joint focus of attention to shared emotions: laughing together, crying together? What are these interactions like for you? For your child?
8. While setting limits, what are the joint focus of attention interactions with your toddler? In what ways is the focus on what you want and in what ways is the focus on what your child wants? When are choices useful? For example: "It's time to leave the playground, do you want to walk or get in the stroller?"
9. When do you have frustrating or angry interactions with your toddler? What are they like for you? For your child? When are angry interactions frightening for you? For your child? For your husband/partner? For your child's siblings? When you and your child have angry interactions how is the rupture in the loving feelings repaired?
10. What interactions have you had with your child about diversity? Differences within the family? Differences with others? Language? Race? Gender? Religion? Physical traits? Personality traits?

## Mother-child attachment

*Your child's attachment to you is growing and so is your child's sense of self. Autonomy strivings and attachment needs are sometimes aligned and sometimes clash. For example, autonomy strivings and attachment needs are aligned when a toddler achieves something and is elated by it, and Mommy is proud and delighted. The toddler is self-satisfied with the achievement, pleased to have delighted Mommy, and motivated by both to do it again. Autonomy strivings and attachment needs may clash when a toddler wants to do something, and Mommy says no. In this situation, sometimes toddlers satisfy their attachment needs by doing what Mommy wants and sometimes they satisfy their autonomous needs by doing what they want. Sometimes they cry to be picked up, and as soon as they are picked up, they squirm away. This is often a phase of development with extreme contrasts.*

1. How does your toddler show his or her love for you, attachment? How does your child show a developing sense of self? Autonomy strivings?
2. When does your child want to be close to you? Be held by you?
3. When does your child reject you? Push you away?

130   Child development information and group questions

 4. When does your toddler try to please you? When does your child not do what you want? What do you do? What do you say?
 5. When does your toddler imitate you? Daddy? Others?
 6. When does your toddler seek your approval? In what ways do you show your approval? How does your child react?
 7. When does your child get your disapproval? How does your toddler react when you disapprove? What kinds of disapproval frighten your child?
 8. What is your child's attachment to others? Daddy? Siblings? Grandparents? Caregivers?
 9. What do you do to support your toddler's attachment to others? What do you do to discourage your toddlers attachment to others?
10. What are your child's attachments to toys? Treasured toy? Attachments to other things? Pets?

## *Mother-child communication*

*Mother-toddler verbal communication is increasing. Toddlers are beginning to talk about their feelings, ideas, wishes, and intentions. Both loving and angry communications are increasingly verbal. You may have decided not to lie, trick, or threaten your child, but may at times.*

*Sometimes communications are contradictory. For example, when you tell your child, "Don't do it again" and then say, "If you do it again." Exaggerating or what sometimes seems fake can be a child's way of communicating strong feelings about something and beginning attempts to negotiate.*

*You may wonder about conversations related to death, religious ideas, sex.*

1. When does your child communicate with words? When do you understand your child's verbal communications, when do you not? What do you do when you do not understand? Do other people understand your child?
2. After you and your child have a conflict, and the good feelings between you have been affected, what happens? What happens that helps the good feelings return?
3. When does it seem like your child is exaggerating feelings or faking them? When is it to communicate strong feelings about something? Other meanings?
4. When do you apologize to your child? When do you want your toddler to apologize to you? To others? What does the apology mean? Remorse? Social decorum? Don't be angry at me.
5. When does your toddler need a physical communication in addition to verbal? For example, "There is no writing on the wall. I'm going to put the crayons away until you are ready to only draw on the paper."
6. What are some of the difficult topics you and your toddler have talked about? Death? Religious ideas? Pregnancy? Kissing? Other? How did

your child react? What kinds of things have you decided not to tell your child about? Now? Never?
7. When do you lie to your child about something? Trick your child? Threaten your child?
8. When do you tell your child what to expect? Doctor visits? Separations? How long before an event is going to happen do you tell your child? How does your child react? When do you not tell your child what to expect?
9. What things are you teaching your child not to do?
10. When do you want your child to not think something? When do you want your toddler to not feel something? What happens? For example, when do you say to your child something like, "No, you cannot have another cookie" but what you mean and communicate is "I do not want you to want another cookie?" Or, "Don't even think about it."

## Mothers' childhood memories

*Specific childhood memories may be awakened for mothers with toddlers. Some of the memories may have come to mind frequently during your adult life but have acquired new meanings. Other memories may be new. Childhood memories can help us to be the kind of mothers we want to be.*

*Your mother's criticisms of you as a mother may be triggered by her own childhood memories and by memories of you when you were a child. Her own feelings of guilt or inadequacy may be activated. Sometimes her criticisms of you may be her own self-criticisms. Sometimes the criticisms of others may be aligned with your own self-criticisms.*

*Your child's childhood memories are being created now. Some experiences that your children are having, you may be helping them to remember in adaptive ways with mother-child shared memory narratives.*

1. What childhood memories of yours come to mind? When?
2. How have your childhood memories influenced you as a mother?
3. What do you remember about your mother that was difficult and you needed to adapt to? What about you will be difficult for your child to adapt to? Or is difficult now?
4. What experiences are you helping your child to remember? Which ones are you not helping your child to remember? Which experiences would you prefer be forgotten?
5. What do you remember about when you were learning to use the potty? Being weaned from the breast or bottle? Your treasured toy? A pet? Getting lost? Being punished? What do you remember about the event, what part of your memory is a shared family narrative?
6. What have you been told about your childhood that you don't remember?
7. What kind of grandmother is your mother? In what ways is she the same as a grandmother as a mother? In what ways different?

8. When do other kinds of memories come to mind? Pregnancy? Delivery? NICU? Other?
9. What childhood memories of yours have you told your child?
10. How does your mother remember your childhood? The same as you? Differently? How are your childhood memories and those of siblings the same and different?

## Separation

*Separations from your child may have become routine and go easy, or difficulties separating may have intensified, or fluctuate in response to context. While toddlers have had more experience with separations and reunions, they also have more fears. Their love for you has grown and at times their anger at you has intensified, and your anger at them. These feelings and life experiences can influence reactions to separations. Your children may have had experiences of loss: loss of a toy, a death of a person or pet, or the loss of a babysitter or nanny.*

1. When are you and your child separated? Sleep? Work? Exercise? Social activities? Vacation? Frequency and duration? Your doctor visits, massage, haircuts, etc.? How do you decide when to be separate during these activities?
2. What are separations like for your child? For you? What helps your child with separations? What experiences has your child had that may influence your child's reactions to separations; make separations easier, more difficult? What experiences have you had that influence your reactions to separations?
3. What fears does your child have that may have an impact on reactions to separation? Fears that you will not return? Fears they are not loved?
4. What are good-byes like? When and what do you tell your child about separations?
5. What are reunions like?
6. What contact do you have with your child during separations? Phone? FaceTime?
7. Who takes care of your child during separations?
8. What games of separation do you and your child play? Hide and seek? Pretend play?
9. What were separations from your mother like?
10. How do you decide what is the right amount of separation for you? For your child?

## Play

*Play can tell us what is on a child's mind: their wishes, fears, and efforts to master developmental steps. Aspects of everyday life and unusual experiences are part of their pretend play. Sometimes the underlying meaning of their play is disguised or symbolic.*

*Puzzles, matching games, block building, and construction toys provide cognitive challenges. They also teach life lessons. The world is made up of objects that have component parts that can be assembled, disassembled, and reassembled in the same form or differently. As in language, the same words can be strung together differently to create sentences with different meanings. In contrast, puzzles have one way in which they can be put together and completed. It is a different life lesson. Both kinds of play provide the repeated pleasure that when things fall apart, they can be put back together. Often scattering the pieces of a completed puzzle or knocking down a tower is as much fun as putting it back together. All play has underlying meanings.*

*Beginning winning and losing games are sometimes stressful. Reading to children is an intimate parent-child mental play.*

1. What have you seen in your toddler's play that is related to your interactions with your child? Pretend play related to meals, bathing, potty, separation, sleep, reading? Prohibitions? Teaching-learning interactions?
2. What are your toddler's favorite play activities? With you? Alone? With peers? With others? What were your favorite play activities when you were a child?
3. How do you and your toddler play together? Games of control, for example, start and stop games? Winning and losing games, when do you let your child win? What do you think about competition? High arousal play? Reading?
4. What does your child do while looking in the mirror? What does it mean about a developing sense of self?
5. When does your toddler play alone? Before sleep? Play alone in the presence of another? For example, you are together but each focused on something different?
6. What does your toddler play to master stressful experiences? Doctor visits? Separations? Haircuts? Parental disapproval? Accident? Play with you? Alone?
7. What does your child play that challenges cognitive abilities? Puzzles? Construction toys? Other?
8. What pretend play does your child do that is related to family life? Doll play? Cooking? Mealtime? Disapproval? What have you seen in your child's play that surprised you?
9. When does your child's play frighten you? Frighten your child?
10. What kinds of aggressive play does your child do? Alone? With others?

## Aggression

*Young children may be aggressive when they are angry, frustrated, scared, or overstimulated. A wide range of experiences can trigger these different feelings and aggressive behavior. Toddlers are learning the words for their feelings and gradually discovering that the words can satisfy. For example, "I feel like hitting" eventually can substitute for hitting. "I hate you" can mean, "I am very angry at you." Children are influenced by the aggressive behavior of other children and adults, whether directed towards them or witnessed, whether in person or on TV or video.*

1. When is your child aggressive? How do you respond?
2. When does your child witness the aggression of others? What happens when mommy and daddy have a disagreement or fight? How does your child react?
3. How does your child react to the aggression of others when directed towards your child?
4. When does your child watch TV, video, or books that have aggression in them? How does your child react? What is your thinking?
5. When does your child's aggression frighten you? When do you frighten your child?
6. What kind of play does your child do that has an aggressive component? Pretend play? Punching a pillow? Building a tower and knocking it down?
7. When does your child self-hit, pinch, head bang, or pull hair?
8. When has your child bitten someone? Been bitten?
9. When is your child aggressive with a pet? What happens? When is a pet aggressive with your child?
10. What childhood memories do you have about aggression? Your own, siblings', parents', friends', pets'?

## Body awareness

*Body awareness is increasing. The children are interested in things that come out of the body: poop, pee-pee, vomit, and mucous, and things that grow out of the body: hair, nails, and, whiskers. They may have learned some things about being pregnant, childbirth, and breastfeeding. They have discovered body pleasures and body pain, and the process of healing. They may have had illnesses and accidents. They have experienced growing bigger.*

1. What is your child's awareness of pooping? Peeing? Vomiting? Growing bigger? Where is your toddler in the process of learning to use the potty? Where are you in the process of helping?
2. Sometimes toddlers may want to touch their poop. When has your child wanted to? What happened?
3. What parts of the body does your child touch? To explore? For pleasure? Birth marks? Nose picking? Genitals? Anus? Which have been talked about? Which not? What is your thinking about this?

4. What accidents has your toddler had? Scars? Which have been talked about? Which not?
5. When is your child naked? How do you decide? Naked with siblings? Parents? Friends?
6. What parts of your body does your child want to touch? Hair? Breasts? Genitals? Ear lobes? Nose? What do you do? What parts of Daddy's body? Siblings? What happens?
7. How does your child react to being tickled? What kind of tickling? What do you think about tickling?
8. How does your child respond when touched by you? By others? Touched by strangers? When your child protests touching, what happens?
9. What is your toddler's awareness of growing? Outgrowing clothes?
10. What is your toddler's sense of body-pride? How it looks and what it can do? Jump, run, climb, lift something heavy?

## Children's interactions with other children

*The children may be having more interaction with other children. Maybe friendships are developing. Play with other children is expanding. Sometimes it is pleasurable, sometimes conflictual. Affectionate interactions and aggressive interactions may be occurring. Toddlers may demonstrate their empathy for another child. They may imitate each other. Sometimes their play is initiated by the children and sometimes in response to adult suggestion and supervision. Designated playdate toys and games may minimize conflict.*

1. When is your child with other children? What are their interactions like?
2. What kind of play does your child do with other children? Play initiated and supervised by adults?
3. What does your child learn from other children? What do other children learn from your child?
4. What kind of help does your child need when with other children?
5. When does your child seem to derive social pleasure with another child, or other children? When does your child want all the toys?
6. When does your child withdraw in the presence of other children? Prefer to play alone? With you?
7. When is your child aggressive with other children? When does your child show empathy for another child?
8. When is your child passive with other children? When do you want your child to be more assertive with other children?
9. When does your child eat with other children? Bathe? What happens?
10. How do you plan to celebrate your child's 2-year-old birthday? What are birthdays like for you?

## Emotion regulation

*The children are learning about all their feelings. Sometimes toddlers' feelings frighten them. It is as though there is not a distinction between the feeling and the action. For example, children need help learning the distinction between "I feel like hitting" and the action hitting. Sometimes toddlers are overwhelmed by feelings. They are learning the words for feelings.*

1. What feelings does your toddler know the word for? What feelings do you identify with words? Happy, sad, angry, scared, jealous, shame, pride?
2. When does your child get angry? Scared? Frustrated? Sad? Jealous? Ashamed? Proud? Overwhelmed by feelings?
3. What is it like for you when your child is angry? Sad? Frightened? Overwhelmed? Jealous? Ashamed? Proud?
4. What helps your child to wait? When does your child accept a substitute? Refuse a substitute? When does a shared wish fulfilling fantasy help? For example, I wish it was ice cream time right now. I would eat a big strawberry cone with sprinkles!
5. When does your child persist to master a task? When does your child give up easily? When do you help? How do you decide?
6. When does communicating that you understand how your child feels help to regulate emotions? When does it not help?
7. What helps your child when overwhelmed? What is it like for you when your child is overwhelmed?
8. When does your child suck a thumb to regulate emotions? Use a pacifier? Touch your hair? Cuddle with a treasured toy? Cuddle with you?
9. What kind of play over-stimulates your child? Tickling? Wrestling? What kind of play frightens your child? Pretend play?
10. What kinds of activities soothe your child? Alone? With you? What is it like for you when your child is overwhelmed?

## Gender

*Ideas about gender have changed legally and culturally in recent years. These changes may have influenced your thinking about the development of your child's gender identity and gender role identity. There is a great deal that is not known and a great deal that experts disagree about gender. Young children are interested in boy-girl similarities and differences. You may be observing your child's growing interest in gender. You may agree or disagree with your child's ideas about gender.*

1. Does your son know that he is a boy? Does your daughter know that she is a girl? What does your son do or say that means he knows that he is a boy? What does your daughter do or say that means she knows that she is a girl?

2. How does your son know that he is a boy? How does your daughter know that she is a girl?
3. What does your child think are the differences between boys and girls? Men and women? Their bodies? What they do? What they wear?
4. What is your child's interest in gender?
5. When does your child pretend or try out being the other gender?
6. What does your son do that seems masculine? Feminine?
7. What does your daughter do that seems feminine? Masculine?
8. What gender do people think your child is? What are they responding to? What is this like for you?
9. What is important to you about gender? What is not important?
10. What is important to your husband/partner about gender?

## Underlying meanings of behavior

*A toddler's behavior can be understood in multiple ways. What is observed can be described, what motivated the behavior can be identified, the intention of the behavior can be acknowledged, and what feelings accompany the behavior can be put into words. Helping children to reflect on the meanings of their behavior can promote their ability to regulate emotions, enable them to feel understood, and promote their capacity for empathy. Understanding the meaning of behavior can be the first step towards influencing the behavior. For example: a toddler who cries when getting a haircut may be reacting to the stranger or to losing a precious part of the body. Or a toddler is hitting because of anger or fear.*

1. When has the underlying meaning of your child's behavior influenced your response?
2. When has the underlying meaning of your child's behavior not influenced your response? When does what motivated your child's behavior not matter?
3. When does identifying how you think your child feels help to address behavior? When has it not? When is it not clear what motivates your child's behavior?
4. When has your child awakened in the middle of the night crying, and you thought it was because of a nightmare? What happened? How have dreams been explained to your child?
5. When is it difficult to understand what your child's behavior means?
6. When does identifying what you think your child is remembering help to understand behavior?
7. When has helping your child understand the feelings of someone else helped your child to control behavior? When has understanding the feelings of someone else not helped?
8. When does your child do something dangerous to master being scared? When does your child laugh when frightened?

138  Child development information and group questions

9. When has your child imitated aggression that had been witnessed between other people or on video?
10. When has your child shown empathy for you, for someone else?

## Internal conflict

*Toddlers' wishes to please their mothers, share pleasurable interactions, and be understood are powerful. Toddlers wishes to please themselves are also powerful. Sometimes toddlers have conflict among their wishes. For example, afraid of the noise the blender makes and wishing to avoid it, but also curious about turning it on and off.*

*Sometimes mother-toddler conflict with each other is related to the mother or the child's internal conflict. For example, a mother may be in conflict between setting a limit or pleasing her child. A toddler may be in conflict between pleasing Mommy or pleasing oneself. Identifying internal conflict can be helpful. For example, "I think that you want all the toys for yourself, and you also want to play with your friend."*

1. What internal conflicts do you think your child has? Or is beginning to have? For example, a conflict between continuing to play or going to the potty?
2. When does it look like your toddler has the impulse to do something that you disapprove of, and stops? Or signals you the intention, a way of asking for help to stop? What do you do?
3. When does your child do something to please you?
4. When does your child not do what you want? Why? When do you acknowledge this? For example, "I guess it was important to you to try making pee-pee in the bathtub, but you know it goes in the potty."
5. What conflicts do you have with your toddler that will become internal conflicts for your toddler? For example, brushing teeth. When and how will Mommy's disapproval, become your child's own self-disapproval? What evidence do you see of this happening?
6. What do you do to help identify internal conflict for your child when it is contributing to interpersonal conflict with your child? For example, "I know you really want to jump on the bed, and you also want to do what I said, no jumping on the bed. I'm going to help you get down. Do you want to get down yourself, or should I help you?"
7. When do you use approval and understanding to promote your child's resolution of internal conflict? When do you use guilt, fear, or shame to promote your child's resolution of internal conflict? When is one more effective than the other?
8. What conflicts do you have with your child that are also internal conflicts for you? Separating? Taking medicine? Eating? Pacifier? Limits? Sleeping alone?
9. What conflicts do you have with your husband or partner that create internal conflict for your child?

10. What conflicts do you have between being with your child or your partner? Gratifying your child or your husband?

## Mother-child differences

*Mother-child differences can be physical, personality traits, birth order. Mothers have reactions to the differences and the similarities. Mother-child differences may make it easier or more difficult for a mother to understand or empathize with her child. Traits that are like Daddy may be especially pleasing or disliked by you. Children also have reactions to the similarities and differences between themselves and their parents. Some differences may have been talked about, some not.*

1. In what ways are you the same as your child? In what ways different? Gender? Physical traits: hair color and texture, eye color, skin color? Personality traits? Birth order?
2. When do the differences between you and your child make it more difficult to empathize with your child? When do they make it easier?
3. When do the similarities between you and your child make it more difficult to empathize with your child? When do they make it easier?
4. What differences and what similarities is your child aware of? Gender? Race? Language? Physical traits? Personality traits?
5. What impact do differences between you and your husband/partner have on your child? Physical traits? Personality traits? Behavior? Race? Language? Child rearing ideas? In what way do the differences benefit your child?
6. In what ways does your child try to be like you? In what ways does your child try to be like Daddy? Siblings?
7. What differences and what similarities between you and your child have been talked about with your child? What differences and similarities between you and your child have not been talked about?
8. In what ways is your child like you imagined? In what ways different?
9. What traits does your child have that you think will change? What traits do you think will remain?
10. Which traits that your child has do you think were inherited? Learned? How?

## Learning

*The children are learning many things: emotional, cognitive, social, and physical. Some things they learn by observation, some by instruction, some by trial and error. Learning is more difficult when feelings of anger, anxiety, fear, or shame are intense. Mothers do many things to support their children learning. Some things the children seem to learn through osmosis. You may be seeing some evidence of your child's developing sense of humor.*

1. What are you teaching your child now? How?
2. Where are you and your child in the process of learning to use the potty? Drink from a cup? Self-feed?
3. You may not remember but what do you imagine learning to use the potty was like for you? What have you been told?
4. What readiness has your child shown to learn the things you are teaching? Transition from highchair to booster seat? Potty? Talking? Weaning? Pacifier?
5. What are you teaching your child that your child does not want to learn? When are you explaining something to your child and it seems like you are being ignored? Your child walks away? When does your child looking away from you help your child listen?
6. What is your child learning independent of you?
7. What is your child learning by imitating you? Siblings? Daddy?
8. What is your child learning about the values that are important to you? Empathy? Honesty? Generosity? Manners? A sense of humor? How are they being learned?
9. What is your child learning that you do not want learned?
10. What do you and your child talk about that is increasing learning about death, birth, danger, money, religious ideas? What related experiences has your child had?

## Vignettes

Following are two vignettes. The mother-child dyads were in different groups. Darcy and Millie is about a mother who acquires insight about her complete denial of her 22-month-old daughter's ability to think and to feel. Specific interventions are described that helped to identify the links between the mother's own childhood memories and the discovery of her child's mind.

Roberta and Jade is about a mother and her 24-month-old daughter who was uncontrollably hitting. Exploration of the mother's childhood memories and their link to Jade's hitting and mother-child frightening interactions are described. Interventions leading to self-reflection and new shared meanings about denied and disavowed fear are delineated.

## Darcy and Millie

**Vignette summary**

**Child's age** – 22-months

**Mother-child interaction** – No social referencing or physical proximity

**Presenting problem** – No intersubjective mother-child interactions, mother's denial of her child's capacity to have thoughts or feelings, "She's just a happy baby"

**Childhood memory** – Mother dismissing her wishes, feelings, and thoughts.

**Mother's core theme** – Denial of child's developing mind conflicted with wishes to feel "close" to her child

**Primary defense mechanism** – Mother's enactment of childhood memory; denial of child's thoughts and feelings

**Organizing fantasy** – "She's just a happy baby, she doesn't have any thoughts or feelings yet."

**Intervention** – Interpretation of the link between mother's childhood memories and current denial of child's thoughts and feelings

**Resolution** – Mother's recognition of her child's mind; mother-child intersubjective interactions

*Millie was a cheerful, socially engaging 22-month-old little girl with two mothers. She was in a mother-toddler group with her mother Darcy. Millie participated joyfully in all play activities. Her language was well developed for her age. Turn-taking was easy and her shared fun in activities with other children was apparent. Millie looked mature for her age with long dark wavy hair and thick bangs. She frequently wore a pretty, smocked dress.*

*Millie did not touch base with her mother during the group, but quickly began turning to the play-leader to process events that had occurred, to share the pleasure of her play, and to get help when needed. Her verbal and non-verbal communications about her thoughts and feelings were clear. She initiated shared smiles while delighting in the pleasure of completing a puzzle or block construction. When a child tried to take a toy away from her, she asserted, "My turn," and held on tight. She looked to the play-leader, signaling what was happening and her need for help. When the play-leader described interactions, Millie focused on her. For example, when a child grabbed a toy from Millie, the play-leader said, "It's Millie's turn now. Laura, you need to wait. I am going to help you to wait."*

*Millie's mother Darcy was an active participant in the group that had been meeting weekly since October. It was now mid-November. Darcy's view of Millie was markedly different than mine described above. Millie's inner world was completely denied*

by Darcy. She frequently commented, "She's just a happy baby. She doesn't understand anything. I don't think she has any thoughts or feelings yet, she's only 22-months old. She's just a happy baby." Darcy was highly motivated to deny Millie's developing mind and to assert her happiness, but it was not clear why. Perhaps for Darcy, not having any thoughts or feelings was required to be "... a happy baby."

Millie's other mother did not participate in the group and Darcy rarely talked about her. She was a lawyer at a large firm that Darcy had also worked at before maternity leave. I had never met her and knew little about their relationship or her relationship with Millie. Darcy had given birth to Millie and primarily took care of her.

When a child's inner world is unacknowledged by her mother, as Millie's was by Darcy, and the motivation to deny it is strong, the depth of their relationship and the pleasures for each are limited. Darcy had expressed her wish to be "close" to Millie but maintained her view, "Millie is just a happy baby. She doesn't really know me yet. She doesn't understand anything." I wondered about the childhood memories contributing to Darcy's ideas about Millie's developing mind, her unexpressed sadness related to "She doesn't really know me yet" and how Millie having two mothers influenced Darcy's insistence that "She's just a happy baby." Perhaps Millie's other mother had a different view of Millie's inner world which contributed to Millie's thriving development.

During the sixth week we were meeting, a little girl grabbed a doll from Millie. Millie signaled a need for help to the play-leader who put into words what had occurred, "Heidi grabbed the doll from you, let's tell her it's your turn to play with the doll and you want it back." She said to Heidi, "I see that you wanted the doll, but it's Millie's turn now. I'm going to help you to give it back to Millie." A few minutes later Millie grabbed a puzzle away from Heidi. The play-leader then said, "Millie, do you know what I think happened? You grabbed from Heidi just like Heidi grabbed from you." Millie then handed the puzzle back to Heidi. For Millie, grabbing the puzzle and then handing it back herself seemed to be a way for her to process again what had happened when Heidi had grabbed the doll with which she had been playing and to integrate that the "no grabbing" rule is for everyone. She was also learning that social interactions can be talked about and understood.

At the same time these complex interactions were occurring among the children and the play-leader, Darcy was describing Millie: "I'm going away next month; Millie won't even notice. I don't think she's that aware, she's just a happy baby." The following intervention highlighted the underlying, disavowed feelings in Darcy's statement: "It seems hard for you to imagine that Millie notices or cares about anything, including you. It seems hard for you to imagine that Millie will miss you and feel sad." Darcy looked thoughtful and perhaps moved but did not say anything. I wondered whether Darcy also believed that Millie did not notice that she had two mommies. Nothing more was said. As the group was ending, in front of her mother, Millie grabbed a cookie from Heidi. Heidi cried, Darcy giggled, and Millie ate the cookie. Heidi's mother was angry.

During our next group, when the other women were describing their children's typical 2-year-old oppositional behavior, Darcy restated, but this time with a meaningful difference, "Millie's just a happy baby. She never opposes me. She always does what

*I want her to do. She always wants what I want. She never has her own thoughts or feelings."* Darcy's revised statement, a more direct statement of her wish, provided a new meaning of Darcy's belief about Millie being *"just a happy baby."* The following interpretation highlighted her wish: *"Being just a happy baby seems to mean Millie is at one with you and shares all the same thoughts and feelings that you have."* Darcy remained quiet.

The meaningful shift in Darcy's narrative might have reflected Darcy's wish that Millie and she think and feel the same way about having two mommies. Darcy's awareness of her concern that Millie might have different ideas and feelings about having two mommies may have been emerging.

Highlighting for Darcy the importance to Millie of knowing her mother's thoughts and feelings, I described the grabbing sequence among the children that had occurred the week before: *"I wonder whether Millie grabbed the cookie from Heidi in front of you because she wanted to know what you thought about grabbing."* Darcy now seemed pleased with the possibility that Millie cared about her thoughts. The idea that Millie wanted to know her mother's thoughts and feelings, and that Millie could be influenced by her mother's thoughts, was dawning on Darcy and seemed to interest her. She became quietly introspective. Although it was an example of Millie being influenced by her mother, it was not necessary and would have been accusatory to have mentioned that Millie ate the cookie after Darcy had giggled.

A turning point occurred the following week when Darcy began to preface statements that denied Millie's inner world with the phrase, *"I wonder why I think...?"* This major shift represented Darcy's emerging interest in what motivated her conviction that Millie was unaware of everything, had no thoughts or feelings of her own, and was *"just a happy baby."* It also demonstrated that Darcy was thinking about thinking; she was reflecting on her own thoughts. Insight was now possible.

Two weeks later Darcy began, *"I don't know why I think Millie doesn't know anything or think about anything. Why do I think she's just a baby?"* I responded, *"That is an important question. Who was the baby in your family?"* Darcy quickly remembered, *"My self-esteem is from my dad. He always said that I could do anything, be anything, and have anything. My mother always said that I couldn't do anything. What I wanted didn't count. I was too young for everything. I was just dismissed."* Using Darcy's own words to connect her childhood memory to her attributions to Millie, I said, *"Maybe your mother saw you as just a baby."*

The following week, Darcy told us that her view had changed. *"Millie knows more than I had thought. She needs me to tell her more about what's happening and what I think. I can influence her thoughts, but she also has her own thoughts."* Darcy now believed that Millie might miss her while she was away on vacation and planned to FaceTime with her. New shared meanings had emerged.

Several things contributed to Darcy's insight. First, Millie developed a trusting, supportive relationship with the play-leader who responded to her social referencing and helped her to seek direct contact with her mother when she needed to feel connected with her for reassurance, shared pleasure, information, or validation, *"Let's tell Mommy what happened."* When Millie approached her mother, I said things like, *"Millie wants to show you what she did*, or *Millie wants to know what you think about Heidi grabbing the doll*." This helped to demonstrate to Darcy that Millie did care about what she thought and how she felt. More importantly, it helped Darcy and Millie to feel more emotionally connected. Second, the conviction of the other mothers in the group that their children were aware — think, feel, know, and have intentions — increased Darcy's self-questioning about her denial of Millie's thoughts and feelings. Third, my description that the grabbing sequence among the children was motivated by wishes and feelings, and evoked reactions in the mothers, increased Darcy's awareness that not only did Millie have complex thoughts and feelings, but also that she cared and needed to know what her mother thought and felt. Triggered by the exploration of her childhood memories, Darcy began to question her motivation for the denial of Millie's inner world. She connected her memories about her own mother devaluing and dismissing her abilities, feelings, and wishes to her conviction that Millie was "just a baby." She realized that she was treating Millie the way she remembered her mother had treated her. Another important theme remained.

The ways in which Darcy's view of Millie as "just a happy baby" had been related to Darcy's thoughts and feelings about Millie having two mothers had not yet been explored. If Millie was "just a baby" Darcy could more easily defer thinking about and talking to Millie about what it meant to have two mommies. Darcy's discovery that Millie cared about what her mother thought and felt, and that she could influence what Millie thought about having two mothers, made thinking and talking about it possible. Darcy began to talk about the different kinds of families that were portrayed in the picture books she was reading to Millie and Millie's developing awareness of having two mommies. Darcy also began to reflect on her own newly emerging feelings and ideas about being happy and having two mommies.

## Roberta and Jade

> **Vignette summary**
> 
> **Child's age** – 24-months
> **Mother-child interaction** – Angry, frightening reprimands
> **Presenting problem** – Child hitting uncontrollably, often
> **Childhood memory** – "My father taught me to be tough, not scared like my mother"
> **Mother's core theme** – Frightening mother-child interactions conflicted with the denial of fear
> **Primary defense mechanism** – Disavowal of her own fears and denial of her child's fears. Re-enactment of childhood fears
> **Organizing fantasy** – My child and I are never afraid
> **Intervention** – Exploration of mother-child frightening play, identification of child's fears, and interpretation of mother's disavowed fear
> **Resolution** – Mother-child frightening play and interactions decreased; child's fears were acknowledged. Child stopped hitting.

*Roberta reluctantly scheduled a pre-group visit with Jade. She did not think a warming-up visit was necessary, "Jade is 2 years old, she's not a baby." During the visit, Roberta mentioned that Jade had been hitting, but did not elaborate. Roberta wanted to talk about other things: learning to swim, sleeping in a bed, and beginning to use the potty filled our half-hour visit while Jade played comfortably with the play-leader.*

*The following week the mothers all arrived early for the first group of the year. The surroundings were familiar to the children; they had been in groups since they were a few months old. Through my office door, I heard a loud cry and then quiet.*

*It was time to start the group. As soon as I opened the door, three of the children bounded into the play-area and gathered around the sandbox confident that their mothers would remain close. Two other children entered the play-area more cautiously holding their mothers' hands. Their mothers helped them to sit at the table and play with puzzles. When the children were comfortable, their mothers joined the others on the banquette. As Roberta entered, she was reprimanding Jade for hitting one of the children and warning her not to do it again. Jade chose a toy at the far end of the room, distant from the other children and the mothers. Roberta joined the other mothers.*

*No sooner had we settled and begun to talk about developmental changes that had occurred over the summer, one by one the children came to their mothers either crying because they had been hit by Jade, disturbed by what had happened to another child, or worried about whether they would also be hit. In turn, several of the mothers went into the play-area to get a closer look at what was happening and to protect their children. The hitting happened so fast and unexpectedly it was difficult to anticipate, or to* see what had triggered it. Roberta's warnings had been unsuccessful. Our pleasure in watching the children play as we talked was replaced with vigilance and anger. The mothers were sympathetic to Roberta, but they were also angry. Jade, who had been an easy-going, well-adapted little girl before the summer, was now hitting everybody, mostly her mother and father.

Roberta was perplexed by Jade's seemingly unprovoked aggressive behavior and frustrated by her own inability to "discipline" her: "I've tried everything: time-outs, no iPad, I even threatened to take her special teddy bear away. I would never really do that. Nothing helps. It's been going on for two weeks. She won't stop hitting." While Roberta was focused on disciplining Jade, I was struck with how frightened of her mother Jade might feel by the harsh reprimands and warnings.

Jade was a physically sturdy, intelligent little girl. She was tall for her age and competent. She had short dark hair and was always dressed in blue jeans and a T-shirt. As physically robust, cognitively competent, and socially capable she had been, her play was now inhibited. Except for hitting, she avoided the other children.

To understand more about Jade's inner world and what might be motivating the hitting, I asked Roberta about Jade's play at home. She mentioned games of hide and seek, chase-and-catch, tickling, and a collection of videos. When asked, Roberta described the details: "Hide and seek is great. I hide behind the door and when Jade enters the room, I jump out at her and shout 'boo.' She always startles. I played it with my dad." The videos Jade watched included a selection of action stories and fairytales often frightening to 2-year-old children. The chase game was primarily played with her father. He ran after Jade and when he caught her, he tickled her while she squealed. Roberta called the game "tickle-torture."

The following elements of Roberta's description of their play were significant: "She always startles," "I played it with my dad," and "tickle-torture." A startle is a noticeable indication of psychological and physiological hyperarousal, "tickle-torture" alludes to pain and horror, and "I played it with my dad" suggests that childhood memories were being enacted. The following child development information about high arousal play included typically associated feelings, "These sound like exciting games which are important, but sometimes scare little children." Roberta quickly disagreed and contradicted me: "Jade never gets scared." With subtle surprise and disbelief, I confronted Roberta: "Really? Never?" I had gently challenged Roberta's denial of Jade's fear and awakened childhood memories.

Roberta's memories of her own father when she was a little girl flooded out. She told us, almost bragging, "My father wanted a son. He taught me to be tough like he was, not scared like my mother. He taught me to do scary things like climb trees and ride my bike down a steep hill with no hands. We always watched horror movies together. At the amusement park near our house, we went on the big roller coaster and sneaked around the haunted house avoiding the moving skeletons and booby traps. My dad always got me past the ticket collectors because he lied about my age. I guess I was a tomboy."

The vivid details of Roberta's carnival memories reminded me of the crackles on the smooth surface of a juicy candy apple that can cut your tongue: the pain beneath the sweet surface. The following interpretation integrated Roberta's childhood memories, *disavowed fear, and current mother-child interactions, "It seems like appearing not scared and sharing frightening experiences with your father helped you to feel loved and accepted by him. I wonder whether Jade might be feeling some of the same things." This was a new way for Roberta to think about her memories, but it seemed to strike a chord. Recounting her memories may have triggered remnants of scared feelings. The following child development information highlighted Jade's experience: "Sometimes children hit when they are frightened. Discipline won't help them to stop hitting if they're scared. Acknowledging scared feelings and feeling protected and safe might."*

*As we began to consider the activities and situations that might be frightening to Jade, a distant memory of Roberta's began to emerge. At first the memory was vague and then increasingly distinct. Her memory of a small music box with a twirling ballerina and a lilting melody began to surface and frequently come to mind. When she was a little girl the music box was kept on a high shelf in her bedroom: it was rarely taken down. It was fragile and delicate, the opposite of brave and tough. Roberta longingly tried to recall the name and melody of the music box lullaby.*

*At the same time the music box memory was coming into focus, Roberta began to recognize moments when Jade was scared. She began to limit the frightening videos and modified the scary games. She also began to help Jade talk about her scary feelings. The distant melody of* Für Elise *and the twirling ballerina were now shining bright. By the next week, the hitting had stopped. The joy returned to the group and the warm support among the mothers was restored. The music box memory that had remained in the shadows emerged with all its delicate details. It represented the little girl who had frightening feelings that Roberta had needed to keep far away, on a high shelf, out of reach, out of memory.*

*Roberta had not thought about her play with her father for many years. She had never thought about the music box. There was much to understand about her relationship with her father and his attitudes about gender. There was also more for Roberta to understand about herself, her feelings about being a woman, and having a daughter.*

# Chapter 7

# 29 to 36-months

Mothers with children 29 to 36-months have participated in groups for 1, 2, or more years. Important aspects of the children's development and the evolving mother-child relationship have been shared. Strong bonds have been created among the mothers, and mutual respect and caring between the group-leader and each mother have developed. The mothers continue to feel increasingly competent, confident, and self-aware. They have become more self-reflective and help each other with empathic astute observations of the children and of each other. During this phase of groups, the mothers more frequently raise topics for discussion, and generate shared meanings of the children's behavior, and of the links between mothers' childhood memories and mother-child interactions. The following child development information and group questions support and further the group-process.

## Child development information and group questions

### Mother-child interactions

*Your interactions with your child have become more complex in terms of the intermingling of their surface meaning and their underlying meanings. Your interactions include moments of approval and disapproval. The teaching-learning interactions may be deeply gratifying at times and painfully frustrating at others. Your sense of humor and your child's developing sense of humor may have created moments of mutual laughter. You have a history together of shared memories. Both your affectionate interactions and angry interactions may have become more intense and may also cycle. In other words, there are ruptures and repairs in your ongoing affectionate interactions. You may have discovered the ongoing fluctuating process of feeling like a good mother, a bad mother, and what we have called a good-enough mother. Your wish to be a good mother and the actual mother you think you are, are increasingly more aligned.*

*The value of parenting consistency is often emphasized. There is also value in inconsistency: changing one's mind, the ability to adapt to change, and the awareness of*

DOI: 10.4324/b23150-11

*nuance. Two parents with different ideas can create conflict for the parents, but can be an asset to the children.*

*Watching a mother lovingly care for her child can arouse envy. Watching the pleasurable intimacy between a mother and young child can stimulate uncomfortable feelings in others. Sometimes criticisms of mothers are triggered by those feelings. Sometimes the criticisms of others resonate with mothers' self-criticisms.*

1. When are interactions with your child pleasurable? Angry? Boring? Exciting? What interactions are you having with your child that worry you? What about your child worries you? What have you been told not to worry about? What interactions are related to your child's developing sense of humor?
2. When you and your child have angry interactions, how do you return to affectionate interactions? When is it ok to tell your child that you are angry? Sad? Afraid? Bored?
3. When do you feel like a good mother interacting with your child? When do you feel like a bad mother?
4. What impact are your interactions with your child having on your relationship with your husband/partner? With others?
5. When are your interactions with your child criticized? By whom? When might the criticism be motivated by envy, guilt, or childhood memories? When are the criticisms aligned with your own self-criticisms? When are your interactions with your child admired? By whom? What is admired?
6. How are interactions with your child during our group the same as at home and how are they different?
7. When do you show approval to your child? How do you show approval? How does your child react? When do you disapprove of your child? How do you show disapproval? How does your child respond?
8. What consistencies in mother-child interactions are important to you? What inconsistencies are valuable for your child to learn to adapt to change or nuance, and to adapt to and to enjoy different relationships? When do you change your mind because something is important to your child?
9. What would be your child's definition of a mother? What will become your child's self-description?
10. What are interactions with your child related to sleep? Meals? What are interactions with your child that are related to weaning, learning to use the potty?

## Mother-child attachment

*The foundation of your mother-child attachment relationship emerged from birth to around 1-year. Your attachment relationship has continued to evolve, deepen, and expand. Your child may seek closeness to you physically and emotionally to feel safe, to* be soothed, to understand when uncertain, to share experiences, and to be understood. Feeling understood is at the core of feeling loved.

Your child's autonomy is also more developed and clearer than it was: special interests and abilities may be emerging.

1. How would you describe your attachment to your child and your child's attachment to you? What would be your child's definition of a mommy?
2. How does your child show growing love and attachment to you?
3. When does your child try to please you? When not?
4. When does your child want to be close to you as a secure base? When scared? When in an unfamiliar situation? When over-stimulated? When hurt?
5. When does your child push you away? Reject you?
6. How does your child react when you are sick or get hurt?
7. When does it seem as if your child does not care about you? Go too far away? Laugh when you get hurt? Not do what you say?
8. When and why does your child call to you or come to you in the middle of the night? What happens?
9. When do you know what your child is thinking, feeling? How do you know? When does your child know what you are thinking, feeling? How do you know? When are you on the same wavelength?
10. When does your child show a preference for you? For someone else? To hold? To bathe? To push on the swing? To read? To play? What happens?

## *Mother-child communication*

*Understanding and feeling understood are at the core of communication. Communicating in words what a child has communicated in action can help them to feel understood, can promote their ability to use words when intense feelings are aroused, and can facilitate their self-reflection. Experiencing your empathy can promote your child's ability to empathize.*

*Being told what to expect can be like an inoculation; a bit of the anxiety and protest is triggered and processed before the raw intensity of a painful or unpleasant event. When the event occurs, it does not have the same painful impact that it might have had.*

*Children are learning about death. They may have seen adults and children with disabilities. They may participate in religious ceremonies. The children may be learning about pregnancy and breastfeeding. You may be thinking about what you want to tell your child about these discoveries and what they already know.*

*You may be increasingly aware of what you can control and what your child controls. For example, while there are always foods available that your child likes, what is cooked for dinner may be a Mommy decision. What a child eats is the child's decision. Bedtime is a Mommy decision, what bedtime story is read may be the child's decision. When a child falls asleep is determined by the child's state of relaxation or readiness for sleep. Communications with your child can reflect these distinctions and may be useful.*

*Sometimes communications are contradictory or paradoxical. Sometimes their underlying meanings are disguised.*

1. When does saying "I'm sorry" to your child mean "I don't want you to be angry at me"? When does asking "Who do you want to read to you?" mean "I don't want to read to you"? Other examples?
2. When do you lie or trick your child? When do you use threats? When do you use humor? Guilt? Teasing?
3. When do you want your child to feel differently or think differently? What do you do to try to change what your child thinks or feels? How is changing a child's thoughts or feelings the same as and different than changing behavior?
4. When do you try to change what your child thinks or wants rather than say no?
5. When do you put into words for your child what has been communicated in action?
6. When do you share a wish fulfilling fantasy with your child to substitute for having the thing? For example, "Having all the toys in the world might be fun."
7. When do you plead with your child? Try to convince your child of something?
8. When does your child tell a lie that may be a wish? For example, "I did not write on the wall" can mean "I wish I did not write on the wall."
9. When does your child whine? When is a whining voice a compromise between pleasing Mommy and not asking for something, and pleasing oneself by asking for it?
10. What does your child know about death? What has been said? What does your child know about pregnancy, birth, and breastfeeding? Religion? Disability? Race? Money? How do you decide what is age-appropriate information?

## Mothers' childhood memories

*Mothers' childhood memories are triggered in interaction with their children. Your childhood memories can help you to be the mother that you want to be. Mothers' emerging fears and predictions about their children may be related to childhood memories. Interactions you have with your child now may be related to your childhood memories. Your children's childhood memories when they grow-up are being created with you: the things they will want to do the same as you, the things they will want to do differently.*

1. What memories does your child talk about? What memory narratives are you and your child creating together?
2. What fears do you have about your child? How might they be related to your childhood memories?

3. What are your predictions about your child? How might they be related to childhood memories? How do your predictions influence your interactions now?
4. What interactions with your child trigger your memories? What interactions do you think are enactments of a memory?
5. What experiences that your child has had are reflected in play, but not talked about?
6. What experiences are you helping your child to remember with a shared memory narrative?
7. What experiences do you want your child to forget?
8. What have you been told about your child that pops into your head sometimes?
9. What experiences has your child had that pop into your head sometimes? Delivery? NICU? Accident? Illness? What parts of these memories have you told your child? How do these memories relate to your child's behavior? Your interactions?
10. How have your childhood memories been influenced by having a child?

## Separation

*Some mother-child separations may have become routine and go easily. Some may continue to be difficult, and others may be variable. Saying good-bye and reunion patterns may have been established. Games of separation, like hide and seek, may have been created. The children's confidence that separation is followed by reunion has grown. The children may have found ways to cope with the stress of separation, for example walking you to the elevator and pressing the button or keeping a treasured toy close.*

*The knowledge that abrupt separations are more stressful than those where there has been some preparation may have contributed to how you help your child know what to expect about separation. The idea that longer separations are more stressful than shorter ones and that unfamiliar surroundings and caretakers add to the stress of separation from Mommy may have guided your decisions about separations. Increased angry mother-child interactions typical of this age can increase the stress of separation. Sometimes reactions to separations affect sleep.*

1. When are you separated from your child? Work, leisure, exercise, doctor visits, hair salon, daycare, vacations? Your child's playdates and other activities?
2. What are good-byes like? What are reunions like?
3. Who stays with your child when you are separated?
4. How long are you separated for?
5. What were separations from your mother like for you when you were a child? When were they stressful? When were they pleasurable?

6. How does your child react to separations?
7. When do you tell your child about an upcoming separation? How long in advance? When do you conceal impending separations from you child? How does your child react?
8. When does your explanation about a separation help you to feel better, but not help your child? For example, "I played with you all morning, now I need to go to the doctor." Or "I need to go to work to make money."
9. What contact do you have with your child during separations? What contact do you have with caretakers?
10. What games of separation do you and your child play? Hide and seek? Pretend play?

## *Play*

*Pretend play with dolls, animal figures, and cars has greatly increased for children this age. Beginning role play and everyday life experiences including separations, a bus or car ride, mealtime, bedtime, and bath time are frequent themes. Pretend play related to stressful experiences like doctor and dentist visits, haircuts, and taking medicine are popular scenarios that are sometimes initiated by the children and sometimes by mothers in preparation for an event. For example, play related to an impending hospitalization and surgery, or a family move. Alternating roles occurs. For example, driver and passenger, doctor and patient, Mommy reading a book and baby listening.*

*Winning and losing games may have become more stressful. You may have developed ideas about competition. Puzzles and construction toys have become more complex. Water play is a frequent pleasure. Aggressive play themes evolve. Rough and tumble play may be more vigorous.*

1. What are your child's pretend play themes? With dolls and figures? Food, books, sleep, or potty themes? With you? Alone?
2. What high arousal, rough and tumble, and tickling does your toddler like? Not like?
3. How does your child play with a treasured toy?
4. What pretend play does your child do to help cope with stressful events? With you? Alone? With others? Separation? Doctor? Haircut? Disapproval?
5. What manipulative toys does your child like? Construction toys? Puzzles? Water play? Sand play? Paint? Glue?
6. What interaction play does your child like? Throwing a ball and catch? Hide and seek? Beginning games, Candy Land? How does your child react to winning? Losing? When do you let your child win? What do you think about competition during play?
7. What kind of scary play does your child like?
8. What videos does your child watch? Music? How does your child react?

9. What kind of books do you read to your child? Themes, plots? Characters – gender, race, family constellations?
10. What kind of play during meals, a way of socializing, does your child enjoy? In bed before sleep? Nap time, quiet time? Car rides?

## Aggression

*Aggressive behavior of young children is common and can be alarming to adults. It can also be pleasing. Aggressive behavior may be triggered by anger, fear, or overstimulation. It may be reactive to having witnessed aggression in person or in a video. A child's self-assertiveness may seem aggressive, and at times may be aggressive. Competition can be self-assertive or aggressive. Mothers' aggressive thoughts about their children and interactions with them may be surprising and frightening*

1. When is your child aggressive?
2. When do you support your child's aggression, when do you limit it?
3. What aggressive interactions occur between your child and siblings? With pets? When has your child been aggressive with you? When have you been aggressive with your child?
4. When are others aggressive with your child? Physically? Teasing? How does your child react? What do you do?
5. What kind of aggressive play is ok with you? What kind is not ok? When is competition aggressive in a positive way? A negative way?
6. What kind of aggressive words are ok with you? What aggressive words are not ok?
7. When does your child witness aggression? Angry interactions between parents? How does your child react?
8. When have you seen your child inhibit an aggressive impulse? When have you seen an affectionate gesture turn aggressive? When does a kiss become a bite, or a hug become a shove?
9. When has your child been able to use words instead of aggressive behavior?
10. When is your child assertive?

## Body awareness

*Children at this phase have learned many things about their bodies. They have experienced body pleasures and body pains. They have acquired body skills: walking, jumping, riding a scooter. They are beginning to dress and undress themselves. They participate in washing their bodies and brushing their teeth. During this phase of development, their body exploration has increased. Their interest in their parents' bodies may have also increased. Families have different patterns of nudity. The children's awareness of male-female differences and adult-child differences may be communicated in a variety of ways.*

The children's curiosity about their noses, genitals, anus, and bellybuttons may have intensified. Their interest in what goes into their bodies and what comes out fascinates them. They may have vomited and had diarrhea and had strong reactions. You may have seen them start and stop a urinary stream, pick their noses, inhibit the impulse to poop. They may stimulate genital sensations in a variety of ways, including straddling your ankle.

1. What body skills is your child practicing? Enjoying?
2. How does your child react to vomiting? Diarrhea? Constipation? When does your child spit?
3. When is your child naked? What does your child do when naked? When is your child naked with others? Parents? Siblings? Friends? Others?
4. What body pleasures does your child seek?
5. When have you seen your child start and stop a urinary stream?
6. What have you communicated to your child about genital pleasure? Exploration? Interest?
7. Where is your child in the process of learning to use the potty?
8. What parts of his genitals does your son identify with words: penis, scrotum, testicles, erection? What parts of her genitals does your daughter identify with words: vagina, vulva, labia, clitoris, lubrication, scent?
9. What accidents, surgeries, scars, birthmarks, or illnesses has your child had? What does your child say about them? What impact do they have now?
10. How does your child respond to being touched by you? By others? When does your child protest touching? What do you do?

## Children's interactions with other children

The children's interactions with other children may be increasing at this age. They may have beginning friendships. Their interactions with each other may be joyful, angry, and at times quietly content. They may talk about a playmate when they are not together.

When conflicts arise between the children, the adults may intervene. Sometimes the children need more time and space to process what has occurred before apologies are exchanged. Sometimes they need help to inhibit or get control of aggressive behavior. Sometimes they need help transitioning back to friendly interactions.

1. When is your child with other children? What are your child's interactions like with other children?
2. How is it decided which toys will be shared and which toys not shared?
3. When with another child, when does your child play alone? When do they play with each other with and without adult supervision?
4. What kinds of conflicts emerge between the children? When do you intervene to help? How?

156    Child development information and group questions

5. How do you decide whether to intervene or to let the children resolve the conflict themselves?
6. When are apologies socially indicated, when are apologies contributing to the development of remorse? When do apologies interfere with the development of remorse? When can making a distinction between accepting an apology and accepting a behavior help to resolve a conflict?
7. What are your ideas about birthday celebrations? For your child? For you? What were birthdays for you like when you were a child?
8. When your child is with another child how does it influence eating?
9. When your child is with another child how does it influence learning to use the potty? Same sex? Opposite sex?
10. During playdates what toys are available? What toys or activities are designated for playdates only? If a child is visiting, what toys is your child able to put away: not to be available during the playdate? Who decides?

## *Emotion regulation*

*During the first three years of her child's life, a mother's ability to understand and to tolerate her child's intense and at times ambivalent feelings evolves. The children are learning about intense feelings and how to regulate them. They are learning to use words to communicate their feelings and to feel understood. Sometimes it may seem like your child is dramatizing or faking feelings. This may be a child's way to communicate that the feelings are strong.*

1. How does your son or daughter react when hurt?
2. When does your child feel shame? Guilt? Pride? Fear? Anger? How does your child tell you about having these feelings? How does your child know that you understand? What feelings does your child have that are difficult for you?
3. When is your child overwhelmed by feelings? What happens?
4. How does your child react to making a mistake? How does your child react to losing a game or race?
5. When do you try to conceal your feelings from your child?
6. When is your child not able to use a word to describe a feeling? When does your child deny having a feeling?
7. What fears does your child have?
8. Does your child have any habits that you believe are triggered by feelings? Nose picking? Masturbation? Nail biting? Hair pulling? Rocking?
9. When does your child seem to be faking or dramatizing a feeling?
10. How does your child react to doctor visits? Haircuts? Dental procedures? Disapproval? Frustration?

## Gender

*Ideas about gender in our culture continue to evolve. Some of your ideas about gender may have been influenced by becoming the mother of a boy or of a girl. The meaning of gender to your child may at times reflect your ideas and at times not. Your children may be learning about male-female similarities and differences, transgender, same-sex and opposite-sex marriages. They may identify who is a girl and who is a boy, what is for boys and what is for girls.*

1. Does your son know he is a boy? Does your daughter know she is a girl? How?
2. What gender do people think your child is? Why?
3. When does your child talk about gender? What is said? What do you agree with? What do you disagree with? What does your child know about same-sex and opposite-sex marriage, having two mommies, two daddies, or a mommy and a daddy? Transgender?
4. What have you told your child about gender? What is important to you about gender? What is not important to you about gender?
5. What does your child think is the difference between boys and girls? Men and woman?
6. What about your son is masculine? Feminine? What about your daughter is feminine? Masculine?
7. What has your child done that reveals thoughts or feelings about gender? For example, a girl trying to pee standing up, a boy pretending to breastfeed or be pregnant.
8. What has your son wanted to do that you consider for girls or women? For example, wear lipstick, a dress, nail polish? What did you do?
9. What has your daughter wanted to do that you consider for boys or men? For example, shave her face, wear a tie? What did you do?
10. When does your son pretend to be a girl? Dress up as a girl? When does your daughter pretend to be a boy? Dress up as a boy? How do you respond?

## Underlying meanings of behavior

*Behavior can have underlying meanings, feelings, motivation, and intentions. Understanding the underlying meaning of a child's behavior may provide important information about how you want to respond. A toddler who is learning to use the potty may refuse to eat sausage because it looks like poop. A young child who is struggling to inhibit impulses to grab every toy that a baby sibling has may quickly relinquish toys when other children come close.*

*Mothers intuitively and empathically discover toddlers' fears about losing Mommy's love. When mothers are angry at their children or disapprove of their behavior, they sometimes want to reassure their children that they still love them. This may be a response to their recognition of not having their usual loving feelings towards their children and a way to revive the loving feelings. Mothers may also be remembering their own feelings when they were reprimanded as children, or currently when criticized.*

*Some problematic behavior of toddlers may signal a need to create a mother-child memory narrative about an event. For example, a way to think about and talk about the death of a grandparent, when a nanny leaves or a pet dies, or when the child has an accident.*

1. When has your child's behavior been triggered by an event that frightened or confused your child? When did talking about it help? When did talking about it not help?
2. When do you apologize to your child? When does the apology mean, don't be angry at me, when is the apology a statement of remorse?
3. When is your child's aggression motivated by fear? Anger? Imitation?
4. When is your child's whining an indication of a compromise between asserting or demanding something, and pleasing you by not saying it?
5. When do you reassure your child by saying "I love you"? What motivates you? How does your child react?
6. When do you fear losing your child's love? What happens?
7. When do you see traits in your child that you can imagine when an older child, teenager, adult? Which will be assets, which liabilities? What impact does this have on your interactions with your child?
8. When do you use triggering fear to control your child's behavior? For example, "If you climb on the table you will break your neck." When does triggering your child's anxiety help to control behavior? When does it not? When does it promote the behavior you want to limit?
9. When is it difficult to understand the underlying meaning of your child's behavior?
10 When is knowing the underlying meaning of behavior useful? For example, "Even when you are so angry, you cannot bite." Or "Even when your friend is so sad, he cannot take your special bunny home with him. His mommy will help him to feel better." When is knowing the underlying meaning of behavior not useful?

### *Internal conflict*

*Children need to learn to tolerate ambivalent feelings, and to process conflicting wishes. For example, I love Mommy and I am so angry at her. Autonomy strivings and attachment needs may clash. For example, I want to be close to Mommy and I want to run away fast.*

*Many conflicts that you may have with your child now will become internal conflicts for your child. For example, drawing on the table or drawing on the paper. Young children gradually learn to resolve internal conflicts, usually in favor of Mommy's wishes. Sometimes the first step is to identify the conflict.*

*Mothers and children this age often have an increase in conflict with each other. For mothers, being angry at and disapproving of the child you love can be stressful and frightening. For the children, increased conflict with Mommy, though sometimes painful, is part of the process of developing internal conflict: the mother's disapproval becomes the child's self-disapproval.*

1. Sometimes a child is in conflict between pleasing Mommy and self-pleasing. When does this happen?
2. When does your child whining indicate your child's internal conflict between asking for something and giving up wanting it to please you?
3. When does identifying your child's internal conflict help to resolve the mother-child conflict and the whining? For example, "I know you really want to go to the park, and I told you we cannot go now, so you are using your squeaky voice instead of your big strong voice." When does it not help?
4. How does your child signal an intention to do something you disapprove of and get your help to control an impulse and stop? For example, your child pushes a stool next to the counter with a plate of cookies on it, starts to climb up, gets your attention, and then climbs down.
5. When are you in conflict about setting a limit for your child?
6. What advice have you been given that you are conflicted about following?
7. What child rearing conflicts do you and your husband or partner have with each other that reflect each of your own internal conflicts?
8. What conflicts do you have with your child that reflect your internal conflict? For example, conflicts with your child about sleeping in your bed related to your internal conflict about allowing it.
9. When have you seen your child's attachment needs clash with autonomy needs? For example, when struggling to do something, asks for your help, and then is angry when you help?
10. When does your child seem to be conflicted between pooping in the potty or continuing to play? Wanting to poop in the potty and afraid? Wanting to poop in the potty, but not wanting to flush it away? Or wants to flush the toilet, but not poop in it?

## Mother-child differences

*Mother-child differences and similarities may have crystalized. Their impact may be clearer to you now. Your child also may be aware of some of the similarities and differences between you, as well as similarities and differences with Daddy and siblings. Some may have been talked about, some not. Some of the traits may be physical, some may be talents, and some personality. Some traits may be considered assets, some liabilities, and others neither or both.*

1. What traits does your child have that are like you? Different? Like Daddy? Like your mother or father? Like your siblings?
2. Which traits do you think will be assets, liabilities? Both?
3. What reactions has your child had to differences? Gender? Race? Physical traits like eye color? Hair? Personality? Which have been talked about, which not?
4. What reactions has your child had to the similarities between you? With Daddy? With siblings?
5. When does your child imitate you?
6. What traits do you have that you do not want your child to acquire? What do you do to prevent your child from acquiring the trait?
7. What traits does your child have that are alien to you?
8. What traits does your child have that you had as a child but no longer have?
9. When do the differences between you and your child make it easier to empathize with your child? When do the differences between you and your child make it more difficult to empathize with your child?
10. When do the similarities make it easier to empathize with your child? When do the similarities make it more difficult to empathize with your child?

## *Learning*

*The children are learning many things, all the time: cognitive, social, physical, moral, and emotional. Some things you may be focused on teaching them, other things it is not clear how they were learned.*

*Learning to use the potty is an achievement with practical and developmental significance. The details of the process vary for each mother and child. Language acquisition and fluency are gradual and often are being evaluated. The importance of consistency is often emphasized for parents. The value of inconsistency is also important. Certain inconsistencies contribute to children learning to adapt to change, the nuances of specific relationships, and particular environmental demands.*

1. What are you in the process of teaching your child? What things does your child learn quickly? What things require many repetitions to learn? When do you think consistency is important? When is inconsistency of value?
2. Where are you and your child in the process of teaching-learning to use the potty?
3. What did you expect your child to have learned by now, but has not? What has your child learned that you would not have expected?
4. What has your child learned about you and needs to adapt to? What did you need to learn to adapt to your mother?
5. How do you decide what limits to set? How do you set them? How does your child respond?

6. What words has your child learned that may be ok to say in some settings but not in others? What other things has your child learned that are ok in some settings, but not others? What do you do that you do not want your child to do?
7. What is your thinking about the transition from the crib to the bed? Highchair to booster seat?
8. What are non-negotiable limits for you and your child? Which limits are repeatedly negotiated? When do you show disapproval of your child? How? How does your child respond?
9. What is your thinking about punishing children? What is your thinking about spanking?
10. What is your child's response to learning to use the potty? How do your child's needs to feel in control influence learning to use the potty? How do your child's impulses to touch poop or pee influence learning to use the potty?

## Vignettes

Following are five vignettes. The mother-child dyads were in different groups. Sally and Cliff is about a mother who wanted her 30-month-old son to sleep in his own bed, but every morning awoke surprised to discover him in her and her husband's bed. Interventions that linked her childhood memories to current interactions with Cliff enabled her to hear him and help him sleep through the night in his own bed.

Judy and Derrick is about 30-month-old Derrick's behavioral difficulties after his nanny quit and his mother was unable to talk with him about his painful feelings that were related to her own unresolved childhood loss of which she was unaware.

Claire and Beverly is about a mother's reactivated childhood sexual memories that triggered fears about her 3-year-old daughter being sexually abused. Interventions are described that helped to identify her childhood memories of excitement and unsafety that triggered her current fears of sexual abuse.

Elise and Ajax is about the meaning of 3-year-old Ajax's recent refusal to poop in the potty. Elise was 8 months pregnant and her efforts to protect Ajax from feeling displaced by a younger sibling contributed to his fantasy that he was pregnant.

Kathleen and Amber is about the impact of a mother's reactivated childhood sexual guilt that prevented her from telling the pediatrician about her daughter's masturbation that had caused superficial irritation and urinary tract infection symptoms, and the pediatrician's recommendation to catheterize her daughter, all contributing to Kathleen feeling like a "bad mother."

## Sally and Cliff

**Vignette summary**

**Child's age** – 30-months
**Mother-child interaction** – Child climbing into parents' bed in the middle of the night
**Presenting problem** – Mother wanted child to sleep in his own bed, but believed there was nothing she could do about it: "I don't hear him"
**Childhood memory** – "I slept on the floor outside my parents' bedroom"
**Mother's core theme** – Wish to protect her own mother, conflicted with getting comfort from her mother
**Primary defense mechanism** – Enacting a childhood memory, dissociation
**Organizing fantasy** – "There's nothing I can do; I sleep through it"
**Intervention** – Interpretation of a link between childhood memory and current mother-child interaction
**Resolution** – Mother heard child climb into bed; mother provided needed comfort to her child and helped him to sleep through the night in his own bed

*Cliff was a thriving 30-month-old little boy. He ate well, spoke well, played well, and slept well. For the past three weeks he had awakened happy every morning in his mother and father's bed. Every morning his mother, Sally, was surprised.*

*Sally did not think that this was a good pattern for Cliff. Sally's husband did not share her view but deferred to her. Sally was convinced there was nothing she could do about it; she never felt or heard Cliff enter their bed. She only discovered him in the morning: "What can I do about it? I sleep through it." The discrepancy between Sally's conviction that it was not good for Cliff to come into their bed and her equally strong conviction that there was nothing she could do about it suggested that there might be childhood memories connected to what could be understood as her unconscious conflict.*

*Given Sally's determination to have Cliff sleep in his own bed, Sally responded surprisingly fast when asked about the value of having Cliff sleep in bed with them: "I'm providing him with needed security, and we all get a good night's sleep." While Sally described what she believed to be of value in having Cliff sleep in their bed, she still insisted that she wanted him in his own bed, "But what can I do? I sleep through it."*

*When someone insists that they want something, but they themselves create the obstacle, something is being obscured. Sally's repeated phrase, "What can I do, I sleep through it*" offered a possible way to understand her insistence that there was nothing she could do. Sally believed that "sleeping through it" was happening to her, not that she had any agency to influence it. The following question related to childhood memories provided the first step: "Who slept through what when you were a child?" Sally responded, "When I was a child, I had nightmares about our house burning down. I was terrified. Every night I would sneak to my parents' bedroom and sleep on the floor outside their closed door. I didn't want to wake them. My parents suffered enough. They slept through it every night."

Sally protecting her mother was a major theme in their relationship. She had always been determined to be a "good girl" and keep her fears to herself. She remembered her mother having severe migraines, and her parents' constant dread that a migraine would be triggered. When Sally was a little girl and awoke in the middle of the night, she dared not enter her parents' bedroom, no matter how frightened she felt.

The following intervention summarized Sally's dilemma: "The current situation sounds like a repetition of your memory of sleeping on the floor outside your parents' bedroom when you were a little girl." Sally looked surprised and curious. I continued, "The roles are now reversed, and Cliff is getting something you did not get. You are now the parent sleeping through your child's distress rather than the scared child sleeping alone on the floor. And Cliff is the scared child getting something that you did not get." I then added a confrontation: "In spite of this, like you, Cliff's distress is not being addressed directly." Sally looked stunned with the connection between her past and the present and recognized that in some ways, Cliff was alone with his distress as she had been. New shared meanings were emerging.

The following week Sally told us that she had begun to hear Cliff when he got into her bed in the middle of the night. It was not known how this happened. Sally not hearing Cliff, a dissociation, had enabled her to unknowingly enact a childhood wish. The interpretation of a link between the past and the present, and a confrontation with the idea that Cliff's distress was not being directly addressed, had enabled Sally to hear him. She wanted to comfort him knowingly and directly. Sally was able to discover, from fragments of Cliff's description, that he was being awakened by frightening dreams. Sally was now able to walk him back to his own bed and to comfort him. During the day, they talked about the frightening dreams.

An explanation of dreams that is empowering to young children is the following: "Your dreams are stories that you make up and tell yourself while you are sleeping." Additional elements are: "The stories have pictures. Dreams are happy, sad, scary, and sometimes silly stories. Everyone dreams. Things that happen during the day may be hidden in your dreams at night. Your wishes and fears during the day are part of the stories. We can talk about dreams." The empowering core of this explanation is that the dreamer is the author and the director of the dream.

Within two weeks, Cliff was sleeping through the night in his own bed again. Sally's insight that her childhood memory was being enacted, combined with her wish to comfort Cliff, enabled her to hear him in the middle of the night. Now a mother, her revived memory of sleeping outside her parents' bedroom helped her to differentiate her own childhood wish to get into her parents' bed, or second-best to sleep on the floor outside* *their bedroom, from her current interactions with Cliff. She recognized that what Cliff needed was understanding and comfort that could be provided out of her bed. In addition, Sally now believed that her childhood memory was about what she thought her mother wanted. She entertained the possibility that her mother would have wanted to know about her distress and to soothe her: "I didn't want to disturb my mother. I'm not sure what she would have wanted." Sally's childhood memory had slightly, but meaningfully changed.*

## Judy and Derrick

> **Vignette summary**
>
> **Child's age** – 30-months
> **Mother-child interaction** – Escalating mother-child conflicts
> **Presenting problem** – Nanny had quit, mother refused to talk to child about his loss
> **Childhood memory** – Family dog died, nobody would talk about it
> **Mother's core theme** – To ward off erupting painful feelings
> **Primary defense mechanism** – Reaction formation, anger to mitigate feeling rejected and betrayed
> **Organizing fantasy** – "Talking about feelings does not help"
> **Intervention** – Interpretations about her wish to ward off her child's grief

*During a group that had been meeting for about two years, Judy announced that Nora, her 30-month-old son Derrick's nanny since his birth, had quit. Judy was angry and felt betrayed. Judy worked more than full-time and was totally dependent on childcare help. She had believed that Nora loved Derrick: "If that's how she really feels, I'm glad to be rid of her." When asked what she had said to Derrick about Nora leaving, Judy replied, "Nothing. Talking to Derrick will only make things worse. If he wanted to talk about her, he would." Furthermore, according to Judy, "There is nothing to talk about."*

*Since Nora had left, Derrick, who had been an easy, cooperative little boy, had become increasingly "difficult." His mother said that Derrick had become, "...demanding, oppositional, and crying all the time. He's impossible." Yet, Judy refused to talk to him about Nora. Derrick was throwing things, hiding until his mother was screaming in desperation to find him, protesting even brief separations, and pooping in his underpants. It was easy to understand the specific behaviors Judy was describing as Derrick's reactions to the loss of Nora and to his inability to organize his thoughts and feelings into words to adapt. In addition, he was reacting to his mother's rage.*

*The women in the group suggested to Judy that maybe Derrick's behavior was linked not only to Nora leaving, but also to the fact that nothing had been said about it. Judy rejected this possibility: "There is nothing to say." Judy's anger at Nora, Derrick, the group, and me predominated her state. The following interpretation addressed both Derrick's and Judy's grief underlying the anger: "It sounds like the thought of Derrick being sad about losing Nora is so painful to you that you need to deny its significance and focus on Derrick's angry behavior. Maybe you are avoiding talking to Derrick about Nora because you think not talking is the best thing to do." I suggested what she might say to Derrick if she changed her mind.*

The following week Judy told the group that Derrick's behavior had become "more difficult." She said, "Three days ago when I was tucking Derrick into bed, I decided to talk to him about Nora. I had to try something; he was impossible." Perhaps the impending separation from Derrick at bedtime, and her feelings related to separation that were evoked, triggered Judy's decision to talk to him about Nora. Judy told us about their conversation: "I wonder what you are thinking about Nora and why she left. I guess you miss her. We haven't seen her for a long time. She doesn't work here anymore. I guess you think about her sometimes. I probably should have said something sooner, I was too angry." Judy continued, "Derrick began to sob, I felt so terrible for him. For the first time he was crying in grief like a grown-up, not like a child wanting his own way." It was as if, until this moment, Judy had not realized that a child could have intense, authentic painful feelings of loss. Her dismissing attribution that children cry to get their own way had dominated her thinking and her interactions with Derrick. The following interpretation highlighted her empathy for Derrick's painful feelings of loss and implicitly her own: "It sounds like you were able to recognize and tolerate Derrick's painful feelings and that helped him." I wondered to myself what had been Judy's personal experiences of loss that she was not discussing, or even remembering.

The next day Derrick asked his mother if the scrape on Nora's knee was better. The last time Derrick had seen Nora her knee was covered with a large bandage after a fall. The injury had occurred when Nora tripped over Derrick's firetruck that had been left in the hall. Derrick's mother reassured him, "Yes, her knee is all better."

Part of Derrick's reaction to Nora leaving seemed to have been his concern that she left because of her injury that had been caused by his firetruck. Derrick may have also been worried that it was his fault his mother was angry, and that talking about Nora was not allowed. His mother talking to him about Nora opened the conversation and helped Derrick to ask about Nora's sore knee.

For a while, Derrick and his mother talked about Nora, the games they had played, and the books they had read together. Memories about the happy times they had shared were being co-constructed. At times they talked about Derrick's sadness and anger when Nora left, and his concerns about her tripping on his truck, which was an accident. Shared memories of love, loss, sadness, anger, and recovery were being created together. A distinction between family and non-family was made. Derrick's "impossible, difficult behavior" ended. In a short while, they only talked about Nora on occasion.

About a year later some light was shed on Judy's reaction when Nora had left. A woman in the group had a dog that died. Her dog was very old, sick, and in pain. She was describing how she, her husband, and their two children had a special goodbye before the dog was taken to the vet to be given an injection, only for dogs, when it is time for them to die. Judy recalled the loss of her own dog when she was a little girl. She remembered going to sleep-away camp for 1 month when she was 11-years. When she returned home, her dog was not there. She was never told what happened, but remembered some of her thoughts: "I didn't know if she was hit by a car, ran away, or was given away. Nobody would talk to me about it. I guess last year when

*Nora left, my memory about my dog was influencing me not talking to Derrick. I didn't think about it then."* Judy's memory and her new insight about repeating with Derrick what she remembered her parents having done with her promoted her conviction about the importance of talking with children about events and creating shared memories.

## Claire and Beverly

> **Vignette summary**
>
> **Child's age** – 36-months
> **Mother-child interaction** – Mother teaching child how to protect herself from sexual abuse
> **Presenting problem** – Mother's emerging fear of her child being sexually abused
> **Childhood memory** – Father's friend kissing her with his tongue, and mother's accusation that she liked her brother's bathroom peeping
> **Mother's core theme** – Sexual conflict and guilt
> **Primary defense mechanism** – Disavowal of sexual feelings and projection of sexual impulses
> **Organizing fantasy** – A girl needs to be taught to protect herself from sexual abuse
> **Intervention** – Linking childhood memories of sexual guilt to current fears of abuse, and highlighting the importance of protecting children, empowering them to say no, and normalizing childhood sexual feelings
> **Resolution** – Mother became more protective of her children, empowered them to say no, and became more accepting of their childhood body pleasures

*Claire had three children: a 14-year-old daughter, an 8-year-old son, and Beverly, a 3-year-old little girl with whom Claire was in a mother-toddler group. Claire had been a practicing attorney in a small law-firm until her second child was born. She had a busy home, with beginning teenage sexual excitement that set the stage for the emergence of her childhood sexual memories.*

*The group had been meeting for over two years. The women had shared many intimate details about their children, themselves, and their marriages. The mothers and I had just settled on the banquette when Claire mentioned a recent newspaper article about the sexual abuse of a young girl. Claire declared her intention to teach Beverly how to protect herself. She wanted to ensure that Beverly would never be sexually abused. Claire's focus on Beverly and the omission of any reference to her 14-year-old daughter, or 8-year-old son in this context was noteworthy. While the newspaper story was disturbing, Claire's related memories may have triggered her concerns.*

*Claire described how she was warning Beverly about potential dangers and teaching her self-protective strategies: "Never talk to strangers, never take candy from strangers, never get into a car with strangers." I could imagine how frightening these warnings might be to a 3-year-old and how unsafe and unprotected they could make Beverly feel.*

*In addition, 3-year-old children are rarely alone with strangers, and the parents of a sexually abused child often know the abuser.*

*In the middle of enumerating her instructions to Beverly and appearing startled, Claire remembered a kiss when she was 14 years old. Her father's friend put his hands on her bottom and kissed her in a way that tickled the inner edges of her lips with his tongue. She never told her parents, or anyone, and had not thought about it for many years.*

*Claire's older daughter was approaching 14-years; the same age Claire remembered having been when kissed and fondled. And while Claire thought the newspaper story had triggered her concern, her daughter being the same age as she was when inappropriately touched and kissed may have created the personal context for her emerging memory and worry. From Claire's description of the kiss tickling her lips, I wondered about the sexual arousal, shame, and guilt Claire might have felt and whether any of these feelings motivated her to keep the kiss secret. I also wondered whether as a child Claire felt unprotected in other ways.*

*The following child development information highlighted parents' protective role: "It is the parents' responsibility to protect their children. Little children cannot protect themselves. I wonder when else you felt unprotected." Claire responded, "When I was 10 years old, my little brother who was 8 always spied on me when I was in the bathroom. When I told my parents, they accused me of teasing him and said that I liked the attention." Claire's memory of her parents' accusations and disdain, and her associated shame and guilt, had motivated her to keep the kiss secret and contributed to her anxiety about Beverly being sexually abused.*

*The following clarified Claire's memory: "Not only do you remember your parents not protecting you, but in addition you remember being blamed for your brother's peeping and being criticized for any excitement or pleasure you got from it." Claire repeated, "I never told my parents about the kiss." Claire's statement was a confirmation that in some ways she thought the kiss was her fault and she felt ashamed. I continued, "Maybe you thought it was your fault that your father's friend kissed you with his tongue and touched you on your bottom. Maybe it is part of the reason for not telling your parents." The room was quiet. I added, "Little children cannot protect themselves. They learn to protect themselves when they feel protected by their parents and when they feel entitled to say no. In addition, when their body pleasures are recognized and accepted by their parents, they learn when and with whom pleasurable touching and kissing are desirable, and when and with whom they are not."*

*To discuss the ways in which parents can lay a foundation for young children to protect themselves from sexual abuse when they are older, two main themes were addressed: the children's entitlement to childhood body pleasures and their entitlement and support to say no to their bodies being touched. To promote group discussion to explore the mothers' attitudes about body pleasure, the following questions were useful: "What are some of the body pleasures your children are learning about now? Which are ok with you, which are not? Which do you support, with whom, and how?" To explore the children's protests to being touched and ways to support them, the following questions were posed: "What are some of the different ways in which* the children are currently trying to avoid being touched by family members, and by others? When do they say no to kisses or handshakes: or recoil when a stranger touches them? When do you support your child and say things like, "You didn't like it when the man in the elevator touched you, I told him not to touch you"? Or "It's ok you don't want to shake hands now"? I also asked, "When do you insist that the children be touched, or bribe them with treats to be touched? When are the children asked to be nice and kiss someone so as not to hurt their feelings?" The allusions to child sexual abuse scenarios in these questions about what happens between parents and young children were obvious, as was the implied protection of both being entitled and empowered to say no, and entitled to have body pleasures in safe, acceptable ways. The questions confronted the mothers to make the point clear that there are many everyday opportunities to support the children saying no to unwanted touches in contrast to frightening hypotheticals in the future. The women appreciated the potential importance of supporting both body pleasure and saying no. We also discussed situations when the children are required to be touched in ways they do not want and ways to give them more control in those situations. For example, when being examined by the doctor, or getting haircuts: "I know you don't like it when the doctor examines you, do you want me to hold you when you get your check-up?"

The following week, Claire told the group that she had decided to discontinue the male babysitter in his early 20s she had hired recently and with whom she did not feel "quite comfortable." It was not clear whether Claire's discomfort was in response to the babysitter's gender, age, or behavior. The babysitter was a surprise to us. The other women in the group believed that the babysitter also might have posed a threat to Claire's 14-year-old daughter, and her 8-year-old son. This had not occurred to Claire. She had denied what was a glaring possibility to the other mothers.

Claire now recognized that a 3-year-old is not able to protect herself. She also understood that in certain situations, the best way to teach Beverly now and lay the foundation for the future was to support her when she said no to being touched. When Beverly protested, but needed to be touched, for example by the doctor or when getting her nails cut, Claire recognized the importance of acknowledging and accepting her feelings and supporting communications about them. Beverly was no longer required to do high-five with their neighbor, sit on her uncle's lap whom she saw only on occasion, or to be kissed when she did not want to be. In some ways, Claire realized that while she had been hyper-vigilant about teaching Beverly to protect herself, at the same time she was denying her own protective and supportive role. She also recognized that she did not feel protected by her own parents when she was inappropriately kissed and touched by their friend, and furthermore did not feel safe enough to tell them.

Claire became more accepting of the normal body pleasures children enjoy. In addition, Claire began to address her reactions to her teenage daughter's developing sexuality and the revival of her own teenage sexual memories. Claire stopped bathing Beverly with her 8-year-old brother. She now believed that bathing her children together had been linked *to her memories about her brother peeping at her in the bathroom when she was a little girl, her conflicted feelings about it, and her parents' accusations. Claire's childhood memories now had new meanings. Her feelings about her brother spying on her now included both her excitement and not liking it. The memory of her parents' accusations and the shame she felt had shifted.*

## Elise and Ajax

> **Vignette summary**
>
> **Child's age** – 36 months
> **Mother-child interaction** – Mother preparing her son for the birth of a sibling
> **Presenting problem** – Child stopped pooping in the potty
> **Childhood memory** – Being "displaced" by the birth of her sister
> **Mother's core theme** – Wish to protect son from sibling rivalry
> **Primary defense mechanism** – Enactment of childhood memory, denial of impact on her child
> **Organizing fantasy** – "It's his baby too"
> **Intervention** – Interpretation of the connections between childhood memory of feeling displaced by the birth of her sister, her wish for her son to think the baby is his baby too, and his refusal to poop in the potty

*In the middle of a lively group discussion about learning to use the potty, Ajax's mother Elise mentioned, "Ajax just is not into it anymore. I think I'm going to put him back in diapers." Ajax was now 3-years and had been using the potty for 3 months. He wore underpants all the time. Several days earlier he had begun to refuse to use the potty. The women were surprised; learning to use the potty had gone smoothly for Ajax. I wondered what the connection might be between Elise being 8 months pregnant and Ajax beginning to protest any use of the potty, her apparent nonchalance about Ajax refusing to use the potty, and her readiness to put him back in diapers. A possible meaning was a wish that Ajax would remain the baby.*

*Elise believed Ajax was well prepared for the arrival of his baby sister. She had read him many books about babies, their crying, and the attention they need. I wondered what Ajax was being told about his mother's pregnancy and what he thought about it. The following child development information added a ripple to our discussion: "Regardless of what information young children have been given about the birth of a sibling, they may have their own theories about who can get pregnant, and how a baby gets in and how it gets out of Mommy's body. When mothers are pregnant, their children Ajax's age, boys as well as girls, often have thoughts and feelings about a baby being inside their own bodies – just like Mommy. Children may think that a baby can get in if they eat something and get out when they poop. These ideas can have an impact on their eating and pooping." The women remained quiet and curious. Ajax was the oldest in the group; two other children were also in underpants, and another mother was pregnant.*

*I asked Elise about Ajax's reactions to this phase of her pregnancy. Rejecting the connections that I was beginning to make between her pregnancy and Ajax refusing to* use the potty, she asserted, "He's never said anything, we just read books about babies. I don't think he thinks about it." The following idea about children's play related to pregnancy was an attempt to broaden the discussion: "Sometimes children communicate ideas or fantasies they have about pregnancy through their play. For example, they may put a pillow or stuffed animal under their shirts." Elise said she thought "It would be weird for Ajax to do that," and then said, "I want Ajax to feel that the baby is his baby too. I don't want him to feel displaced by the baby as I did by my sister. I just don't talk about it." Elise's childhood memory of feeling displaced and her reaction to the idea of Ajax pretending to be pregnant captured the intensity of her feelings about a sibling being born and were motivating her interactions with Ajax.

Elise's solution to ensure that Ajax would not feel displaced by the baby the way she had felt about her sister was "I want him to think that the baby is his baby too." I began to question with Elise whether her concern that Ajax would feel displaced by the baby, and her wish for Ajax to feel "The baby is his baby too," might motivate her to communicate ideas to Ajax that he could misinterpret as there is a baby in his tummy too, just like Mommy. Elise appeared thoughtful but did not say anything.

The following week Elise reported that "Ajax played being pregnant for the first time. He stuck out his tummy and said, I have a baby in my tummy." Elise took the opportunity to clarify for him, "The baby is only in Mommy's tummy. You will be the big brother." The next day Ajax resumed pooping in the potty.

It is not clear whether Ajax had played being pregnant before but his mother had not noticed, or hearing us talk during the group had been useful to Ajax, or whether Elise communicated something different to Ajax that enabled him to clarify something in his own mind that enabled him to use play to cope with his worries. Pretending to be pregnant is different than unprocessed worries about being pregnant. For Elise, the image of seeing Ajax pretending to be pregnant allowed her to differentiate her wish that Ajax not feel displaced by the baby, from a fantasy that he was pregnant. Elise also understood the importance of Ajax making this distinction. Ajax's ability to play being pregnant revealed in a clear way some thoughts that were on his mind of which his mother had been unaware. New shared meanings had emerged.

## Kathleen and Amber

> **Vignette summary**
>
> **Child's age** – 36-months
> **Mother-child interaction** – Child screaming whenever mother took her to the potty
> **Presenting problem** – Terror of potty
> **Childhood memory** – Childhood masturbation and parental prohibitions
> **Mother's core theme** – Conflicts about childhood sexual guilt reactivated when her daughter began to masturbate
> **Primary defense mechanism** – Medical procedure trauma and guilt enacted with child
> **Organizing fantasy** – "I am the worst mother"
> **Intervention** – Interpretation of links between childhood sexual guilt, medical procedure for child, and taking child to the potty

*Sometimes memories haunt parents because of painful associated guilt. The lingering residue of feeling like a bad mother can spread and invade mother-child interactions. Kathleen was unaware this was happening to her when she was trying to teach Amber to use the potty.*

*Kathleen and 3-year-old Amber had been in a group since Amber was 12-months. Amber was as competent verbally as she was athletic. She was generally easy-going and well-adapted. Developmental steps from bottle to cup and crib to bed had gone smoothly. However, none of these abilities or traits was helping Amber learn to use the potty.*

*Kathleen described her hopelessness to the group, "I will never teach Amber to use the potty. She just won't do it. She seems terrified. She screams every time I take her." Listening to Kathleen, I was reminded that when Amber was 16-months she had symptoms of a urinary tract infection. After a week of home remedies of cranberry juice and crying when she urinated, the pediatrician convinced Kathleen that catheterizing Amber was necessary to make a diagnosis. Kathleen had not thought that Amber had an infection and was concerned about the impact of this painful and invasive medical procedure.*

*The procedure was even worse than Kathleen had anticipated. She and two nurses held Amber down while she screamed, and Kathleen wept. The lab results confirmed that Amber did not have a urinary tract infection. Kathleen felt excruciatingly guilty for having agreed to the procedure even though the doctor had said it was essential.*

*Several weeks after the procedure, feeling very guilty and like "...the worst mother in the world," Kathleen had confided in the group that she had not told the doctor about Amber's "genital rubbing." She had believed it had caused some superficial irritation and had triggered the urinary tract infection symptoms. In retrospect she had wondered* whether her own embarrassment about Amber's genital pleasure, "she was only 16-months," had prevented her from telling the doctor. Kathleen thought that if the doctor had known, he might not have suggested the catheterization. Kathleen believed she was "the worst mother," not only because she had not told the doctor, but also because her daughter was masturbating. In some ways, Kathleen agreeing to her daughter being catheterized, and her guilt about it, represented self-punishment for her own masturbation guilt.

As Kathleen described the current struggle wrestling Amber to the potty screaming, I reminded her about the medical procedure when Amber was 16-months: "It sounds like when you take Amber to the potty, in your mind you are taking her to be catheterized again. It is as though you are not remembering but you are re-living all the terror, horror, and guilt you experienced. In addition, there may be more for us to talk about children's sex-play." Even though it is not clear how or whether all that was in Kathleen's mind was communicated to Amber, and it is not known what Amber's own associations were between the potty and her medical procedure when she was younger, there seemed to be some connections.

The relief Kathleen and the entire group experienced upon hearing we could talk more about sex-play was palpable. Understanding what was happening in the present in terms of memories of the past was liberating. Taking Amber to the potty felt to Kathleen like a re-living of the medical procedure and all the associated feelings. Furthermore, her guilt about the catheterization was compounded by her own childhood sexual guilt that had been reactivated. I asked, "What childhood memories do you have about masturbation?" Kathleen remembered that when she was around 10-years her parents forbid her to touch her genitals. However, she secretly masturbated to orgasm in her bed before falling asleep and felt deeply guilty and ashamed.

Kathleen's unrecognized lingering sexual guilt and shame, which was embedded in her story, could now be discussed in the group. Each woman recounted experiences of her own childhood sex-play, teenage sexuality, and her parents' reactions. We also talked about attitudes the women had towards their children's current genital curiosity and pleasure. Amber began to routinely use the potty. Kathleen became more self-forgiving.

As an adult, Kathleen knew that childhood genital exploration, stimulation, and masturbation are considered normal; yet her own feelings of sexual guilt had been activated. The way in which Kathleen's new understanding of her memories changed her interactions with Amber is unclear; however, Amber no longer cried about the potty.

# Section IV

# In conclusion

Chapter 8

# Individual sessions with a group mother

There are a variety of indications for short-term individual sessions with a group mother and her child. The primary purpose of individual sessions is to promote group participation for the mother and the child. When individual sessions occur, it is important to assess, and when needed to discuss, the additional gratification for the mother that individual sessions may provide, and their impact on her and on the group. When a mother wants an individual session because of discomfort discussing something in the group, this is explored. Either her difficulty will be resolved or a referral for individual treatment or couples therapy in addition to the group may be needed.

The following vignette is about Ricky and 20-month-old Brianna who were seen for 12 mother-child sessions because of the distress Brianna experienced throughout the group, and her mother Ricky's minimal participation in the group.

## Ricky and Brianna

> **Vignette summary**
>
> **Child's age** – 20-months
> **Mother-child interaction** – Mother unattuned, intrusive, and directive
> **Presenting problem** – Child softly sobbing throughout group, delayed language
> **Childhood memory** – Not reported
> **Mother's core theme** – Conflicts between mother-child relationship and career ambitions
> **Primary defense mechanism** – Isolation of affect, splitting
> **Organizing fantasy** – A constant focus on child when with her was required
> **Intervention** – Individual mother-child sessions to promote child's comfort during groups, and attuned mother-child interactions. Exploration and interpretations to integrate mother's relationship with her child and work
> **Resolution** – Mother's focus shifted from attention to her child's external behavior, to emotional connecting

*Ricky had waited to become pregnant until she felt that she could not wait any longer. She had worked hard since getting her MBA and had built a successful business. She loved her work and was eager to keep growing her business. Ricky was now 43 years old, and Brianna was 20-months. Ricky thought the mother-toddler group was "perfect," but she was not sure how often she would attend because of work. Work may have been one of her reasons; being a single mother, though not mentioned, may have been another. We arranged for Brianna's babysitter to remain available to Brianna in the observation area when Ricky did not attend.*

*Ricky did everything fast. She talked, moved, and thought fast. Everything she said and did had a lively, exuberant style. Her eyes twinkled and her golden hair bounced, reflecting the light as she moved. She repeatedly gave directions to Brianna, "Say hello." "Give your friend a kiss." "Go play." She also posed many rhetorical questions to me: "Isn't she adorable?" "Don't you think she's the cutest?" "Isn't she so smart?" Brianna, trying to keep up with her mother, looked dazed.*

*Ricky and Brianna had been in the group since September. It was now early December. Ricky had brought Brianna to every group, stayed about 10 minutes, and then left. Brianna's slight smile rapidly faded when her mother slipped out the door. Throughout the group, Brianna softly sobbed and wandered aimlessly, often gazing out the window into the courtyard where she had seen her mother walk away. She was unable to play or to be comforted. Since the group is for mothers with their children, Brianna's babysitter* remained in the play observation area to be available to Brianna, but mostly she spent the hour on her phone. Ricky preferred that the babysitter and Brianna not have a "close relationship." They appeared emotionally disconnected. There was no physical or intersubjective interactions between them during the group. Brianna's language was delayed for her age. Ricky had repeatedly refused any additional help for Brianna or for herself.

We had just returned from winter vacation and for the first time Ricky attended the entire group. She had become concerned about Brianna after observing a friend's child who was the same age: "My friend's little girl can do so many things Brianna can't do. I'm worried." Brianna was now 23-months. Ricky agreed to supplement the group with weekly individual play sessions for Brianna with the play-leader, Alyson McCormick, and at the same time, in the same room, Ricky and I would talk. With her mother present and available, Brianna would be able to build a relationship with Alyson that would be helpful when she needed someone with whom to feel emotionally connected during the group when her mother was not there. In addition, my talking with Ricky might help us to understand more about Brianna, Ricky, and the babysitter.

During our first three sessions, Ricky and I talked while we watched Brianna begin to play with Alyson. Alyson's exclusive attention to Brianna, the lowered stimulation without the other children and mothers, and most importantly Ricky remaining close and available, enabled Brianna to feel more comfortable and to begin to play with Alyson. While Ricky remained available to Brianna and attentive to watching her, she described the details of her enjoyable interactions with Brianna. She highlighted bath-time games, reading, and breakfast time. Ricky also talked about her pride in Brianna's physical appearance. Brianna had long blonde hair, a rosy complexion, ice blue eyes, and delicate features. While talking about these positive gratifying aspects of Brianna, the pleasures in their interactions, and Brianna's pretty appearance, Ricky was implicitly asserting some positive feelings about herself as a mother. Ricky conveyed her anxiety about Brianna's development and her mothering by her repeated rhetorical question, "She's so smart, isn't she?" Since Ricky's work was important to her and often kept her away from Brianna, the absence of any mention of work was potentially meaningful. In addition, her avoidance of mentioning anything about being a single mother was noteworthy.

At the end of our fourth session there was a shift. Ricky began to comment on the significance of our conversations together: "It's amazing how we talk about all the little things Brianna does." Focusing with me on the "little things" she knew about Brianna and enjoyed with her enabled Ricky to begin to talk about her conflict and guilt about time away from Brianna when at work, the anxiety she felt when separated from her, and her conviction that she was a "terrible mother."

Upon arriving the following week, Brianna refused to enter. She was kicking and screaming. Ricky was reprimanding her and threatening to leave without her. Clearly disturbed by Brianna's behavior, Ricky began to tell me about the fun they had together on the bus and her belief that Brianna did not want their play together to end. I thought this was also true about Ricky, who preferred to continue to play with Brianna rather than to resume our conversation about her feeling like a "terrible mother."

I asked Ricky what it had been like playing with Brianna on the bus. She responded, "We have a lot of fun. I exaggerate everything. I speak loud and fast, it's exhausting, but it helps me to stay focused on her and not to be preoccupied with my work." In the same way Ricky tried to keep work out of her mind when with Brianna, she also kept work and being a single mother out of our conversation.

Ricky's ability to reflect on aspects of herself when she was interacting with Brianna was impressive and provided an opportunity to address something that might be important. My next comment targeted her core theme – her conflict between work and Brianna: "The kind of play you are describing, although a strain, also sounds like it is serving an important function. It seems vital to you to keep a constant focus on Brianna while you are with her. What would it be like to be with Brianna if you were not talking to her for a moment, if you were thinking about something you needed to do at work and Brianna was quietly looking out the window? Work is important to you." In a quiet voice Ricky affirmed, "You mean that could be okay." Ricky's statement echoed her recognition that she could be a good mother even while thinking about work. Her statement was about her conflicted painful feelings, not her intellectual understanding. Ricky's statement also affirmed that we were thinking together about both work and Brianna. Such an integration of work and Brianna, rather than the split she had created, helped Ricky to be more attuned and emotionally available to Brianna, rather than blindly or in a way compulsively focused on her.

The next session Ricky and Brianna entered ready to play. The change in Ricky was telling. She seemed more relaxed, her pace had slowed down, and her voice was gentle. She made no demands on Brianna or on me. She described their bus ride as "pleasant," "Sometimes I talked to Brianna and sometimes I was thinking about work."

Ricky became more aware of and attuned to Brianna's inner world and to her own. Her focus shifted from external behavioral attending to Brianna, to emotional connecting with Brianna. These changes in Ricky remained and expanded. These changes also enabled Ricky to help the babysitter to be more emotionally available to Brianna. Ricky's feelings about being a "bad mother" no longer influenced her rivalry with the babysitter in a way that had prevented her from helping the babysitter to be more attentive to Brianna. Ricky insisted that the babysitter not use her cellphone while taking care of Brianna and limit screen-time for Brianna. In addition, Ricky's increased attunement to Brianna provided a useful model for the babysitter.

We met for six more sessions. Brianna's play became more focused and organized. She no longer cried during the group; her relationship with Alyson was secure which helped her when her mother left. Brianna turned to Alyson when she needed help and to share the pleasures of her play. She always chose to sit next to Alyson during snack. Brianna also was able to remain emotionally connected to her babysitter, who had put her cell phone away. With a glance across the room or up-close touching base they stayed connected. With her mother and babysitter's support, and her relationship with Alyson, Brianna was able to participate with the other children. Her pleasure in her social interactions and delight in play activities was apparent. Expressive language began to emerge. The individual sessions with me and Alyson were no longer needed.

*In addition to work, Ricky had been reluctant to participate in the group in part because of her general devaluation of women – she had more important things to do, as well as her competition with them that was related to her painful feelings about being a "bad mother." Pleased with Brianna's development and feeling more supported in both her work and her mothering, Ricky became less self-critical. She began to attend the group occasionally. In time, Ricky began to talk about her childhood memories and her experience of being a single mother, both of which were related to career ambition struggles. Feeling like a "good-enough mother" had needed to occur first.*

*Our individual mother-child sessions to supplement the group had enabled Ricky to share with me the details of the pleasurable moments she had with Brianna and her sense of pride in Brianna's physical appearance – both of which reflected some positive although fragile feelings about herself as a "good-enough mother." These enhanced feelings about herself enabled Ricky to reflect on aspects of her interactions with Brianna that were over-stimulating, emotionally disconnected, and unsatisfying to them both. My recognizing the importance of her work and acknowledging her professional achievements supported another important part of her life which she had felt she needed to keep out of her mind while she was with Brianna. Raising the question about what it would be like to be with Brianna while thinking about work prompted her to question what had been an unconscious tenet: I must be completely focused on Brianna when I am with her. Ricky was now able to relinquish that notion and to better integrate these two parts of her life, being a mother and her career. Brianna began to thrive.*

# Chapter 9

# Ending groups

In anticipation of the ending of a group, a month before the last session, the group-leader announces it. The children are around 3 years old. While the mothers have had the schedule, the announcement often triggers a reaction of surprise and loss. The mothers' attachment to and autonomy from the group and the group-leader are evidenced during this time.

Asking the mothers about their children's expected reactions to groups ending is useful. The mothers' descriptions of their children's anticipated reactions reflect aspects of their own reactions and reveal their emerging awareness. A version of the following statement opens the group discussion and may trigger unexpected comments: *"I have enjoyed working with you and watching your children grow. We have talked about many important topics. There are many things we have not talked about."*

At the last session, mothers shed tears, but there is also satisfaction and eagerness to move into the next phase of development and mothering. There is a looking forward to the children growing. Saying good-bye is a celebration of a milestone. The mothers feel empowered to go forward and cherish having shared this important phase of life.

DOI: 10.4324/b23150-14

# Glossary

This glossary defines terms as used in this book

**Adaptation:** responsiveness to internal and external opportunities, stresses, and demands with the aim of personal well-being and optimal interpersonal outcomes

**Age categories:** Infant, birth to 3-years. Baby, 2-months to 12-months. Toddler, 12-months to 3-years. Child, 2-months to 3-years

**Attachment:** the mother-child relationship bond that promotes the child's safety and development, and the mother's caretaking and well-being

**Childhood memories:** the significance of childhood memories during psychodynamic mother-baby-toddler groups is that their meanings influence mother-child interactions, can be understood, and lead to change

**Conflict, internal:** opposition within the mind between opposing wishes, values, impulses, and feelings

**Consciousness:** a mental state of awareness: the subjective experience of knowing

**Defense mechanisms:** mental processes employed to mitigate painful thoughts and feelings

**Denial:** mental repudiation of an aspect of reality

**Development:** the process of physical and mental growth that includes the role of the environment; *see Maturation*

**Disavowal:** repudiation of one's own thoughts and feelings

**Displacement:** feelings, fantasies, attributes originally directed towards or about one person, are re-directed towards another

**Dissociation:** disruption of connections between mental processes, including conscious perception, for the purpose of defense

**Emotion regulation:** mental processes that determine the expression of emotions, and the maintaining and returning to a state of equilibrium when intense feelings have been aroused that disrupt the equilibrium

**Empathy:** a process of feeling, imagining, thinking, or sensing the experience of another; central for all human relationships and vital for child development

# 186 Glossary

**Expectancies:** adaptive mental predictions based on experience that influence future experience and promote awareness

**Good-enough mother:** a term coined by Donald Winnicott that refers to the mother providing sufficient amounts of gratification needed to buffer frustrations, and promote healthy development

**Group-process:** mothers' support for each other; questions and concerns about their children; group-leader support and interventions linking childhood memories to mother-child interactions; child development information and group questions to promote discussion, self-reflection, and new shared meanings

**Historical truth:** a reported occurrence, (memory) that is verifiable; *see Narrative truth*

**Idealization:** the attribution of perfection to someone or to an experience; the denial of any negative thoughts or feelings about the person

**Inner world:** each person's subjective perceptions, thoughts, and feelings, including sense of self, fantasies, wishes, conflicts, intentions, fears, and memories

**Insight:** a formulation of an aspect of one's own mental process from a new perspective; *see New shared meanings*

**Intergenerational transfer of trauma:** the traumatic impact of events in one generation affecting subsequent generations

**Interpretation:** a statement that postulates the meaning of behavior, including thoughts and feelings, and links between a mother's childhood memory and the way in which it is being enacted, of which she is unaware

**Intersubjectivity:** an interaction between two people where each is aware of the subjective experience of the other; *see Social referencing*

**Maturation:** the unfolding of predetermined growth that lays the foundation for the emergence of more organized and complex physical and mental functions, and structures; *see Development*

**Memories:** **explicit** or declarative memories are mental constructs related to actual events, include associated wishes, fears, conflicts, and feelings, and are organized into narratives; **implicit** or procedural memories include the evocation of an emotion, bodily sensation, body procedures, or interpersonal ways of being with another that are connected to past relationships or events, not narrated

**Mental representations:** the ways in which the self, others, and self-with-other, ideas and feelings are symbolized in the mind or mentally portrayed

**Mother's core theme:** a psychodynamic construct about primary conscious and unconscious conflicts

**Mother's expanding sense of self:** a facet of a mother's capacity for insight derived from her attachment to her baby, pride in being a mother, the pleasures with her child, and her mothering goals

**Narrative truth:** the personal meaning of a reported occurrence – a memory aiming toward internal conflict resolution, adaptation, and positive sense of self: *see Historical truth*

**New shared meanings:** an expansion of the term insight to include the mothers' and the group-leader's emotionally significant experience with each other leading to change

**Non-verbal:** aspects of communication that include gesture, facial expression, tone of voice, affect, and physical interaction

**Projection:** the attribution of an unacceptable or shameful idea, impulse, or feeling of one's own to another person

**Psychoanalytic approach:** exploration and interpretation of conscious and unconscious multiple meanings of behavior – actions, thoughts, feelings, wishes, memories, and fantasies

**Psychodynamic:** the mental processes underlying behavior and their impact on behavior; included are conscious and unconscious thoughts, feelings, intentions, memories, fantasies, wishes, and the conflicts among them

**Reaction formation:** conscious thoughts and feelings that are the opposite of and defend against their unconscious meaning

**Reflective functioning:** ability to think about and to understand one's own and others' feelings, wishes, and intentions

**Secure base interactions:** mother-baby and mother-toddler interactions that enable the child to comfortably explore and play away from Mommy, return to her, or social reference from a distance with her when needed, *see Social referencing*

**Security of attachment:** the mother-child relationship bond that promotes the child's development and the mother's caretaking

**Self-constancy:** an ongoing, relatively stable, and reliable sense of self regardless of emotional state or interpersonal interaction

**Self-reflection:** contemplation of one's thoughts, feelings, and behavior from varying points of view; an element of what has been called reflective functioning

**Sense of self:** evolving thoughts and feelings about oneself that grow out of bodily, mental, and interpersonal experiences beginning in infancy

**Social referencing:** babies' and toddlers' non-verbal signaling to their mothers to get information to guide their responses when they are uncertain about the meaning, safety, and threat of things, persons, and situations; to share pleasures, and to support attachment

**Splitting:** mentally separating aspects of the self, other, perception, and experience for the purpose of defense – usually into good and bad

**Support for mothers:** interventions that affirm, corroborate, and validate mothers' interactions with their babies and toddlers that promote infant mental health: recognition of the challenges and stresses of mothering

**Trauma:** the experience of being overwhelmed and unable to adapt

**Treasured toy:** described by Donald Winnicott as a transitional object: an object like a teddy bear or blanket to which a child creates a strong attachment, especially important during times of stress and separation from mother, and endows with emotion regulation capacities, that thereby promote the child's development of those needed mental capacities including emotion regulation, frustration tolerance, the ability to tolerate ambivalence, and the capacity to be alone

**Unconscious:** memories, thoughts, and feelings without awareness which yet have influence

**Unresolved trauma:** ongoing feelings of anxiety, helplessness, and fear in response to a past event

**Working alliance:** an aspect of the group-leader's relationship with each mother, leading to their interactions with the shared aim of exploring and understanding together the conscious and unconscious meanings of the mothers' childhood memories, the developmental meanings of their children's behavior, and mother-child interactions

**Working models:** *see Mental representations*

**Working through:** the mental processes of resolving trauma and conflict with the aim of adaptation, including the assimilation of child development information and support

# Suggested reading

Alvarez, A. (2012). *The Thinking Heart*. Abingdon: Routledge.
Baradon, T. (2016). *The Practice of Psychoanalytic Parent-Infant Psychotherapy: Claiming the Baby*. Abingdon: Routledge.
Baradon, T. (2018). New Beginnings: A Time Limited Intervention for High-Risk Infants and Mothers. *Handbook of Attachment-Based Interventions*. Steele, M. & Steele, H. Eds. New York and London: Guilford Press, pp. 174–197.
Beebe, B. (2014). *The Origins of Attachment: Infant Research and Adult Treatment*. London and New York: Routledge Press.
Beebe, B. Cohen, P. & Lachman, F. (2016). *The Mother-Infant Interaction Picture Book*. New York: WW Norton & Company.
Coates, S. W. (1998). Having a Mind of One's Own and Holding the Other in Mind: Discussion of "Mentalization and the Changing Aims of Child Psychoanalysis" by Peter Fonagy and Mary Target, *Psychoanalytic Dialogues*, 8: 115–148.
Coates, S. W. (1998). Can Babies Remember Trauma? Symbolic Forms of Representation in Traumatized Infants. *Journal of the American Psychoanalytic Association*, 8: 115–148.
Dozier, M. & Bernard, K. (2019). *Coaching Parents of Vulnerable Infants*. New York and London: Guilford Press.
Fraiberg, S. (1959). *The Magic Years: Understanding and Handling the Problems Early Childhood*. New York: Scribner
Fraiberg, S. (1975). Ghosts in the Nursery: A Psychoanalytic Approach to the Problem of Impaired Infant-Mother Relationships. *Journal of the American Academy of Child Psychiatry*, 14: 387–421
Fraiberg, S. (1980). *Clinical Studies in Infant Mental Health*. New York: Basic Books.
Gold, C. (2011). *Keeping Your Child in Mind*. Boston: Da Capo Lifelong Books.
Gold, C. (2016). *The Silenced Child*. Boston: Da Capo Lifelong Books.
Harrison, A. & Tronick, E. Eds. (2022). Intersubjectivity: Conceptual Considerations in Meaning-Making with a Clinical Illustration. *Frontiers in Psychology*. https://doi.org/10.3389/fpsyg.2021.715873
Lefcourt, I. (2021). *Parenting and Childhood Memories: A Psychoanalytic Approach to Reverberating Ghosts and Magic*. London and New York: Routledge Press.

Lefcourt, I. & Bergman, A. (1999). Self-Other Action Play. *Children at Play*. Slade, A. and Wolf, D. Eds. Oxford and New York: Oxford University Press, pp. 133–147.

Lieberman, A. (2005). Angels in the Nursery. *Infant Mental Health Journal*, 26: 504–520.

Lieberman, A. (2017). *The Emotional Life of the Toddler*. New York: Simon and Schuster.

Lieberman, A. Diaz, M, Castro, G. & Bucio, G.O. (2020). *Make Room for Baby*. New York and London: Guilford Press.

Mahler, M. Pine, F. & Bergman, A. (1975). *The Psychological Birth of the Human Infant*. New York: Basic Books.

Nachman, P. (1998). Maternal Identification: A Description of the Process in Real Time. *Journal of the American Psychoanalytic Association*, 46 (1): 209–228.

Nachman, P. & Carr, E. (Issue Eds.) (2017). Daniel Stern: Contributions to Psychoanalysis and Developmental Psychology, Part 1, *Psychoanalytic Inquiry*, 37 (4). Abingdon: Routledge.

Nachman, P. & Carr, E. (Issue Eds.) (1019). Daniel Stern: Contributions to Psychoanalysis and Developmental Psychology, Part 11, *Psychoanalytic Inquiry*, 38 (2). Abingdon: Routledge.

Olesker, Wendy. (1990). Sex Differences During the Early Separation-Individuation Process: Implications for Gender Identity Formation. *Journal of the American Psychoanalytic Association*, 38: 325–346.

Olesker, Wendy. (1998). Female Genital Anxieties: Views from the Nursery and the Couch. *Psychoanalytic Quarterly*, LXVIL: 276–294.

Olesker, Wendy. (2014). A Developmental View of Hostile Aggression. *Journal of Infant, Child and Adolescent Psychotherapy*, 13: 298–307.

Schechter, D. (2017). On Traumatically Skewed Intersubjectivity, *Psychoanalytic Inquiry*, 37 (4): 251–264.

Schechter, D. & Willheim, E. (2009). When Parenting Becomes Unthinkable: Intervening with Traumatized Parents and Their Toddlers. *J. Am. Acad. Child and Adolesc. Psychiatry*, 48: 3.

Scheftel, S. (2009). The Children's Books of William Steig: A Creative Representation of Early Separation and Resiliency. *The Psychoanalytic Study of the Child*, 66 (1): 251–278.

Scheftel, S. (2012). Why Aren't We Curious About Nannies? *The Psychoanalytic Study of the Child*, 66: 251–278.

Seth, A. (2021). *Being You: A New Science of Consciousness*. Westminster, London: Dutton.

Shapiro, T. (2011). Infant Psychiatry: Infants, Mothers and Dyads. *Journal of the American Academy of Child & Adolescent Psychiatry*, 50 (3): 207–209.

Shapiro, T. & Makari, G. (1994). A Linguistic Model of Psychotherapeutic Listening. *Journal of Psychotherapy Practice and Research*, 3 (1): 37–43.

Steele, H. & Steele, M. (2018). Group Attachment-Based Intervention: A Multifamily Trauma-Informed Intervention. *Handbook of Attachment-Based Interventions*. Steele, H. & Steele, M. Eds. New York and London: Guilford Press, pp. 198–219.

Stern, D. (1995). *The Motherhood Constellation*. New York: Basic Books.

Stern, D. (2004). *The Present Moment in Psychotherapy and Everyday Life*. New York: Norton.

Stern, D. & Brushweiler-Stern, N. (1998). *The Birth of a Mother: How the Motherhood Experience Changes You Forever*. New York: Basic Books

Tronick, E. Gold, C. (2020). *The Power of Discord*. New York, Boston, London: Little, Brown Spark.

Winnicott, D. (1953). Transitional Objects and Transitional Phenomena: A Study of the First Not-Me Possession. *International of Psychoanalysis*, 34: 89–97.

# Index

acknowledgements xiv
adaptation 23, 185; and expectancies 23; and inconsistency 54–55; and shared memory narratives 24, 131; to what cannot be known 18
age categories 185
aggression 23; Child Development Information and Group Questions: 11 to 19-months 114–115; fear of Vignette 122–124; 29 to 36-months 154; 20 to 28-months 133–134; 2 to 10-months 92
Alvarez, A. 189
attachment 22, 27–28, 185; and mothers' expanding sense-of-self 31

Beebe, B. 189
baby's name 81–82
beginning groups 67; babies and toddlers 80–82; child development information and group questions 82–84; group composition 70–71; group schedules 70–71; group sessions 80–82; pre-enrollment visits 69–70; pre-group mother-child visits 71–73
Bergman, A. 190
body awareness, child development information and group questions 23, 39–43; Child Development Information and Group Questions: 11 to 19-months 115–116; 29 to 36-months 154–155; 20 to 28-months 134–135; 2 to 10-months 93
breastfeeding conflict vignette 125–127; career conflicts 71; and mother-child interactions vignette 180–183

Child Development Information and Group Questions, 2 to 10-months 4, 17–20, 83–84; aggression 92; body awareness 93; children's interactions with other children 93–94; emotion regulation 94; gender 95; internal conflict 96–97; learning 97–98; mother-child attachment 89–90; mother-child differences 97; mother-child interaction 87–88; mothers' childhood memories 90–91; play 91–92; separation 91; underlying meanings of behavior 95–96
Child Development Information and Group Questions, 11 to 19-months 4, 17–20, 83–84; aggression 114–115; body awareness 115–116; children's interactions with other children 116; emotion regulation 117; gender 117–118; internal conflict 119–120; learning 120–121; mother-child attachment 110–111; mother-child communication 111–112; mother-child differences 120; mother-child interactions 109–110; mothers' childhood memories 112–113; play 113–114; separation 113; underlying meanings of behavior 118–119
Child Development Information and Group Questions, 20 to 28-months 4, 17–20, 83–84; aggression 133–134; body awareness 134–135; children's interactions with other children 135; emotion regulation 136; gender 136–137; internal conflict 138–139; learning 139–140; mother-child attachment 129–130; mother-child communication 130–131; mother-child differences 139; mother-child interactions 128–129; mothers' childhood memories 131–132; play 132–133; separation 132; underlying meanings of behavior 137–138

Child Development Information and Group Questions, 29 to 36-months 4, 17–20, 83–84; aggression 154; body awareness 154–155; children's interactions with other children 155–156; emotion regulation 156; gender 157; internal conflict 158–159; learning 160–161; mother-child attachment 149–150; mother-child communication 150–151; mother-child differences 159–160; mother-child interactions 148–149; mothers' childhood memories 151–152; play 153–154; separation 152–153; underlying meanings of behavior 157–158
childhood memories 185
children's interactions with other children 23, 43–44; Child Development Information and Group Questions: 2 to 10-months 93–94; 11 to 19-months 116; 20 to 28-months 135; 29 to 36-months 155–156
Coates, S. 189
Cohen, P. 189
consciousness 185
core themes, mothers' 5, 72
Covid pandemic 13

defense mechanisms 11, 185; summary 56
denial 185
development 185
disavowal 185
displacement 185
dissociation 185
doll-play mother-child secure base symbol, vignette 122–123
dreams: explanation for children 119; mother reports 60

emotion regulation 23, 44–46, 185; and co-constructed memory narratives 58, 166; Child Development Information and Group Questions: 2 to 10-months 94; 11 to 19-months 117; 20 to 28-months 136; 29 to 36-months 156
empathy 185
expectancies: development of 89, 186

Fraiberg, S. 189

gender 23; Child Development Information and Group Questions: 2 to 10-months 95; 11 to 19-months 117–118; 20 to 28-months 136–137; 29 to 36-months 157
glossary 185–188
Gold, C. 189
good-enough mother 13, 148, 186
grief, re-activated 34, 100
group goals and group-process, summary 17
group-leader: approach 1, 9–12, 17; and empathic failures 10; and personal feelings 10–11; summary 12; vignette 78–79
group-notes outline 72
group-process 186
groups ending 184

historical truth 49, 186

idealization 186
individual sessions with group mother vignette 180–183
inner world 186
insight 186
intergenerational transfer of trauma 9, 186
internal conflict 25, 31, 50, 119–120, 127, 138, 158, 186; Child Development Information and Group Questions: 2 to 10-months 96–97; Child Development Information and Group Questions: 11 to 19-months 119–120; 20 to 28-months 138–139; 29 to 36-months 158–159; and core themes 9
interpretation 186
intersubjectivity 77, 186; and limit setting 109; and pointing 109

kidnapping, fears of 23–24

Lachman, F. 189
Lefcourt, I. 190
learning 23, 25; Child Development Information and Group Questions: 2 to 10-months 97–98; 11 to 19-months 120–121; 20 to 28-months 139–140; 29 to 36-months 160–161
Lieberman, A. 18, 58, 190
limit setting and joint focus of attention 24, 42

maternal depression, vignette 104–106
maturation 186
memories: explicit, implicit 186

memory narratives, co-constructed, vignette 24, 58, 165
mental representations 186
mother-baby avoidant interaction pattern 59
mother-child body-play 40
mother-child communication 22, 28–30; Child Development Information and Group Questions: 2 to 10-months 89–90; 11 to 19-months 111–112; 20 to 28-months 130–131; 29 to 36-months 150–151
mother-child differences 23; Child Development Information and Group Questions: 2 to 10-months 97; 11 to 19-months 120; 20 to 28-months 139; 29 to 36-months 159–160; vignette 51–54
mother-child interactions 3, 9, 22–26; Child Development Information and Group Questions: 2 to 10-months 87–88; 11 to 19-months 109–110; 20 to 28-months 128–129; 29 to 36-months 148–149
mother-child proximity 57–62; vignette 63–66
mothers' childhood memories 3–5, 22, 31–34, 80; Child Development Information and Group Questions: 2 to 10-months 90–91; 11 to 19-months 112–113; 20 to 28-months 131–132; 29 to 36-months 151–152
mother's core theme 186
mother's description of her baby or toddler 81
mothers' emerging fears, injury to baby: kidnapping 23–24; spoiling 168–170
mothers' envy of children 14
mother's expanding sense of self 24–25, 186
mother's experiences of childbirth 83
multi-lingual families 53

Nachman, P. 190
narrative truth 31–32, 49, 187
new shared meanings 187

Olesker, W. 190

play 22, 36–37; Child Development Information and Group Questions: 2 to 10-months 91–92; 11 to 19-months 113–114; 20 to 28-months 132–13; 29 to 36-months 153–154
pointing 60; to a future event 61; and joint focus of attention, 185, 187; to a past event 62

projection 187
psychoanalytic approach 187
psychodynamic 187
psychodynamic themes: aggression 23, 37–39; body awareness 23, 39–43; children's interactions with other children 23, 43–44; emotion regulation 23, 44–46; gender 23, 46–49; internal conflict 23, 50; learning 23, 54–56; mother-child attachment 22, 27–28; mother-child communication 22, 28–30; mother-child differences 23, 51–54; mother-child interaction 22, 23–26; mother-child memories 22, 31–34; play 22, 36–37; separation 22, 34–35; underlying meanings of behavior 23, 49–50

reaction formation 187
reflective functioning 49, 187
Reiswig, R. 190
reunion after separation: and expectancies 56–57, 81–82; and peek-a-boo 21

Sackler Lefcourt Center 47
Schechter, D. x, 190
Scheftel, S. 190
secure base interactions 187
security of attachment 187
self-constancy 187
self-reflection 187
sense of self 187
separation 22, 34–35; Child Development Information and Group Questions: 2 to 10-months 91; 11 to 19-months 113; 20 to 28-months 132; 29 to 36-months 152–153; separateness of minds 35, 78
Seth, A. 190
sexual guilt, vignette 174–175
Shapiro, T. 190
sibling rivalry, vignette 172–173
sleep 55; vignette 162–164
sexual abuse fear, vignette 168–171
social referencing 187
splitting 187
Stern, D. 191
suggested reading 189–191
summaries: Defense mechanisms 56; Group-leader approach 9–12; Group-leader support 12–17; Group-notes outline 72; Mother-baby-toddler group goals 20; Mother-baby-toddler group-process

20–21; Mothers' core themes 9; Psychodynamic themes 22–23

toilet, fear of vignette 42–43, 55, 174–175
trauma 187
treasured toy 34, 37, 89, 92, 114, 188
Tronick E. Gold C. 191

unconscious 188
underlying meanings of behavior: Child Development Information and Group Questions 17–21; 2 to 10-months 95–96; 11 to 19-months 118–119; 20 to 28-months 137–138; 29 to 36-months 157–158
unresolved trauma 188

vignettes: Child Development Information and Group Questions: 11 to 19-months 121–127; 29 to 36-months 161–175; 20 to 28-months 140–147; 2 to 10-months 98–108

working alliance 188
working models 188

# Taylor & Francis eBooks

www.taylorfrancis.com

A single destination for eBooks from Taylor & Francis with increased functionality and an improved user experience to meet the needs of our customers.

90,000+ eBooks of award-winning academic content in Humanities, Social Science, Science, Technology, Engineering, and Medical written by a global network of editors and authors.

## TAYLOR & FRANCIS EBOOKS OFFERS:

- A streamlined experience for our library customers
- A single point of discovery for all of our eBook content
- Improved search and discovery of content at both book and chapter level

## REQUEST A FREE TRIAL
support@taylorfrancis.com